To Craig
Best wishes
Nicholas Kinloch

From the Soviet Gulag to Arnhem

From the Soviet Gulag to Arnhem

A Polish Paratrooper's Epic Wartime Journey

Nicholas Kinloch

Pen & Sword
MILITARY

First published in Great Britain in 2023 by
Pen & Sword Military
An imprint of
Pen & Sword Books Ltd
Yorkshire – Philadelphia

Copyright © Nicholas Kinloch 2023

ISBN 978 1 39904 591 9

The right of Nicholas Kinloch to be identified as Author of this work has been asserted by him in accordance with the Copyright, Designs and Patents Act 1988.

A CIP catalogue record for this book is available from the British Library.

All rights reserved. No part of this book may be reproduced or transmitted in any form or by any means, electronic or mechanical including photocopying, recording or by any information storage and retrieval system, without permission from the Publisher in writing.

Typeset by Mac Style
Printed in the UK by CPI Group (UK) Ltd, Croydon, CR0 4YY.

MIX
Paper | Supporting responsible forestry
FSC
www.fsc.org
FSC® C013604

Pen & Sword Books Limited incorporates the imprints of Atlas, Archaeology, Aviation, Discovery, Family History, Fiction, History, Maritime, Military, Military Classics, Politics, Select, Transport, True Crime, Air World, Frontline Publishing, Leo Cooper, Remember When, Seaforth Publishing, The Praetorian Press, Wharncliffe Local History, Wharncliffe Transport, Wharncliffe True Crime, White Owl and After the Battle.

For a complete list of Pen & Sword titles please contact

PEN & SWORD BOOKS LIMITED
47 Church Street, Barnsley, South Yorkshire, S70 2AS, England
E-mail: enquiries@pen-and-sword.co.uk
Website: www.pen-and-sword.co.uk

Or

PEN AND SWORD BOOKS
1950 Lawrence Rd, Havertown, PA 19083, USA
E-mail: Uspen-and-sword@casematepublishers.com
Website: www.penandswordbooks.com

Contents

Maps		vii
Preface		xi
Chapter 1	The Eastern Borderlands	1
Chapter 2	The Farm	5
Chapter 3	Hitler and Stalin	8
Chapter 4	Father Szymanski	11
Chapter 5	Old Piotr	14
Chapter 6	Storm Clouds Gathering	19
Chapter 7	War	22
Chapter 8	Soviets in the Village	25
Chapter 9	Journey to Another Village	30
Chapter 10	Siberia	38
Chapter 11	Vassili	45
Chapter 12	Russki Narod	51
Chapter 13	Roubles and Kopeyki	55
Chapter 14	Freedom	60
Chapter 15	Uzbekistan	65
Chapter 16	The Polish Army	71
Chapter 17	The Middle East	77

Chapter 18	Billy	83
Chapter 19	The Mariposa	89
Chapter 20	Scotland	97
Chapter 21	Paratrooper Training	104
Chapter 22	The Coasters	112
Chapter 23	1943	115
Chapter 24	The First Polish Independent Parachute Brigade	120
Chapter 25	1944	123
Chapter 26	The British First Airborne Division	127
Chapter 27	Operation Market Garden	131
Chapter 28	Driel	138
Chapter 29	Crossing the Rhine	142
Chapter 30	For the Memories	147
Chapter 31	The Crossroads	154
Chapter 32	The House with the Red Cross	163
Chapter 33	Escape	169
Chapter 34	The Dutch Underground	176
Chapter 35	Last Chance	183

Epilogue 193

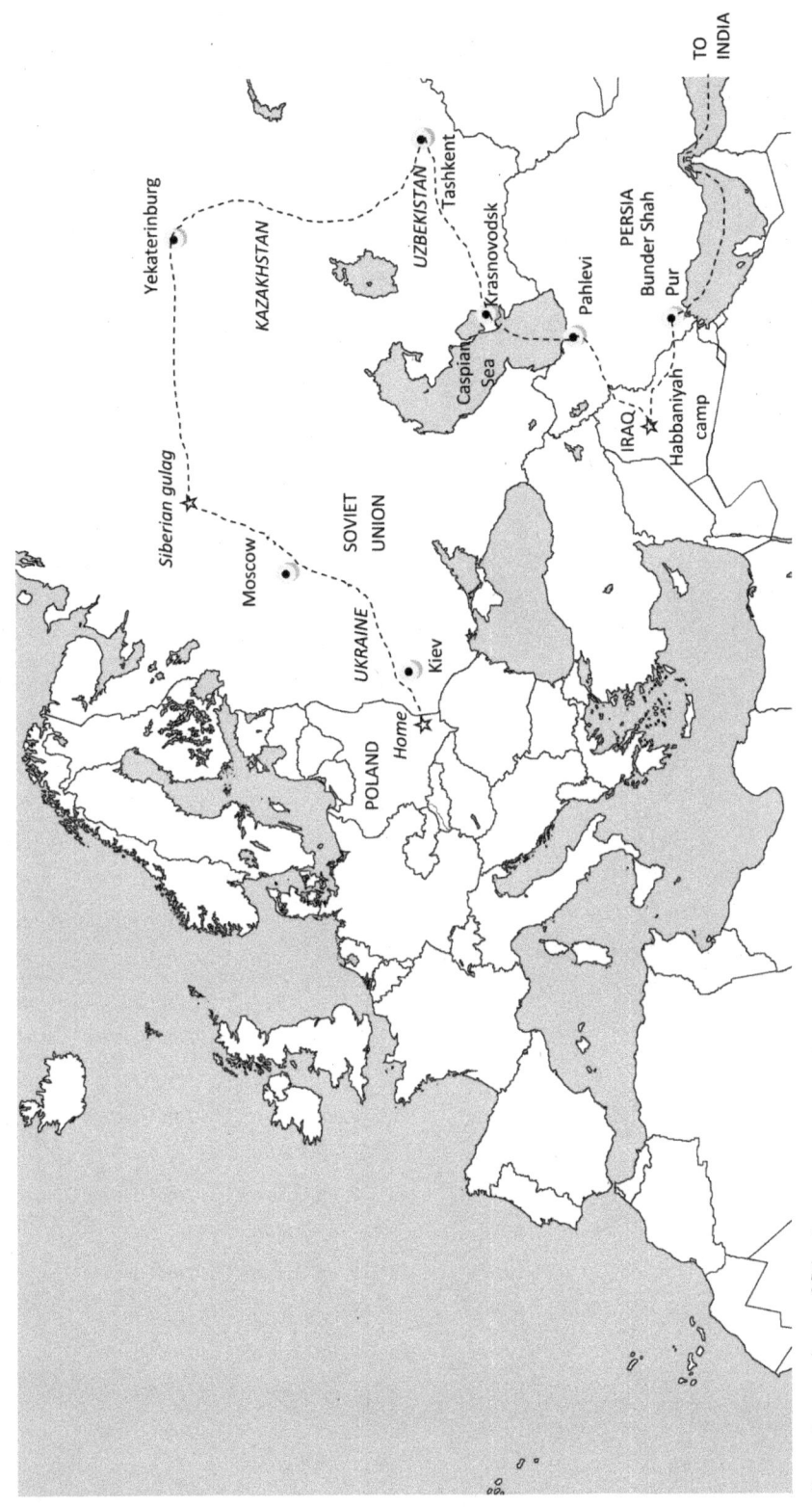

Route into and out of Siberia.

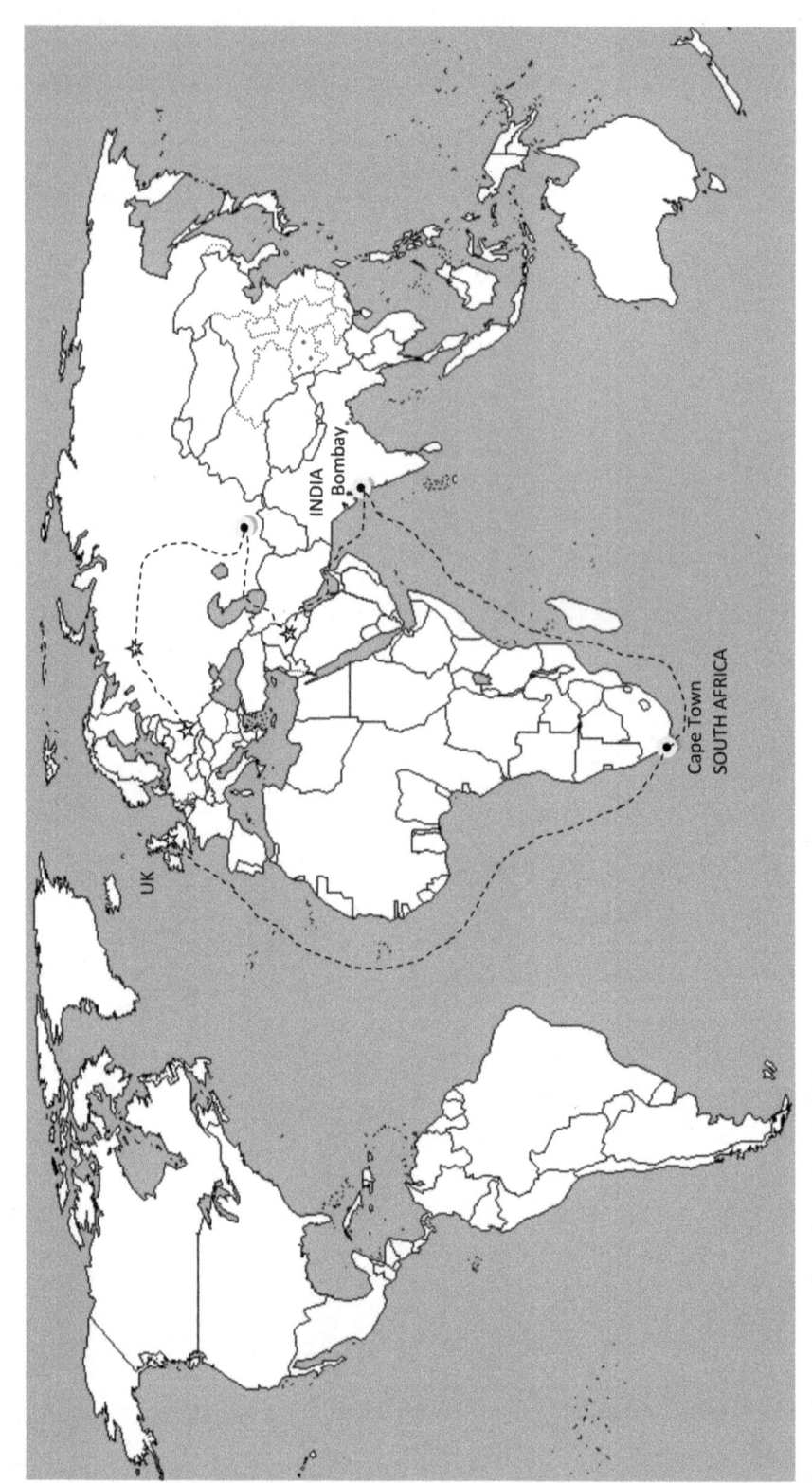

Route of my journey from Poland to the UK.

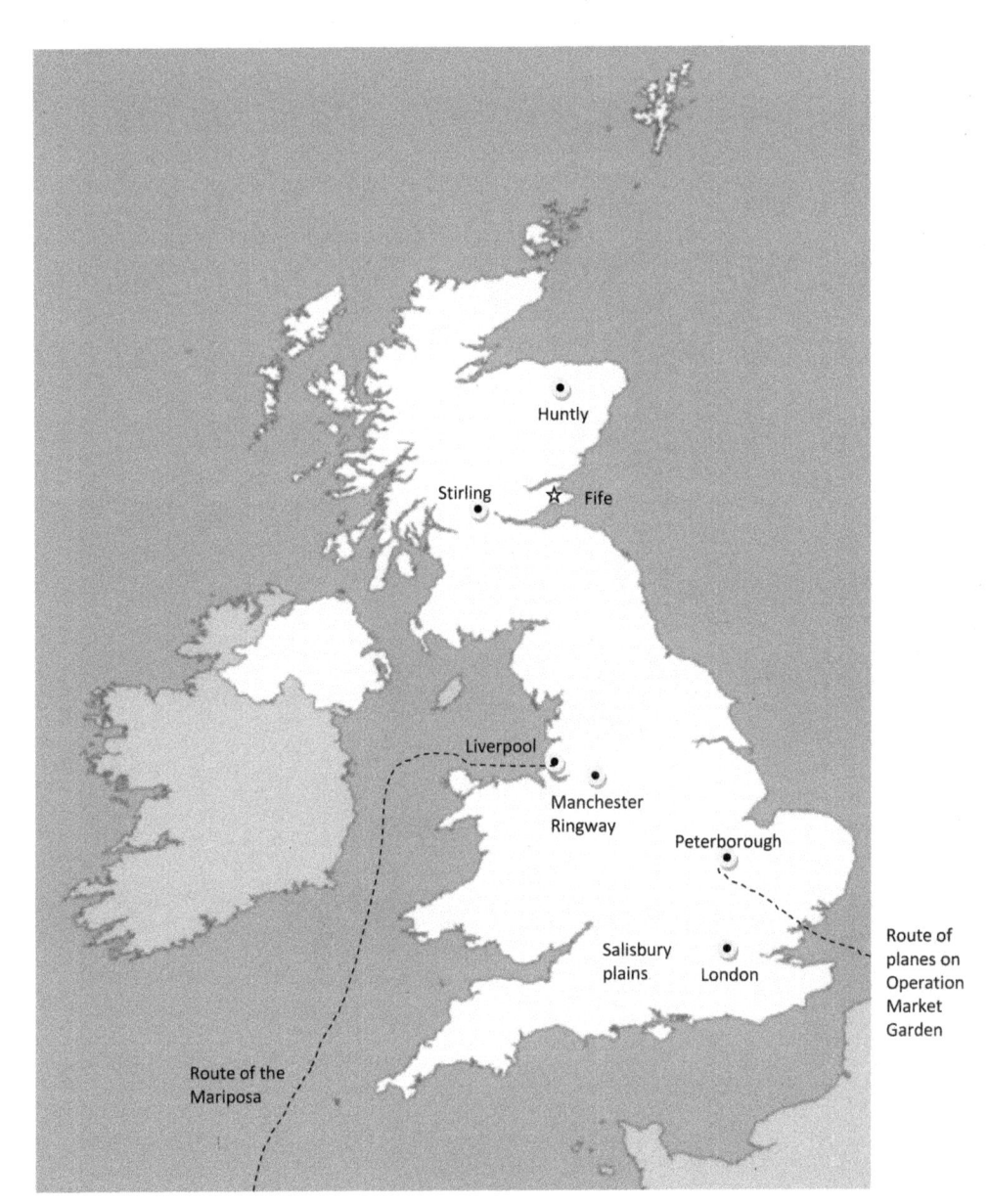

Polish paratroopers in the UK.

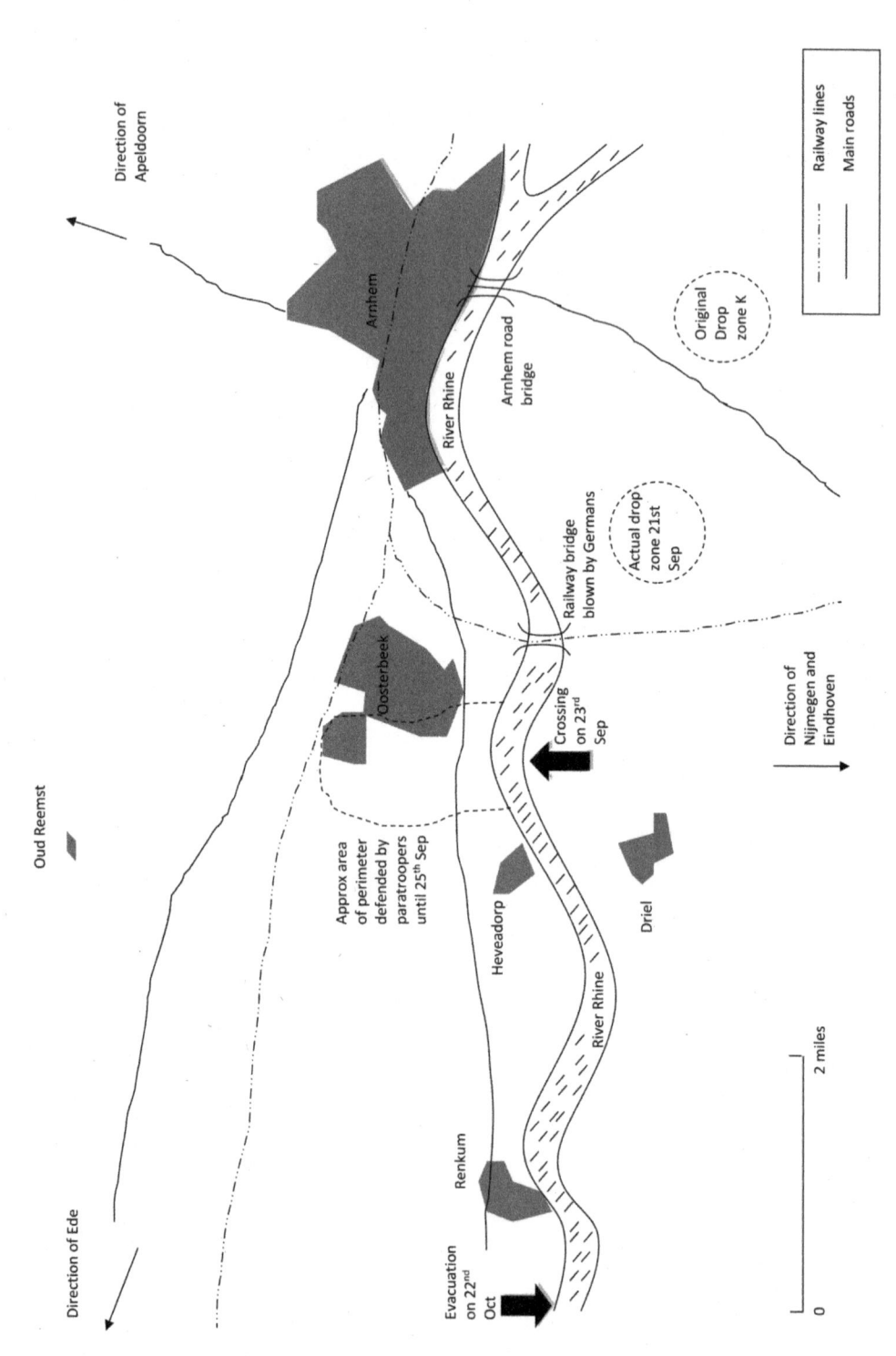

Operation Market Garden.

Preface

Stanisław Kulik was my grandfather and, in a sense, I have always known his story. Some of my earliest memories are of him telling me small snippets from it: about Siberia, about hiding from the Nazis in the Netherlands, or being chased by a knife-wielding Arab in Iraq, but I had never heard the whole story before.

It was only in 2007 when I sat down with him to take detailed and organised notes. He was then aged 83 and, over the course of six months, I drove to St Andrews every week to talk with him. Many journalists had come to him before wanting to write his story, but he had always turned them down. I think he had only wanted a family member to write it.

I made a start on writing, but then work and other commitments took over. My notes lay untouched for almost thirteen years, until 2020, when I finally found myself with the time to attempt the project.

This book is a true story, although at times it may appear incredible. Some of the names of protagonists have been changed in order to protect their privacy. It has been an honour and privilege to give a voice to my grandfather and to share his story.

I would like to thank my parents for supporting and encouraging me through the long book-writing process. My dad helped to proof-read my drafts and it was my mum who found Pen & Sword, the eventual publishers of this book. I would also like to thank Henry Wilson at Pen & Sword for reading my submission, finding the story as fascinating as I do, and agreeing to publish it.

Thanks also to Gordon Elliott for his regular gentle prompting and enquiring about the book; it was a meeting with him in July 2020 which led to my re-engagement with the project. Thank you to the Colinton Library Book Group, and to everyone else who read my drafts and gave feedback.

I would also like to thank the Dutch underground for risking their lives to save my grandfather, and the Dutch people for commemorating each year what happened at Arnhem.

Most of all I should thank my grandparents. Stanisław passed away in June 2016, and his wife Isa in October 2020. My only regret is that they are not here to see the published book.

Chapter 1

The Eastern Borderlands

We were a typical Polish family in the 1930s, and that meant large, and poor and Catholic. I can still picture us all in our wooden house with the thatched roof in a village in the east of Poland.

It's a little house with a concrete floor and beside the fire we have potato sacks for a rug. On the walls there are pictures of soldiers from the Polish-Soviet War, fighting the Soviets in 1920, and a picture of Pilsudski, the leader of Poland. In the bedroom there is a small cross hanging over the bed where I sleep head to feet with my two older brothers. Their feet poke me in the face all winter, so that we are glad when summer finally comes and we can go out to sleep in the hay shed. Next door there is another bedroom where my two sisters and little brother sleep, and then down a short hall to the living room which is also the kitchen and the bedroom for my parents.

Growing up there, I never would have believed you if you had told me what would happen to me just a few years later.

We lived in a village called Obrentchuvka. It was made up of about ten small farms, or holdings, stretching over a distance of a couple of miles. Surrounding us was farmland, forest and rivers. The nearest town was called Ichrovitsa where a few hundred people lived, and where all the shops were. The city, Ternopol, was approximately ten miles away which took two hours by horse and cart, but I hardly ever went there. Our village was close to the border with Soviet Ukraine which was only around seven or eight miles away.

You know, for many years, Poland hadn't existed. It had been divided between various empires – Austrian, German and Russian. But Poland became an independent country again after the First World War. In those days the Polish borders were different to how they are nowadays. In the west it had been given territory from Germany by the Treaty of Versailles in 1919 after a Polish uprising against German rule. And in the east the

2 From the Soviet Gulag to Arnhem

Poles had been engaged in a series of messy and complicated conflicts until 1921, for control of disputed land after the collapse of the empires of Russia and Austria-Hungary. These conflicts were mainly against the Soviet communists; but also against, then alongside Ukrainians, and even against the Lithuanians at times.

It was in this land called Kresy or the Eastern Borderlands, in the east of Poland where we lived. We lived in the south-east of this area which had belonged to the Austro-Hungarian Empire before the First World War, and there were people of all backgrounds and ethnicities who lived there. There were Poles and Ukrainians, Catholics, Orthodox Christians and Jewish people. Some of the Ukrainians there campaigned for independence, and rightly or wrongly the Polish government encouraged Polish people to move there in order to dilute the Ukrainian influence.

My father had been able to buy the land for half price because he had been in the Polish army and my parents had moved there a couple of years before I was born. My grandparents originally came from a different part of Poland, but I never met them. They were as mythical to me as the saints in the church in front of whose statues my mother used to light candles and say fervent prayers.

My parents came from the region around Krakow, where my father had been a railway engineer. My mother had come from a wealthy family with servants, or so the story went. Apparently they had a much better life in Krakow and children there could go to school every day without being pulled away for harvest or because of bad weather like we were. My aunt was a teacher who had stayed in Krakow, and the one time she visited us everyone said she looked like a queen next to my mother in her country clothes. My aunt said that we should go back to Krakow but my father was a stubborn man. He wanted to persist with his farm and the business that he had set up drilling wells, which the local people paid him for, and which over time started to make more money.

My parents' first child was Stefka and she was born in 1914. A couple of years later came Edek and then Billy, who was five years older than me.

I had a younger brother called Mietek, born two years after me, and finally Rozia, my youngest sister who was born in 1932. My parents had other children too but they died as babies or as young children and I only found out about them later. Child mortality was high in those days, and they were buried in Ichrovitsa cemetery. Well, that's a lot of names and dates… still with me?

So, a large family. But big families were common in those days; a big family was needed to work the land as there weren't many machines, mainly just horses and people.

As for me, I was born in 1924 in Obrentchuvka. It might sound strange but I don't really remember what day my birthday is, as we didn't celebrate birthdays in our house; we didn't have the money for it, but I remember my name day is on 8 May. Namedays are celebrated a bit like birthdays, but we call this day *imieniny* and your name day corresponds to the feast day of the saint of the same name. My name was Stanley, or Stanisław in Polish; it was the name of a Polish king from the olden days, but everyone called me Staszek for short. So my name day was on the feast day of Saint Stanisław who is one of the patron saints of Poland.

* * *

When I was about nine years old, my oldest sister Stefka married a local Ukrainian man. Everyone said he was a good catch; he was a good man and he had a big farm. When she got married she received the traditional gift of some land from our father's holding, as well as presents for her house, like pots and jugs from other guests. She lived about five miles away in her husband's village.

Actually, she almost didn't get married at all. Just before the wedding one of our older neighbours told Stefka that she was making a mistake and that he would like to marry her instead. She liked him and almost changed her mind, but our father said no – it was too late in the day, she was already engaged and too much money had been spent organising things. He didn't want to be a source of local gossip and scandal, thank you very much. Stefka had a traditional white wedding in the local Catholic church. They travelled to and from the wedding by cart as it was a special occasion. They put straw in the back of the cart, and covered it with sheets and blankets so that people could sit on it.

On the way, the 'wedding gate' blocked their path, a Polish tradition. Our neighbours had blocked the road with a rope, hung with decorations, and wouldn't let anybody through until the groom had paid the ransom.

Money is no good for this though, you can only get past after you pay with bottles of vodka.

Afterwards, there was a party outside the house with a band and dancing. My father could play the clarinet and fiddle, and there was also an accordion and drums in the band. When Stefka and her husband arrived they were greeted by our parents with bread, salt and a shot of homemade vodka. The bread and salt symbolize wealth and love. Vodka, well it just symbolizes the start of the party! There were lots of toasts to the newlyweds with the homemade vodka; every five minutes somebody different would stand up and then make a toast, or sing songs like *sto lat*.

> *One hundred years, one hundred years, let us live, one hundred years!*

The band got drunk, as did some other men who hadn't even been invited, and my father had to throw one out. The wedding party went on all night and then started again the next day; the tidying up went on for even longer afterwards.

The next to marry was Edek, my oldest brother. He married a rich, older local Ukrainian woman, although the gossip was that he later tried to dump her for a younger one. Edek got married in wintertime with the snow all around, in his wife's Russian Orthodox church. The Orthodox priests had long grey beards and the women would cover their heads with a headscarf; there were mosaics on the walls, shining in the candlelight, and lots of icons of saints which people would kiss.

Edek said that he didn't want land from our father for the marriage, just money. My father agreed, as he had found out that Edek had been stealing money from him to buy his wife presents. Edek went round organising his wedding on horseback, but the horse died because he made her work too hard. In fact Edek was a big source of regular scandal, despite the best efforts of my father!

But we would soon find out that Edek would be the least of our worries.

Chapter 2

The Farm

When the weather got warmer, my younger brother Mietek and I slept on the hay in the shed. It was better than all of us sharing the bed, where it was a battle each night to not be stuck in the middle between your two brothers. We often used to stay up late in the summer, running around and playing and if we didn't wake up in time, my father would come and throw a bucket of cold water over us. I would jump to my feet, gasping for breath with the shock of the cold water; somehow most of it always seemed to land on me.

Mietek and I had to help look after the animals on our farm holding. Our two horses had to be fed a couple of hours before they started work, which meant at 5am for a 7am start. Each winter, my father would sell one of the horses to save money and feed, and then buy another one in spring for the harvesting and ploughing. We gave the horses hay and corn to eat, changed the straw and took away their dung, which would be used as manure. I always managed to get Mietek to do the dung part, as he was a few years younger than me; he would carry shovelfuls of it out of the shed with his nose wrinkled up.

We also had two cows on the farm and Mietek and I had to milk them by 9am each morning, before it got too hot and all the flies came out. We brought the cows in from the grass and milked them in the shed. When we brought them back out to graze afterwards, we tied them down so they wouldn't wander away, as there were no fences; we would tie one of the cow's horns to one of its feet, or tie it to a post, so that it could only walk in circles.

Each year, I wondered whether we would keep the calves or the cow. My father would get the local bull round to service the cows, as he called it, and when a new calf was born he would either keep or sell the calves or the older cow depending on which one he thought had more potential. I was always sad if he sold the calves as they were very cute, and I would play with one and get attached to it. 'Don't get so fond of them, it's just an animal,' my mother would say to me. She made butter from the cow's milk using a churn, and would show my younger sister Rozia how to pat the butter so that it got a nice pattern on it; or she would boil the cow's milk to make fresh cottage cheese.

After the cows, we went to the pigs. Mietek and I fed our two pigs on barley meal, and when the pigs were fat enough that they could barely stand up, then my father would decide it was time to slaughter them. To kill a pig, he used to knock it out with an axe or hammer and then quickly cut its throat. Then, one year, he turned to my older brother Billy, and told him that he was now old enough to try it himself. Billy, white-faced, took the hammer, hesitating; he had never done it before. When he brought the hammer down onto the pig's head, he only did it gently, so that the pig was just a bit dazed. When he tried to cut its throat, it got up and started running about with Billy chasing it around with a knife!

After that, my father would hang up the pig to bleed, so that its blood collected into containers that were placed on the ground under the carcass. He would put boiling water over the carcass, and use burning straw to singe the skin, and then wash it with a special stone to take all the hair off. Next, he would open up the pig into two halves and cut the head off. That was what life was like in the countryside in those days. We had to do everything for ourselves.

My mother would rub salt into the cuts of the ham and store it in barrels. We didn't have fridges back then, so that was the only way you could keep food for long periods of time. She would turn them every so often in the salt and then hang the hams from the roof of the storeroom. Pork was the main meat that we ate and almost all of the pig would be used – my mother would use the blood to make black pudding and the fat was used like lard for cooking. The meat had to be washed by soaking it overnight in water to remove the salt before cooking. For breakfast some days my mother fried up pig's fat, then poured off the excess and we would eat the crispy bit on bread; or she made jajecznica which mixed bacon with scrambled eggs. She would make potted meat; kielbasa sausage; slanina, which is a kind of very streaky bacon; mince and stews with potatoes, carrots, cabbage and so on; and a dish of pork with cream sauce that was out of this world.

My father would pick up the leftover bones from his bowl and suck on them to get all the meat and marrow. We couldn't let anything go to waste. A few years before we had run out of food and had to borrow from our neighbour, then sell more birds to Benjamin so that we could buy supplies.

Benjamin was a local Jewish man, and in those days lots of Jewish people lived in Poland. Many had come from the Soviet Union where they had been persecuted. They were Ashkenazi Jews and they spoke a language called Yiddish, but most could speak Polish too. They would come to the market in Ternopol and buy calves and chickens from us, but not the piglets as their religion didn't allow them to eat pork. Benjamin used to buy birds from us, and he would put them, still alive, into sacks tied on each side of his horse.

We had eggs from the hens that we kept in a coop on the far side of the farmyard. Any eggs that we didn't use, we brought to the local shop in Ichrovitsa, to pay for any supplies that we couldn't make ourselves on the farm, things like sugar, salt, coffee and tea. But we mainly lived off our land and our animals.

As well as the chickens we also had ducks, geese and turkeys too, although they were hard to rear. My mother showed us how to stuff our duvets and pillows with the feathers from the birds. We plucked the feathers and pulled out the hard bit in the middle, leaving the soft feather to make into the stuffing. We used the geese feathers for the duvet, and duck feathers for our pillows as the duck feathers weren't quite so good.

We were born and raised for country life. Our days were governed by the weather, and the seasons, by the cycles of ploughing, planting and harvesting crops and by the needs of the animals. We didn't have a lot, but we had enough and all of our neighbours were in the same boat, so it was the only life that I knew. Little did we know, however, that everything was about to change forever.

Chapter 3

Hitler and Stalin

In the summertime, my mother decorated the house with flowers from the garden. It looked beautiful at this time of year full of red poppies, yellow sunflowers, pink roses, blue and purple irises and white lilies. She didn't have vases, but put the flowers into clay pots round which she then stuck coloured paper to decorate them.

In front of the house, we had a garden laid with grass where we also planted apple trees and vegetables such as peas, carrots and cabbages. We had beehives at the end of the garden where the bees produced lots of honey from all the flowers in the garden.

Summer was hot and sunny and Billy and I would go down to the small stream nearby and dam it up with stones and mud on Friday night. By Saturday morning the water would have risen up behind the dam and it would be like a swimming pool. Billy and I would take our horses and go down to the river. We only had old saddles for the horses, with no stirrups, and you had to make your own stirrups by doubling up a piece of rope over the horse's back.

There would be fish all about, but nobody ever thought to catch them, until my father went once and got nine or ten big fish that we fried and ate. Billy and I would go naked into the river until Piotr, our old neighbour with a stubbly white beard, complained about us; then we went in our underwear instead. We splashed around so much in the river that the water would become dark like coffee, and our hair and faces would be brown and sandy – you came out of that river dirtier than you went in! Afterwards we would go upstream where we had some pails and could clean each other off.

When the weather got colder we brought a metal bath into the living room, which we filled with water boiled in big metal pots on the fire in our house. Someone had to come and scrub your back with a cloth and soap, because the bath was so small that you couldn't do it yourself without getting water everywhere.

In summertime we would sometimes get big thunderstorms and, when the weather broke like this, my mother would be afraid. She would put a candle in the window and take her wooden cross out of the drawer, holding it close to her chest, praying to her picture of the sacred heart of Jesus that the lightning wouldn't hit the house. 'Hail Mary, full of grace,' she would repeat over and over, crossing herself, praying on her knees, in her flowery dress and headscarf and apron, which she always wore when she was in the kitchen; praying with her hands clasped together up at her lips, on her knees, or holding my younger sister Rozia who was eight years younger than me: 'Lord, keep us safe, and bless this family.'

* * *

Harvest time was the only time that I heard my father praying or saw him going to church; when he watched the weather and the crops closely, to decide when to start the harvesting. Our farm holding contained approximately 100 acres. We grew rye, wheat, oats, as well as barley, turnips, potatoes and sweetcorn. We had about twenty acres of each and we rotated the crops each year to ensure the soil stayed good.

During harvest time, all the neighbours came to help each other. No money would be paid, but we would feed those who were helping. My mother cooked a big pot of stew, called bigos, which had chicken, pork, sausage and sauerkraut in it. It stood beside the fire for days on end and people would just come in and take a ladle out of it; nobody worried about food poisoning in those days.

The crops had to be scythed down by the men, working their way slowly across the fields in lines, swinging their scythes rhythmically in front of them. As the men worked the mice would run out of the fields and Rozia and Mietek tried to chase them away with sticks, but they never caught them. The crops would then be tied up into lots of little bundles and they had to be threshed to separate the straw from the grain and chaff.

The threshing machine was powered by a horse or by four men walking in a circle, and used rotating drums with teeth to separate the straw from the grain and chaff. We used the straw to stuff our mattresses. We would change the stuffing every few months and the first night after doing this, the mattress would be so high that you could hardly get onto the bed, but it soon flattened down. Barley straw was the best as it was softer, rye and wheat straw were hard like sticks!

We used the straw for roofing too and my father got our house newly thatched every two or three years. If we didn't need the straw for roofing that year the men would stack it up in the fields, then cover it up, wrap round it with ropes and hold it down with stones in case there were high winds. We could use this straw as bedding for animals when we needed it.

We had another machine that we used to blow off the chaff from the grain. The chaff was the covering of the grain, and we had to get rid of it before we could use the grain. We put the grain in one side of the machine, then turned a handle and it produced a strong current of air which blew the chaff away. The grain that we were left with needed to be taken to the mill. My father would book a time with the miller; sometimes it could even be in the middle of the night, as the mill worked non-stop at harvest time. Then the miller gave us back wheat, barley and rye flour.

* * *

'If we have anything left by the spring, we'll sell it at the market at Ternopol,' my father said at the end of the harvest every year, as he stood eating bigos out of the big pot with the other men. 'But definitely not before; you never know if you're going to run short before the next harvest.' My father had streaks of dried sweat on his face, stained with the dust from the fields, a sign of the hours of hard work. Dusk was spreading across the clear sky, turning red in the west where the sun was reaching the horizon. We had all gathered together beside our cottage as the fields glowed golden in the low light.

It was the summer of 1936 and the topic of conversation soon shifted to what everyone had been talking about that year: Hitler. I was only twelve years old at that time, but the name was already familiar to me. He was the Führer, the leader of Germany, the leader of the Nazi party.

In March 1936 he had sent his army to reoccupy the Rhineland, an area between Germany and France. It had been German, but after the First World War, there was the Treaty of Versailles which said that Germany would not be allowed any military there. He was testing out Britain and France, to see if they would do anything when he broke the treaty. But nobody did anything and Hitler wasn't the only thing we had to worry about – there was also Stalin in the Soviet Union.

Chapter 4

Father Szymanski

I used to walk to school in Ichrovitsa, which was about five miles away. There was a dirt road at the front of our holding which was the main road to Ichrovitsa. It was OK when it was dry, but after rain it just turned into mud. The horses couldn't even lift their feet out of the mud when it was like that. The school was near the doctor's house in the town where he saw you in a room in his own house. In Poland we started school at seven years of age, and there were two classes, one for the older students and one for the younger children.

The children in our village were always being pulled away from school. We couldn't go in the winter months as the weather would be too harsh and dangerous and we couldn't go when work was needed on the farm, such as planting, ploughing or harvesting. Billy and I would help my father plough the fields with the horse and plough, up and down the fields in neat rows, turning over the earth. It would take a long time, days and days, as the horse could only pull a single-furrow plough and we had 100 acres. As we ploughed we used to turn over the plough and sharpen it every so often so that it would be easier for the horses to pull, but our land was so good that you didn't get many stones.

In the spring my father would take us out to the fields to plant seeds by hand and to help cut wood for firewood – we would let it dry over the summer so that it wouldn't spark so much when we burned it in winter. In winter time we would load the firewood onto a sledge to transport it, but if the snow was soft the horse would find it really difficult to move. We got our firewood from a forest that was about ten miles away; my father had bought some of this forest for our own use and our area was marked out by pegs.

When we didn't go to school my father would just write a note to our teacher, excusing us from school. It was possible for months to pass without going to school. Sometimes Billy tried to teach me, but I just ignored him as he was not a real teacher. I'm not going to lie, I wasn't the best student in the world; I never really learned to read or write properly.

When we went back to school after the harvest in 1936 our class had a new teacher. Her name was Pani Kaminska and she had originally been from Krakow, just like my parents. She had bright blue eyes and grey hair tied back in a bun. She was kind, but she gave you the belt on your hands if you didn't listen. We sat in rows at old-fashioned wooden desks, the boys on one side of the room and the girls on the other. We sat in order of age, so that the youngest were at the front.

One of the girls in my class was the daughter of Edek's best man at his wedding. She was called Ania and had an older sister called Kasia. All the men and older boys, like my brother Billy, said Kasia was gorgeous. She went to church every Sunday all dressed up; all the men chased after her and would try to impress her. But she was so picky that they said that she would end up alone, as she said 'no' to everyone, and then one day it would be too late.

Pani Kaminska was our teacher for a couple of years until the summer of 1938. During that time, once a week a Catholic priest, called Father Szymanski, came into the school and would tell us religious stories from the bible. My mother told me that Father Szymanski was a Polish nationalist, which she said meant that he thought a lot about Poland and the Catholic church, but sometimes not so much about other people. Father Szymanski wore a long black robe and had a small white collar around his neck; he smelled of incense, and tradition. After he had read from the bible, if you asked him nicely, sometimes he would tell you other stories. He said that these tales weren't from the bible but they had morals that would help to make you better, so it was OK to tell these tales.

Father Szymanski would also tell us stories about Poland. He told us that Poland used to be a huge country, called the Polish-Lithuanian Commonwealth, that stretched from the Baltic Sea in the north, down towards the Black Sea in the south. It included Kresy where we lived. 'But the Germans and the Russians, and the Austrians,' he said, 'took more and more of our country until eventually there was nothing left.' He sighed, 'but then,' he continued, 'there was a great war, about twenty years ago, and we got our country back after Pilsudski led the Polish forces to victory over the Soviet Red Army at the miracle on the Vistula River.'

On the wall of the classroom there were pictures of soldiers from this 1920 war against the Soviets, and the picture of the former Polish leader Pilsudski just like the picture we had at home. Pilsudski stared down at us with a steely gaze, a moustachioed military strongman. He was very popular in Poland as he had led the Polish army to victory over the Soviets when all had appeared lost, which had safeguarded the new Polish state, but he had died a few years previously. There were also pictures of Polish cavalry from the past, called Hussars, and we were told that they had some kind of item of clothing like wings, that made an incredible noise as they charged which scared the enemy and made them run away.

I worried whether there would be more wars in the future. Earlier that year, in March 1938, Hitler's armies had moved to occupy Austria. His excuse was the need for Germany to secure its borders, but they said the streets of Vienna were lined with celebrating Austrians.

Hitler had fought in the First World War which Germany lost. Millions of men had died. A lot of people in Germany thought that they were betrayed, and they blamed groups like the Jews and the communists. Then, after the war, Germany had to give up a lot of land, and was forced to pay back large amounts of money to other countries. They became a very poor country. A lot of Germans resented that.

'And what about Stalin?' I asked Father Szymanski.

'Stalin? He's a monster. Just look what he has done to his own people. He used to want to be an orthodox priest but now he's a Bolshevik. They don't believe in God,' he replied.

And then, after all of these stories about religion and about morals and history, I got to thinking about the boy who sat next to me in class, and how he was such an annoying person, and always used to pull my hair during lessons. And how three of us boys who all came from my village decided to teach him a lesson after school, and I wondered whether that made me a bad person. But then I remembered that the teacher had brought him out to the front of the class and belted him for pulling my hair, so it maybe didn't really matter what I had done. Maybe the most important thing was just who carried the biggest belt.

Chapter 5

Old Piotr

In the winter it got so cold that the whole house had to be insulated. The temperature was below freezing for months, even during the day, and the snow didn't melt until spring. My father and Billy built a wooden frame right round the house and packed it with straw. Otherwise, after the snow had frozen hard against the walls, the walls would crack and freeze, and when it began melting the walls would get damp. At night in winter the windows had to be covered with straw too, as otherwise they would crack from the severe frost. Sometimes the snow would drift so high that it would block the front door. Then my father would have to climb out the window in order to dig us out.

In the winter of 1938 the thatch on our roof caught fire from sparks from the log fire that had gone up the chimney. It was night-time and we hadn't even noticed until a neighbour came round to warn us, then we all had to run round to his place in our nightgowns. I ran round with just my nightshirt on and not even any underwear. There was no fire brigade in those days, so we had to try to manage the fire ourselves. It was only after many hours that we eventually managed to put out the fire by flinging up water and snow onto the roof.

In winter Billy and I used to make skis. We would cut out the wood and then hold one end over a pot of boiling potatoes which my mother had cooking on the stove. We connected a wire from the front of the ski to a screw in the middle of the ski, and as the front heated up, we both turned the screw so that the wire tightened and the front of the ski curved up. We also made sledges; the runners were iron bands from barrels that had been smoothed out. The other boys in the village copied this design as it was so much faster than the wooden runners that they had been using.

The end of November was Andrzejki. It was an evening of magic, fortune-telling and games, when the women and girls would try to find out about their future marriage prospects. My mother would take Rozia by the hand and show her how to heat up wax, then take a key, and pour the wax through the hole in the key into a bowl of cold water. Rozia watched my mother intently as the wax gradually dripped into the water. After the wax cooled off, my mother held it up in front of a candle and the shadow that appeared on the wall was said to represent your future husband. Every girl I knew saw signs of a good-looking and wealthy husband!

All the neighbours would go round and visit each other's houses, especially in the wintertime. There was an old neighbour, Piotr, who smelt like horses and hard work, who would come round to visit us, and tell stories by the light of our old paraffin lamps in the dark with shadows flickering on the walls. There was no electricity in our house. In those days only the bigger towns had electricity.

Old Piotr told us stories in his low, husky voice; especially stories about the devil, so that Mietek and Rozia were scared stiff, listening with eyes and mouth wide open. Neither of them would want to go to bed alone after he visited.

'Sir Twardowski,' he said, 'made a deal with the devil – he promised to give his soul in exchange for great wisdom and magical powers.' He looked at us intently, pausing: 'Twardowski tried to outwit the devil by making the deal on one condition – the devil could only collect his soul in Rome, where Twardowski had no intention of going. Ha! Twardowski became rich and powerful, but you see, you can never trust the devil! In the end he tricked Twardowski into visiting an inn called Rome, where the devil with his blackened, hideous features and bright, shining red eyes caught him and his soul!' He finished on a crescendo, throwing his arms up in the air and making everyone jump.

It was a good story to frighten children, but I was more worried about real people. Poland was caught in the middle between Hitler and Stalin and I didn't trust them.

When the Bolsheviks and Lenin had taken over from the Tsar in Russia nobody had thought much of Stalin. They used to call him *Comrade Index Card*. He was just an administrator, looking after the files. But nobody else was as ruthless as he was and now he was the one in charge. He had started calling himself *The Man of Steel*.

Stalin had taken over all the farms in the Soviet Union, but this had caused a famine and millions of people had starved to death. Stalin had his NKVD secret police everywhere in his country, spying on people. Even children spied on their own parents. They said that there were only three kinds of people in the Soviet Union: those who had been in prison, those who were still in prison, and those who were going to be in prison.

Piotr took a handful of the peas that my mother had roasted and they cracked like nuts as he ate them. 'If anybody steps out of line in the Soviet Union then they are executed or sent to the gulag labour camps in Siberia. They call it the Great Terror.'

We had a peace treaty with Germany and with the Soviet Union too, but those were just pieces of paper. Some people said that Hitler and Stalin promised there would be no war with Poland as long as Pilsudski was alive, but Pilsudski had died in 1935, and that was three years previously.

* * *

It always felt like Christmas when my mother started to cook the sauerkraut. 'Everyone knows that the secret to good sour cabbage is in the preparation, and giving it enough time to sour,' she would say to nobody in particular. 'You can't rush good sour cabbage! And you can never have too much either,' she would add, before sending me outside to get more.

We kept the sour cabbage in a storage shed, in a barrel with iron hoops which my father had made earlier in the year just before harvest time. The cabbage was cut on a special board containing a series of knives, which cut through it with a scrunching sound so that it fell down into the barrel underneath. A layer of salt was put on top and we then stamped down on it with a piece of wood in order to break it up a bit. This process was repeated until the cabbage reached to the top of the barrel, when it was sealed, and a stone put on top to make the fit airtight. It was kept over the winter until it was ready.

To get to the storage shed I had to walk across the farmyard through the snow which was collecting in drifts against the side of our cottage, and past the water trough now almost covered with snow. The trough was still upside down, after my father had quickly upturned it and hid his shotgun underneath when two policemen came to investigate him for hunting on someone else's land without a licence. And I remembered how Billy and I had to try hard not to laugh when the policemen kept stepping back and forth over the trough with the shotgun hidden underneath.

Our Christmas celebrations would last three or four days, but the main celebration was on Christmas Eve, 24 December, which we called

Wigilia. We decorated the house by twisting coloured lengths of paper into corkscrew shapes and pinning them up to the walls and ceiling. We pinned some up on the Christmas tree too, alongside star-shaped biscuits which my mother had made, wrapped up in silver paper, and sweets and chocolates wrapped with pictures of Jesus from the church. We weren't supposed to eat anything from the tree until it was taken down in the New Year, but I always put some sweets in my pocket to eat earlier.

My father, Billy and I had brought the Christmas tree back to the house a few days before; it was a fir tree which we had taken from the forest at night. The whole tree would be too big, so Billy had climbed to the top of the tree and cut off the top bit with a saw. Normally my father nailed it to wooden legs on the floor, but for Christmas that year in 1938, he had hung it from the ceiling! He wanted to try to hide the dark mark there – a few months before he had accidentally blown a hole in the ceiling when he came back from hunting and pressed the trigger on his gun by mistake!

Sometimes my father would take me out hunting with him. In those days, hunting was just part of life in the countryside where we lived; everybody did it. We would go and shoot wild boar or wild pigs for food. We also used to go hunting foxes. Around February time the foxes would have a really nice thick coat that you could sell for lots of money; the fur was made into women's coats. My father used to work on the gun cartridges so that they would be even stronger than normal; he made small, pea-sized lead pellets and then filled up a normal cartridge with these and extra powder. They were so strong that they would have brought down a horse, not just a fox.

We would put on our heavy trousers, long johns, as well as thick fur coats and fur hats. You could hear the foxes calling across the snow and we would go after them on horseback. For some reason the fox wouldn't be so scared if you were on a horse – maybe it couldn't smell you so well. You never went directly for the fox, as it would just run away, but rather you would circle round it. The fox would just sit and watch the horse like it was hypnotised, as you slowly and carefully circled closer; when we were close enough, my father would shoot.

We started our Wigilia meal when the first star came out at night. It was said to be like the star that guided the Wise Men to find Jesus in

Bethlehem. Every proper Wigilia meal needed to have twelve dishes in memory of the twelve apostles of Jesus.

As well as sauerkraut and mushroom pierogi dumplings, my mother also cooked dishes like fried carp and beetroot soup called borscht, with little *uszka* dumplings that looked like the shape of somebody's ears, and cheesecake. After the meal, we gave each other presents like homemade boiled sweets that were hard outside but soft and fruity inside, or chocolate covered gingerbread. We had to be careful with food the rest of the year, but we always ate well at Christmas.

The evening finished by going to church, for midnight mass. All the families from the surrounding farms and villages would gather and sing traditional carols in the dark atmospheric candlelight, our voices echoing around the church. They were carols which everyone knew from childhood, like *Lulajże, Jezuniu, Hush little Jesus*, as Rozia slept peacefully through it all on the wooden benches of the church.

Chapter 6

Storm Clouds Gathering

'The Jews killed Jesus,' Father Szymanski intoned solemnly from his pulpit at the front of the church, looking down on the congregation. 'But despite this,' he continued, gesturing to the large wooden image of Christ on the cross behind him, 'our Lord forgave us and died for our sins. He was resurrected and whosoever believes in him shall have eternal life.'

I could see some people in the congregation nodding as he spoke, while others sat expressionless looking at the floor, or shaking their heads. I was confused, I whispered to Billy sitting beside me: I couldn't imagine Benjamin, who bought our chickens at the market, killing Jesus even if he was a bit rough with the chickens sometimes. And there were some Jewish children in my class at school who seemed harmless. And didn't our mother always say that 'there is just one God'.

'I heard on the radio that in Germany they are burning synagogues and destroying Jewish property,' Billy replied. 'They called it Kristallnacht. They have even laid down a law that forbids marriage between Germans and Jews.'

The church was full. It was Palm Sunday – the week before Easter 1939. Everyone had gathered 'palm fronds' and brought them to church. These symbolised the palm branches which people scattered in front of Christ as he rode into Jerusalem. Of course it was too cold in Poland for real palms, but we made do with the branches of the trees and bushes that we did have, such as willow, raspberry or yew. I lined up in the aisle with Mietek and Rozia, who was waving her frond enthusiastically and waiting to get it blessed by Father Szymanski. We waited our turn in the line and when we got to the front, Father Szymanski made the sign of the cross over us and then splashed holy water onto the fronds, before Rozia excitedly ran back to show my mother.

On Easter Sunday we ate a big meal: a sour rye soup called zurek made of vegetables, kielbasa sausage, pickles, sour cream and hard-boiled eggs;

as well as ham, sausages and the Easter eggs, called pisanki, that we had decorated on the previous days using our chicken, duck and goose eggs.

Any eggs that we didn't finish would be saved for the next day, Wet Monday – the boys in the village would get the eggs after they had finished going around soaking the girls with water, in a tradition that was supposed to ensure that the girls remained beautiful! When we finished eating, my mother would cross her fork and knife on the plate, to make the sign of the Christian cross, and then Rozia and Mietek would copy her, closely eyeing the babka cake that my mother had made for dessert.

* * *

We went to the Catholic church every Sunday, as did most Polish families; but my father didn't go. Father Szymanski, the priest, came round to visit each family once a year. He always took away lots of gifts for the church from these visits and Billy told me that he had heard there was a rumour going around that Father Szymanski was dating a young woman. Billy seemed to know all the rumours.

'I haven't seen you much in church this year,' the priest would say to my father when he came to our house. My father always excused himself and said that he had been too busy to go to church. 'I'll come next time,' he would say; but he never did.

Then their conversation turned to the news from Germany. After first invading the Rhineland, then Austria, the Nazis had invaded the Sudetenland in Czechoslovakia in the autumn of the previous year, 1938. The British and French had done nothing to stop them, and had made the Munich Agreement with the Nazis which said that if we let the Germans keep these territories then we would have peace in our time.

'I heard that Poland also seized some of the Czechoslovak territory at that time,' my father said.

'Well, that was different...' The priest's voice trailed off, before picking up again. 'Hah! And what did you think when, just last month, March 1939, the Nazis took over more of Czechoslovakia?'

I had heard the news. The radio said that you could see the Nazis parading in the streets of Prague and Hitler walking beside Prague castle, and now the Nazis were demanding that we gave them part of Poland. They wanted access to Danzig and East Prussia. Everyone was nervous about the German demands. The entire western part of Poland had been German before the First World War. It had been taken away from Germany in the Treaty of Versailles and now they wanted it back. Western Poland separated the main part of Germany from the small German state of East Prussia and the free city of Danzig where lots of Germans lived.

You could listen to German radio where we lived, although the signal wasn't good. You could hear Hitler making speeches and shouting out demands. I couldn't understand much, but he said that the Germans were superior to us, to the people living in the east of Europe. He talked about needing more living space for the Germans.

The situation in Danzig was getting worse. It was mainly Germans there and the Poles were being attacked, or being forced to take on a German name, or to go to a German school rather than a Polish school. Polish people weren't allowed into certain restaurants.

I wasn't sure that the Germans would stop with Danzig. In March 1939 they had withdrawn from the non-aggression treaty that Poland had with them. Britain and France had promised they would come to our aid if we were attacked, and some people even said that the Soviets would help Poland if we were invaded by the Nazis, but I didn't know whether to believe them.

'It's an outrage what the Nazis are doing!' Father Szymanski exclaimed. 'Will you fight again for Poland if she needs you?' he asked my father. And my father replied that he had his gun and could use it if he needed to, but he was older than he was when he fought in 1920 and he wasn't joining the army yet. He said that I was too young to join and Edek had his own family now.

Then Father Szymanski turned towards Billy and stared at him and Billy sat silently for a moment, then replied 'I'm going to join the home guard!' before my father could say anything. 'If the Nazis invade Poland, I'm going to fight for our country!' he continued, as my father stared at him wide-eyed.

Chapter 7

War

Our lives started to change forever on 1 September 1939 when I was aged 15. The radio was playing a Polish Radio News broadcast, and we all rushed to gather around our crackly wireless in the kitchen, that ran on a small battery that we had bought in Ichrovitsa.

Polish Radio News. On 1st September 1939 at dawn the German air force and regular army unexpectedly crossed into Polish territory without a declaration of hostilities.

We all looked at each other in shock. My mother had her hand over her mouth and with her other hand had grabbed hold of Rozia. Without realising it she was grabbing Rozia's arm so tightly that it was turning the skin white, and Rozia started to cry with the shock and pain.

German airplanes attacked a number of towns all over Poland. Casualties have been reported among the civilian population.

My heart was in my mouth and beating hard, as I listened to the announcer describe what was happening.

Simultaneously with air attacks, the German army has violated Polish territory by crossing the border in several places. Fighting is going on in the frontier regions. Several tanks have been put out of action.

My mind was in turmoil. Would the British and French come to help us? What about the Soviets? Were they all just going to let Hitler invade country after country without doing anything? We needed to prepare for the Germans coming.

* * *

The Nazis had fabricated an incident to justify their attack. They had pretended to be Poles, and then they had attacked their own German radio station the night before they invaded Poland, claiming that they had been attacked by Poland. In the week following the invasion we heard that the Germans had captured the holy Polish city of Czestochowa and had advanced as far as the outskirts of Warsaw.

The radio said that we were putting up strong resistance. 'Poland is not yet dead! Long live Poland!' the announcer on the radio called out. But you couldn't believe everything you heard on the wireless, nobody knew what was really happening. I heard others say that we were being pushed back too quickly; that the Nazis had thousands of tanks, thousands of aeroplanes, more than a million troops. They called it a blitzkrieg, a lightning fast war.

On 3 September, two days after the invasion, Britain and France declared war on Germany. I couldn't understand why they waited so long. We all hoped that they would attack Germany in the west, but they didn't do much. The British just dropped a few leaflets; it was a phoney war.

Conflicting rumours started to spread. Some people said that Warsaw was the centre of our defence and needed to be held at all costs. Others said that our plan should be to slowly withdraw the Polish forces to the east; first to Lviv, and then further east to take shelter in the hills on the Romanian and Soviet borders, where they could wait and hope for support from the British and French. It was supposed to be good defensive territory where the Polish army had ammunition dumps all set up and where we could resupply the troops through Romania.

Some people said that Hitler gave drugs to his army so that they could stay awake and keep fighting for up to five days at a time; that they were trained by being forced to walk in a circle, carrying rucksacks filled with stones, for days after days without stopping.

Then, soon after the German invasion, Billy was called away by the home army. We all watched him walk away, up the road, accompanied by a couple of other young men from the local villages. I watched his figure become smaller and smaller until he reached a turn in the road and disappeared from view. I wondered what would happen to him and when I might see him again.

* * *

These were days full of doubt and uncertainty. Nobody knew what the Germans might do; whether they would just try to take the parts of Poland that used to be German, or try to take the whole country. And what would they do to us? We had all heard Hitler talk about how the Poles and the Slavic people in Eastern Europe were inferior to the Germans, and we all knew that it hadn't gone well for the Jews in Austria when the Nazis came.

I asked my mother if I could join the home army too, like Billy. 'Of course not,' she answered, washing the clothes in the boiler. She lifted a handful of white clothes out of the brick boiler that my father had made and stoked the burning sticks underneath. Then she transferred some of the soapy water from the boiler to the sink via a pipe and used a scrubbing board to start cleaning the coloured clothes.

She checked that the clothes came out good and clean. A few months ago, Mietek had caught lice from another child at school and I had to comb out dozens of their white eggs from his hair onto a potato sack while he sat on the floor beside me.

'You're too young. You're only 15,' she continued. She told me that I could stay on the farm where it was safe and help look after Rozia and Mietek. 'It's true the British and French haven't come yet, but maybe the Soviets will come and help us.'

We would soon learn that you should be careful what you wish for, as it might not be what you expected.

Chapter 8

Soviets in the Village

I could hear them before I could see them. It was a low rumble that came over the fields from the east, that gradually grew like a never-ending roar of thunder, into a crescendo of noise, until even the ground itself started to shake and convulse with its power.

It was 17 September 1939, sixteen days since the Nazis had invaded and I was outside with Mietek at the far end of our farm holding. When I first saw them in the distance, on the horizon, they looked like small black ants kicking up a haze of dust all around them. As they moved towards us, I could make out more and more details of them; caterpillar tracks, turrets and a long gun pointing out the front: tanks!

How did the Germans get here so quickly! I had thought that they were still fighting with us for Warsaw at the Bzura river. But then I realised that these tanks were coming from the east, while the Germans were in the west of Poland. As they got closer I saw the design on the tanks, a big red star, and I realised that these were Soviet Red Army tanks. They were coming from the direction where Billy and the home army had gone, and I anxiously wondered what was happening to them all. Were the Soviets coming to help us?

The blood was pumping in my head as I tried to decide what we should do, stuck out in the middle of the fields with the Soviet tanks around us. What were they doing here? I grabbed Mietek by the shoulder and pulled him after me as I started running. 'The Soviets are driving through our fields and over all our crops. We need to get back to the house!'

When we arrived back, my father was livid. 'Your tanks drove right over our wheat and rye!' he was shouting at a Soviet soldier. 'I want to bring a complaint against you all!'

'Don't worry, you'll get compensation, comrade,' the soldier replied without expression. He was wearing a khaki uniform with a dark brown leather belt, and on his cap was a red star. 'You'll get compensation in Siberia.'

Siberia. The word sent a chill down my spine. The place where Stalin took all of his enemies. The place where Old Piotr said that they have the gulag labour camps.

The soldier laughed, but it was cold and without humour. He was a young man, maybe mid twenties, with high cheek bones and short hair. His expression never changed; he never smiled. 'We have come to protect you from the Germans, comrade!'

'Are you going to fight them?' my father asked.

'Haha, we are your liberators! This land should never have been Polish in the first place; you just caught the Soviet Union at a moment of weakness in the war in 1920. Don't worry, we know you Poles are not capable of protecting yourselves, so we will protect you and our Ukrainian brothers from the Germans. After all, you are now all Soviet citizens!'

Soviet citizens?! What did he mean? The soldier pulled out a notebook and pencil, and told my father that he was doing a survey of all the houses and farms. He got my father to tell him the size of our farm, and the size of our family; how many crops we had and how many animals. 'And make sure you tell the truth – we can easily find out if you don't and then it would be worse for you.'

The soldier wrote everything down in his notebook. Then on the next page he wrote a few figures and words, then tore out this page and gave it to my father. 'Everything belongs to the Soviet state now; there is no private property. This is the amount that you will give us each week. How much grain, how many eggs, things like that. We will come by horse and cart to collect it each week.'

My father took the piece of paper and his mouth opened as he looked over what had been written there. 'How can we do this?!' he exclaimed to the soldier. 'What if our hens don't lay, or there is a problem with the crop? And now winter is coming! Our family will be left with almost nothing; just bread, water and soup!'

'That's your problem, comrade.'

* * *

Some of the Soviet tanks would stop beside our farm as they passed through on their way further west on their invasion of Poland. The soldiers would make camp, sitting around fires and cooking fish or eating dry bread. They used to fling out this fish from their tanks afterwards. The fish was so smelly, it must have been well out of date. Dry bread and smelly fish; the Soviet soldiers weren't given very good food; they were treated like dogs.

As well as the smell of the fish, the breeze would also carry over the sounds of the soldiers talking. Some nights you could hear them shouting at each other, or singing songs, fuelled by cheap vodka and cigarettes. Sometimes the soldiers would stay overnight at some of the farms; sleeping on the floor with their guns. And sometimes you could hear aeroplanes overhead, firing at some unknown target. People would then go and hide amongst the crops; but nobody tried to run away, as there was nowhere to go to – the Germans controlled the west and the Soviets controlled the lands all around us.

Food and goods disappeared from the shops in Ichrovitsa. They said it was being sent to the Soviet Union or to the Red Army. You had to queue for hours if you wanted anything from the shops, or try to barter some of your belongings for other goods. Clothes were not available in shops anymore, so you had to make do and mend the clothes that you had. My mother was always busy, knitting jumpers for us, or helping to sew and mend our clothes.

In Ichrovitsa there was something like an army camp and there were plenty of Soviet soldiers and vehicles there. The soldiers were always stationed on lorries with double machine guns ready to put down any potential uprising.

By the beginning of October 1939, after the Soviets had been here for a few weeks, I stopped going into Ichrovitsa. It didn't feel safe there anymore and there was a lot of violence. Local communists, who had been suppressed by the Polish government before, started to show their heads, and anyone who thought they had been hard done by before was looking to take advantage of the situation to settle old grudges.

The Soviets had taken over all the important buildings. Their soldiers were everywhere and the NKVD secret police too. They set up a local militia, and they put Ukrainians that they trusted, or communists, into all the positions of power. The militia were given the job of helping to maintain law and order and keeping things under control, like managing all the queues for the shops. But I didn't trust them; I knew how those people felt about the Poles, or anyone who wasn't communist.

I felt like I couldn't trust anyone. I heard that Benjamin, the Jewish man who bought chickens from us at the market, had started to help the Soviets, and that some people had become Soviet informants. I heard there was a woman in Ichrovitsa who informed the local militia about her neighbour listening to a foreign radio station. But we couldn't even get independent Polish broadcasts on the wireless any more. All we could hear was Soviet radio, telling us to welcome the Soviets; telling us that the Soviets had come to make life better; that they were not invading, they were just coming to protect people. They tried to make it sound like it would be bloody heaven.

* * *

One day, after the Soviet invasion, I found a Polish army horse in our shed. It had been branded with an army mark. We had lots of horses in the Polish army, and this horse must have run away or its owner been killed. I wondered if it had come from Billy's army. It was so strong and calm – you could go right up to it no problem. People used to say that chestnut horses with a bit of white on the nose were the best and the most lucky, and this one was just like this. We didn't tell the Soviets about it, but somehow they found out anyway and took it away.

On the same day, 6 October 1939, we heard over the radio that the German and Soviet forces had claimed full control over Poland; the Nazis controlled the west of the country and the Soviets the east. A wave of emotions washed over me as I listened to the announcement and tried in vain to process everything that had happened over the past few weeks. I felt numb at the loss of our country and the land and the culture where I had grown up and I felt scared about what the future would hold for us, and what the Germans and Soviets were going to do next. At the same time I felt an incredible sadness and frustration and weakness and anger at my powerlessness to do anything to control what was happening to us.

We were all worried about where Billy was; we hadn't heard any news about him or the home army since he had left and the uncertainty was dreadful. We hadn't expected the Soviets to attack. The whole plan of our army hiding out at the border and playing for time; waiting on France and Britain to come and help; that was based on the Soviets not doing anything.

Had they all been captured by the Soviets? Or had it been even worse?

* * *

All of us were overjoyed when, a few days later, Billy returned home one morning. He had been away for about a month. 'Billy! Oh thank God you are safe!' My mother cried and ran out to greet him as he walked up the path to our house, then threw her arms around him, kissing him on both cheeks, left, right, left, right, over and over again.

'Thank you Jesus and Mary that you are alive! I would go to light a candle in the church but the Soviets have closed the churches down. They say that there is no God when we tell them we want to pray. Do you know that they have forbidden all gatherings, and now only Russian and Ukrainian are the official languages!' The words tumbled out of her.

Billy looked hungry and tired when he came into the house and sat down in the kitchen. My mother fussed about him, getting food ready. The Soviets hadn't left us with much food, but we had been able to hide some things from them. When Billy finished eating, he explained what had happened to him. He had been ordered to the south-east, to the Romanian bridgehead, the hills on the Romanian and Soviet borders. The plan was to hold out there and wait for the French to attack the Germans in the west, as the French had promised they were going to open a western front. But then the Soviets had attacked on 17 September. They had brought almost one million troops and their tanks too. 'I even heard there was a secret agreement between the Nazis and the Soviets,' Billy said, 'to divide Poland between them!'

I wondered whether we could have held out against the Germans with some support from Britain or France. But that support never came, and what chance did we have fighting against both the Soviets and the Germans, caught in a trap between the two of them. On top of that we were having to deal with revolts from Ukrainian nationalists and local communists.

The Polish officers had no choice but to order an emergency evacuation. The army was ordered to evacuate Poland and to reorganize in France. Many of them crossed over the border into Romania and Hungary to then try to make their way on to France, but Billy had decided to come back here. 'Now they're talking about forming an underground army in Poland,' he told us.

In November 1939 we heard that the Soviets had also invaded Finland in the Winter War. It looked like the Soviets were trying to reclaim territory that the Russian Empire had before the First World War. That winter was one of the coldest that anyone could remember. The Soviets had brought their weather with them as well as their soldiers and tanks. The snow piled up high against the side of our house and the rivers froze.

As the turn of the year passed and 1940 started everyone anxiously wondered what the new year would bring.

Chapter 9

Journey to Another Village

Bang-bang-bang. A sudden noise woke me from my sleep one night in February 1940. In my half-awake state I couldn't immediately identify what it was or where it had come from; had I just been dreaming it? But then it came again, a few seconds later.

Bang-bang! My mind was gradually clearing. It was a rhythmic, insistent, thudding noise. The sound was coming from the other room. Someone was knocking on the door of our house. I sat bolt upright in bed, trying to work out what was going on. Then there were shouts from outside. Russian voices! It was the middle of the night, 3:30am. The house was dark and it was dark outside the window. The middle of winter, very cold, with snow lying outside, 10 February 1940.

'Open the door!' came the shout again. 'Hurry up, Polak!'

I rushed to the door of the bedroom and then I could hear the front door being opened from outside, bringing a chill blast of air into the house. Through the door to our living room, I could see a light being turned on and then my father rushing to the front door, still in his night clothes.

'You're not frightened that you don't lock the door?' came the loud, harsh voice again.

Frightened? I was terrified that a Soviet soldier had barged into our house in the middle of the night! Why on earth was he here? What did he want? I knew it couldn't be anything good. Billy, Mietek and Rozia were standing in the dark beside me and we gradually inched our way forward, until we were standing at the entrance to our living room. At our front door was a Soviet officer. It was the same man who had visited before and had taken the survey of our farm.

'Family Kulik?' he said, looking around the room. 'Six of you, yes? Two adults, four children,' and he quickly counted each of us in turn.

My father nodded and began to reach for the tobacco inside his pocket, but then stopped abruptly and my heart jumped with fear, as the officer

Journey to Another Village   31

suddenly pulled out his gun and pointed it at him. 'Stop! Hands up!' he shouted to my father. 'What are you reaching for? Are you armed, comrade?' My father shook his head, his mouth open in shock.

'You need to be careful, comrade,' the officer said. 'Next time you might not be so lucky. Everyone get your hands up and stand against the wall.' He turned around and called outside to another soldier to come inside and search us. Another Soviet soldier carrying a gun with a bayonet entered the room. Then, as he was entering, I noticed someone else standing just outside the front door. It was Benjamin from the market!

'Benjamin!' I called out in surprise before I could stop myself. 'Benjamin, what are you doing here? Why are you helping them? Don't you remember us from the market? You buy the chickens from us; don't you remember?' But Benjamin said nothing and just slowly moved backwards away from the door.

'Quiet, Polak!' the officer yelled, and he pushed me roughly towards the wall. 'And stop that girl crying!' he yelled, pointing at Rozia.

We were almost all in tears; terrified at what was happening. The officer covered us with his gun, while the other soldier searched us for weapons, then searched the house for weapons too; throwing our belongings onto the floor.

When he had finished the officer lowered his gun and looked around the room one more time. 'This house. This farm. It all belongs to the Soviet state. Pack up and get ready to leave. You have half an hour. We'll be back for you then, and you had better be ready.'

* * *

It was hard to concentrate or to think properly in the panic. My mother was sitting on the floor in tears. Mietek and Rozia were standing near her and she reached out and grabbed them, pulling them in close.

I quickly put on my clothes. What were we going to do? What should we take? My mind was a blur in the confusion and shock of what was happening. My father didn't reply for a moment. He stared with wide eyes at my mother and Rozia sobbing on the floor, then at Billy and me, and then at our belongings that the Soviet soldier had dumped on the floor. He opened and closed his mouth a few times, without saying anything. I had never seen my father like this and it made me even more scared.

Should we just run away? Maybe we could get to Romania and then on to France, just like the army? But it was the middle of winter. I doubted that we could make it, and what about Rozia, or Mietek? They weren't strong enough.

Billy, my father and I gathered what we could. We pulled together some bread, filled some cans with water, gathered winter clothes and blankets, salted meat, and some equipment like a kettle. We packed it all into potato sacks. But in the shock and rush of the situation we didn't have time to organise more, and we couldn't think clearly about where we might be going and what we might need.

I was feeling sick with the worry; everything was out of our hands. It felt like we had no control over what was going to happen to us. We were just flotsam and jetsam caught up in a river that was about to overflow and flood.

* * *

The officer and the other soldier came back in half an hour just as they had said. They were on a large wooden sledge in the snow, pulled by two horses. 'Get out of the house!' the officer shouted out from the top of the sledge. 'Get on the sledge. All of you!'

'Where are you taking us?' my father asked, standing at the door.

'Another village in Poland. You'll be very happy there.' The officer gave a humourless laugh and spat on the ground. 'Oh yes, very happy.'

They stared at us from the sledge. Slouched over, slowly fingering their guns in their hands, in their army uniforms with long winter coats and their army hats with the red star, their breath coming in clouds of steam in the cold night air.

Without energy, numbly, we gathered up the belongings that we had piled in the front room. We slowly climbed onto the sledge behind the soldiers; Rozia sitting on my mother's lap. We covered ourselves with the blankets, to try to keep ourselves as warm as we could.

I looked at the soldier and he seemed barely older than me. He had a young face, blond hair, but vacant staring eyes. I wondered where he had come from, what part of the Soviet Union. Maybe Moscow, or the vast empty plains to the east. I wondered whether he wanted to be here, or wanted to be back home with his family; whether he had chosen to come here or had been forced to come.

The officer whipped the horses and we moved off. Leaving behind our farm and our home, under a cold, starry sky, moving across the snow towards Ichrovitsa. Moving towards an unknown future. The only sounds in the still winter air were the sounds of the horses, the sledge and my mother and sister crying.

* * *

They took us to the railway station at Ichrovitsa. When we arrived there were already hundreds of other people there standing in groups, with little piles of their belongings beside them, packed in potato sacks. Old, young, sick and healthy. All looking dazed, shocked and afraid. Some were looking angry.

The officer told us to get off the sledge. We took our belongings and went to join the others on the platform. We tried to talk to them, to find out more information, but nobody knew any better what was happening. We had all been told the same thing, that we were being taken to another part of the country. We all had the same story to tell – we had been woken at midnight, 1am, 3am, by a knock on the door by a Soviet soldier or local militia. We had all been given half an hour, or if you were lucky an hour, to get ready. Then bundled on a sledge and taken here to the railway station.

There was a large train standing beside the platform, merging into the darkness all around. It was the largest train I had ever seen. It had two steam engines, one at each end; one to pull and one to push. Dark smoke was coming out of the chimneys as the furnaces were stoked by the driver. In between the two engines there were about ten or eleven wagons but they were not regular passenger carriages, they were transport wagons like cattle trucks, wooden wagons, with a large door in the middle of each side to allow goods or animals to be taken on or off.

There were lots of Soviet soldiers on the platform and around the train. Some were just standing around in groups, smoking cigarettes, silently watching or talking amongst themselves. There were Soviet guards on the train, between every second wagon, each in a makeshift small guardhouse from where they could look out. There were a handful of soldiers who made their way along the platform, organising people into the train.

Each cattle truck was divided into two levels by a shelf running along its length and most of its width. Big families might get the whole truck to themselves, while smaller families or individuals would have to share a level with others.

A tall soldier, wearing a padded jacket and mittens, made his way over to where we were standing. 'You get on this wagon.' He motioned with his gun to the next wagon down. Its door was open, like a giant black maw waiting to swallow us up.

'Where are we going? What are you doing?' We tried again with the same question that we had been asking ourselves and everyone.

'Another village. You'll be happy.' The same answer that was told to everyone. The gun motioned again to the wagon.

We clambered aboard. We had a whole wagon to ourselves. My parents and two younger siblings went upstairs, while I was downstairs with Billy. There were no seats, no beds, no toilet, no windows. Nothing except a stove on each truck, but no coal to light it with. Our few possessions in their potato sacks were thrown after us by the soldiers. Then they closed the wagon door. Darkness. Total darkness for a few minutes until our eyes became adjusted to it.

We sat there. Silent. Five minutes, ten, half an hour. Who knows how many hours. Voices outside, some crying and screaming in Polish. Shouted replies in Russian. Insistent and intimidating. The metallic and wooden clanging of more wagon doors being closed. Then the train gave one jerk, then another, then, with the third jerk we started moving.

* * *

There were no windows in the wagon. You could peek out through holes between some of the planks of wood. We had to try to block up many of these, as a cold wind would come in through them, but we left a few open so that we could see out. Soon the morning light started to filter in through these gaps. In the early morning, we arrived at the station in Ternopol. We pulled into the station alongside another train that was already there. The station was in shade, with a number of tall trees blocking out the low winter sun. It was a bigger station than the one we had left in Ichrovitsa. A Soviet soldier banged on the wagon door: 'you can collect water here, Polaks!'

They had a big water pump on the platform and people queued to fill up cans, if they had them, or just to take a drink, or wash their face and hands. A soldier accompanied the people at the pump to make sure that no-one escaped. As I looked out on the scene, I thought again about whether we could escape. I had no desire to be taken to God knows where, in a cattle truck like animals. Could we escape while the guards were distracted and keeping an eye on everyone at the water pump?

I looked around. We had pulled up next to the other train. The tracks were close together and it might be possible to jump over to it from our train; or perhaps we could slip behind the trees that were shading the station, when nobody was looking. The Soviet guards were positioned between every second wagon, but if we could get between the two wagons where there was no guard then perhaps they wouldn't see us.

Perhaps Billy and I could then try to join the Polish underground resistance army that we had heard people whispering about – the Armia Krajowa, or the AK. Maybe we could then help them gather intelligence, or weapons, for a future uprising against the Germans and the Soviets. But when I told it to my mother she broke down and started crying. 'Where will Billy and you go? There is nowhere to go. We are surrounded by Soviets and Germans. I don't want to lose you. I don't want you to leave me alone…'

What could we do? Caught between Soviet bullets and Polish tears, we stayed in the wagon and soon the doors were closed again.

At what used to be the border to Soviet Ukraine the train stopped again. The Polish railway tracks were narrower than the Soviet ones, so this train could not run any further. The soldiers and railway workers used cranes and winches to lift the wagons up, then put them on top of a different set of wheels, which could fit on the Soviet gauge. We were going to cross the border. I realised that the Soviets had lied to us; they weren't taking us to another village in Poland. They were taking us to the place they always took their enemies – to Siberia.

* * *

We travelled for mile after mile. Day became night, then became day again. Days began to blur into each other.

As we travelled, the countryside became bleaker and more desolate. We hardly saw anybody or anything – it was almost like a desert. You see a desert with sun in the Sahara – this was like a desert with snow. There were only a few houses every so often. There were forests, as well as some farms which grew potatoes rather than grain, due to the climate. Sometimes you could see oil drills and oil derricks pumping in the distance and I realised that we must be travelling through oil fields.

There were no seats or beds on the wagons. We had to just sit or sleep on the blankets and coats that we had managed to bring with us. It was very cold. We stayed in our clothes the entire way to try to stay warm, and after a couple of days they started to smell. There was no chance for washing, other than your face and hands, which we could wash in the snow when we stopped.

The Soviets always said that we would stop at a nearby station for food, but we never did. We never knew when we would stop, and if we did stop, it was always in the middle of nowhere. There was no station platform and the ground was about six feet below us, so to get off the train we had to clamber down a short iron ladder, made of rungs that were fixed to the side of the wagon.

When we stopped we would try to gather some wood which we would then attempt to burn in the stove on the carriage, to try to keep us warm, or to melt snow for drinking. But it was always cold in the carriage, you could see your breath as you sat on the floor, huddled in clothes and blankets as close to the stove as you could, with cold sharp gusts of air coming in through the holes in the wagon. After a day or two we started to get really hungry, we only had some bread and salted meat with us, and were only given food by the Soviets once during the journey, some beetroot soup, given by the soldiers at one of the stops.

There was no toilet on the wagon. If you had to go to the toilet, you had to just go out the wagon door. You pulled back the wagon door and, if necessary, somebody would hold your hands while you put your backside out the door. Everyone would turn their head away, so as not to look. The outside walls of the wagons were covered in shit. It was an embarrassment, like the damn Soviets were trying to turn us into animals.

At one stop, I saw a small group of people inside one of the carriages ahead, who looked like they were struggling to carry something large towards the wagon doorway. At first I couldn't see clearly what it was, due to the sun reflecting off the snow, but then the sun went behind a cloud and I stood open-mouthed at what I saw.

It was a body! They were throwing a body off the train! I could see it was an old man, with a grey beard, his body rigid and wrapped up in old clothes. The body landed in the snow at the side of the tracks with a thump. The journey was too much for some people and when they died they would just be thrown away like this. I felt the anger and the fear start to rise up in me. What was going to happen to us?! How long are we travelling for? How many are going to die? Are we all going to bloody die on this damn train?

* * *

I lost track of the number of days, but after almost a week of constant travelling we finally pulled into a station and stopped. The name of the station was Murashi. In Russian they have a different alphabet and it was written Мураши in this language. We were ordered off the train by the Soviet guards and then bundled onto lorries.

We travelled in the lorry for another two or three hours, until we arrived at a small town of a few thousand people, which the soldiers called Noshul. We then gathered up our belongings again and made a final trudge through the snow. After about ten kilometres we could see come into view what looked like some kind of camp, made up of wooden barracks and huts surrounded by a high fence. Waiting for us at the entrance was a Soviet soldier. He wore a cap with the red star like the other soldiers, but his was rimmed with a blue band at the top. He was one of the NKVD, the Soviet secret police.

'This is your new home!' he shouted out to us. 'You are fortunate to have been rescued by us from the Germans. We have helped you, and now you will help us. Your only role here is to work. Your only right is the right to work. If you work hard, then you will get more food and you may get a better job. Don't even think about escaping, as you will die or be caught. Look around you – there is nothing there but snow and forest for hundreds of miles. You won't get far. If you try to escape, or do anything bad, you will be sent to the white bears in the north where it is always winter.'

Chapter 10

Siberia

'You Polak bastards better work hard!' It was one of the guards, unsmiling and surly, mocking us as we went on our way to work. 'If you don't work, you don't eat!'

'Haha, you're right,' his colleague laughed. 'But we've got plenty more where that lot came from. These sons of bitches couldn't even defend their own country from the Germans.' He wiped away the snot from his nose with the back of his mitten. 'The Soviet Red Army would never be beaten like that! Work hard or we'll send you to the white bears!'

Everyone aged fifteen or over was sent out to work, so I was sent out with Billy and my father. We worked six days a week, twelve hours a day; early morning until late at night. Sunday was the only day off but no religious occasions were allowed to be celebrated. 'Pray to Stalin!' the guards shouted at us. 'We have smashed the Tsars, and now we will do the same to the Gods. Where was your God to help you in Poland, huh?'

My father warned us not to react. 'Keep your heads down and don't answer back. Don't argue and don't trust anyone here. These gulag camps are rotten to the core.'

The guards were the dregs of the Soviet Union. They got sent here as a punishment. They didn't want to be here either, stuck in the middle of nowhere in Siberia. I heard that one of the guards had accidentally wounded three prisoners, because he didn't know how his gun worked and I had seen another one drunk at his post with a bottle of vodka. Some of the guards had set up a black market with some of the prisoners to get vodka into the camp.

We had travelled about 3,000km to our new gulag home in Siberia. Noshul was located about 1,000km north-east of Moscow, the capital of the Soviet Union. We lived about 10km outside Noshul. The whole area was full of camps, just like ours, made up of long wooden cabins or dormitories; some surrounded by high wooden fences; some patrolled by armed guards and dogs. We were surrounded by a landscape of forests, rivers and snow. Each camp was called a 'quarter' or 'block'. In Russian the word for this was 'kvartal', and was given a number. So there was Kvartal 192, for example, or Kvartal 155, and so on. Each block was full of people that had been brought there against their will from Poland, or from another part of the Soviet Union. There must have been hundreds of thousands, or even millions of people there, spread all over Siberia.

Our camp was made up of three long wooden dorms in this forest, each housing several families. Inside, there wasn't much. Just some wooden beds, which were no more than planks on the floor, and there was no mattress. Our family shared two beds between us. A big family would get three beds and a small family just one bed. There was also one stove in the dormitory, in the corner, which kept us from freezing.

In the camp there were other Polish people from the same village as us, and from neighbouring villages. We had all been taken from our homes on that same night, 10 February, and taken by train up to here. We shared our overcrowded dormitory with five or six other families. There were no walls and no privacy – the husbands used to have to hold up blankets for the women to change behind.

There was a big kitchen next to the buildings, with a cooker and a shared washroom that contained one pipe. You could have a cold bath in a steel bath, and it was possible to get hot water by boiling water on the stove, but people didn't often get this far as they were exhausted after working all day. The toilet was a wooden outhouse and there was no toilet paper so people would clean themselves with water or with snow.

* * *

I was sent to work with my father and Billy, while my mother stayed at the dormitory to look after Mietek and Rozia. We were taken by the guards into the forest to cut down wood. There were silver birch trees all around stretching as far as you could see. There was snow everywhere, sometimes up to our waists and we had to wade through it to get to the trees.

We had arrived in the middle of winter, February 1940, and it was bitterly cold. The temperature would get down to minus 40 degrees Celsius. We had to wear lots of thick layers of clothes in order to try to stay warm. After our arrival we had been provided by the guards with one pair of winter clothes: a pair of trousers, a jacket and shoes, all of which were padded with cotton for warmth.

Our boots were made of a kind of fur which looked a bit like horse hair, that came to the knee. It was so cold that we stuffed our boots with newspaper to try to avoid frostbite. Some people used to nail their shoes to a piece of wood, to substitute for the shoe's sole, when they got worn down. We wore fur hats with flaps that came down over the ears and wound scarves round the rest of our face so that only our eyes would poke out.

We wore mittens, as they were warmer than gloves and you had to be careful not to touch anything with your bare hands. It was so cold that your hand would stick to anything made of metal and then it would rip your skin off when you pulled your hand away.

The foreman of our group was a Russian man called Vladimir. He was about thirty years old and a short man with a pock-marked face. We found out that he was the son of a minor Communist party official in Moscow who had fallen out of favour with Stalin. His father had been executed and the rest of the family had been brought to Siberia. 'The more you work, the more food you will get. But it will never be enough,' Vladimir told us. But he was a good man, he always said we met our quotas even when we didn't.

Each camp had a quota of work which was allocated to it by the Soviet authorities in Moscow. The camp commander needed to ensure this work was completed. 'If he fails in this task, his punishment might be to end up doing your job!' Vladimir said. The guards were always watching, to make sure that we were working.

'Watch out for the blue tops,' Vladimir continued. The blue tops were the NKVD guards, you could tell them by their blue caps. The NKVD officers were sent to work in the gulag when they were convicted of assault, or extortion, or some other crime; or if they were just stupid or useless or drunk; or if they had families that were deemed to be too rich, or too Jewish or came from the wrong ethnic background.

The other guards came from the Soviet army. They had been found guilty of some real or imagined crime in the army, and had been sent here to the gulag for a few years as punishment.

There were also guards who used to be prisoners – Soviet political prisoners, or criminals, thieves or murderers. They worked their way up from the bottom by being well behaved, or discovered how to use this corrupt gulag system to their advantage, maybe by supplying the guards with what they wanted through the black market. And then there were guards who had become prisoners, through being reported by colleagues who disliked them; or for desertion, for drinking, stealing, or losing their weapons.

* * *

The wood we cut down would eventually be used for things like railway sleepers and telephone poles. You had to shovel the snow away from the tree before you could cut it down. The men would cut down the trees, then the boys stripped the branches off using small axes while others helped turn the tree around. If the branches were too big then we had a big saw that we could use to cut them off. We then chained together three or four trees and a horse would drag them along to the road. The Russian horses were small but incredibly strong. The tree trunks would be piled up in pyramid shapes to a height of two or three metres. You had to be careful that the timber did not move while you were on it, as then you could easily be crushed.

These trunks would then be transferred to a large sledge. This was all done by manpower. The central portion of the sledge ran on ice in ditches that had been ploughed out and filled with water, while 'wings' on the sledge helped stabilise it. The sledge was pulled by a kind of tractor, down to a frozen river, where the wood was dumped. The tractor ran on caterpillar tracks, which allowed it to move more easily over the snow and ice and rough ground. The guards told us that once spring came the ice would melt and the logs would float downstream to a saw machine.

On our team there was one man, Adam, who was about twenty years old. He was a clever man, who had been studying at the university in Ternopol and had had a big future ahead of him. We had been working as usual at felling trees; working in a number of squads, each cutting down the silver birches, before trimming off the branches. Each squad worked on its own tree and there were a number working in the same area. You had to be careful, as the trees could sometimes fall in an unexpected direction or at an unexpected time.

Adam had been watching our tree, which we had been working on for a while and which was now close to falling. He had made sure that he was at a safe distance, but had not noticed that another squad's tree was nearby and also close to falling. One of us spotted it starting to go, the wood creaking and cracking as the trunk began to split and slowly topple over. It was falling directly towards where Adam was standing. We all shouted at him to run, but he ran the wrong way. He looked up in panic as he saw what was happening. He gave out a scream that was cut short and drowned out by the noise of the falling tree. When we got to him he was crushed and dead. But the work didn't stop. Quotas had to be met. We had to keep on working. His family were notified and he was buried in an unmarked grave, while we continued working. After this the guards separated the squads more so that there was less danger of a tree falling onto your squad.

* * *

In our free time there was a guard from the NKVD in Noshul who would come to the dormitory and lecture us about how great the Soviet Union was. It was the same guard who had met us when we first arrived at the camp in February. His name was Alexei.

Alexei had been arrested and sent up to Siberia because he had gossiped about an affair that his commanding officer had been having. Once here, he got in more trouble for putting on a foreign radio broadcast to the camp by mistake. He had been taken to court and one of the prisoners had to be a witness for him, to say that it was just an accident.

'We saved you Polaks from the Germans,' Alexei barked out to the dormitory. 'Never forget that. The Soviet Union is the strongest country in the world. You will see!' Looking around the room, he pointed at the pictures of Lenin, Marx and Stalin, that were hung on the wooden walls. 'Thanks to these men, our lives grow better every year in the Soviet Union. Every year we are more happy and more cheerful. We are going to build a Soviet paradise for everyone!'

It didn't feel like a Soviet paradise to be taken from your home to work in Siberia. I was so hungry. I had no damn energy and I was bloody exhausted. I didn't care about a classless society, I just wanted to have a full stomach. I could almost put my fingers right around my arm, and the others were just as bad; you could see all their cheekbones and ribs.

'Your country no longer exists! Where are your British and your French now, huh? Did they come to help you? No! Comrade Stalin is your leader!'

* * *

We were paid in food: bread and potato soup. Every day there was the same food and the soup was more like water than soup. The food was rationed; all the work that we did was piecework, so that the amount of food you got depended on the amount of work that you did, but we were always hungry. We never got paid as much as the Russians who were also working there, and the NKVD secret police got the best rations, like meat and sugar.

For a full twelve hour day of hard manual work we would only get about a kilo of brown Russian bread. Sometimes we tried to cheat – one of us would stand at the front of the line and get the family's ration of bread. Another one of us would wait in the middle of the line and then ask for the bread again when they got to the front – sometimes the baker couldn't remember if he had served that family already or not.

My mother, Mietek and Rozia got even less food. 'You're not doing any work for us,' Alexei said, when they complained to him, 'so why should you eat.' They got a daily ration of just a couple hundred grams of bread and a bowl of watery soup. Mietek and Rozia were too young to work, so they stayed at home with my mother each day; she would look after them, and do our laundry when she could.

I used to dream about my mother's food back in Poland, like the cakes that she used to make, or about kielbasa, or bigos, or slanina. My clothes were baggy and getting worn out and ragged. I could see my body getting thinner and I could start to see more bones sticking out of my body. I felt tired all the time and had a cough.

'So many people are getting sick,' my mother sighed. Her face looked haunted and haggard; she had dark circles under her eyes, and her cheeks were becoming hollowed out. 'It's the cold, you see, and the lack of food. It's wearing people down... wearing them down... Nobody has any energy anymore.' Her eyes began to tear up: 'Your father has a bad cough; I hope it's not tuberculosis.'

I looked around the dormitory room and a row of skinny faces dressed in rags stared back at me, without emotion. 'They say that there is an outbreak of typhoid over at the next camp,' I said to her. 'Or maybe it's cholera or some other disease, I can't remember.'

In Russia they treated the horses better than us, and gave them more food. At least they got as much hay and corn as they wanted; we were just expendable.

After about two or three months in Siberia I started to find it difficult to see when it became dark. As soon as it became twilight, it was like dark curtains came down in front of my eyes, and I couldn't see anything. It was like I was blind. I was incredibly frightened. What was causing this? How would I ever survive if I couldn't see? I knew that the Soviets had no mercy for people that were not useful for them.

I couldn't even find my way back to the dormitory in the evening. Others had to help me back. They told me that there was a local Russian doctor, who lived not far away in Noshul whom I should go to the next day, to see if she could help me.

'Your eyesight has been affected by your bad diet', she told me. 'If you don't get enough vitamins, then you can get night blindness, like this. You'll get better if you eat the right food,' she continued, to my relief. She gave me about a month's supply of liver and told me that I should boil or fry it. Billy used to joke that it was liver from the white bears, but I didn't care, because it gave me my sight back.

Chapter 11

Vassili

After a few weeks I was put to work on the caterpillar and sledge to carry the wood down to the frozen river. We worked in pairs and Vladimir, the foreman of our working group, placed me with Billy.

The engine was powered by wood; small logs of silver birch that had been dried over the summer in sheds. The wood was burnt inside the caterpillar tractor and the gases produced were fed through filters so that you got a high pressure that could drive the machine. Four or five bags of wood were put into the caterpillar's big furnace and then it had to be sealed so that air wouldn't get in and lower the pressure. This furnace would get red-hot and you could feel the heat on your face from it. You could top it up with extra wood if you were running low, but you had to do it quickly so that air didn't get into the boiler.

It could take twelve hours for a journey to the river and back. Once, during a journey to the river, the caterpillar broke down, and Billy and I had to walk back to the camp. It was a long walk and in the winter time in Siberia the days are very short. Soon it started to get dark. We had heard stories about the animals in the forest there, bears and even tigers. The stable hand at the camp had said that tigers once tried to break into the stables and attack the horses; he said he had seen their prints in the snow. Anxiously, we kept lighting matches all the way home to try to frighten off any animals.

Then one day Vladimir said that Billy had to do a different job, so I would need another partner on the caterpillar. He paired me up with a Russian man from our working group called Vassili. Vassili was tall with dark hollows under his eyes. He had cut his hair short to try to avoid getting lice, but it hadn't worked. Vassili used to be one of the guards himself, but had got in trouble after being accused of stealing and trading petrol on the black market and so he had been made a prisoner like us.

'Listen Staszek you need to be careful with Vassili,' my father warned me, with a worried look, as he left to go to his work. 'He's losing his mind. I don't know where he gets the vodka from. Some moonshine vodka from a local farmer maybe. I think he brews his own vodka too with the help of one of the guards, and… just be careful. If he's drunk…'

Vassili was known as a bit of a maniac who took too many risks. Some people became like that, they thought they had lost everything when they were brought to Siberia, so no longer had any care for what they did, for their safety, or for others.

'Staszek!' Vassili called out to me. The two of us were working in an area away from the others. Vassili came up close to me, stumbling over a tree root and grabbed my head between his hands. I could smell alcohol on his breath, as he shoved his blotched red face close to mine. He had a squashed nose and was missing one of his front teeth, which it was said was due to losing a fight with another Russian over a bottle of vodka.

My job was to connect the caterpillar and sledge together, while Vassili reversed the caterpillar slowly back into position, so that I could get them lined up and attached. 'Careful!' I shouted to Vassili, my eyes watering with the cold air and wind, as he revved the engine, and started moving. 'Slow down Vassili!' He was supposed to do this slowly and carefully to give me enough time to move out the way, but he did it far too quickly.

When he reversed back, he accelerated without warning and suddenly trapped my head between the sledge and the caterpillar, crushing it between them. There was an incredible pressure on my head, squeezing it powerfully like a vice from both left and right. I was trapped and I started to panic. I tried to shout out to Vassili to stop, but I could hardly get air into my lungs and the engine noise from the caterpillar was too loud. I tried to move my head, to move it from side to side, or to use my arms and legs to try to lever myself out of the trap, but it was no good. Colours were flashing before my eyes as the pressure grew higher and higher – reds, yellows, greens, and it was like the world was exploding. Then suddenly everything went black.

When I came to, I was lying on the frozen ground, shaking with the cold and the shock. For a few moments I couldn't remember where I was or what had happened. I lost my memory for a bit. I tried to keep calm, to tell myself that it was going to be OK. I stared up at the sky which was a steely grey overcast day with a few isolated snowflakes coming down.

I was lying between the sledge and the caterpillar, which had been separated. Vassili must have eventually heard my shouts, or realised what was happening, but I couldn't hear or see him anywhere. Maybe he had run off, so that he wouldn't get in trouble. I lay there for a few minutes, gradually feeling my head clearing. I was shaking all over with the shock. I cautiously moved my arms and legs; there didn't seem to be anything broken. I felt my head with a trembling hand, and there didn't seem to be any blood. My head was still ringing and I had a terrible headache.

I stood up slowly, but my legs felt weak and my vision started to darken again, and I wondered for a moment if I was going to faint again. 'Vassili!' I shouted, bending over as my legs started shaking again. There was no answer. Then, louder, I shouted again: 'Vassili! damn you, where are you?' Still no answer. I couldn't see anybody nearby and nobody answered my calls. But I knew that there was a camp nearby; it was the camp where Ania, my friend from school, and her family lived. Ania and her family had been taken to Siberia too, and we would sometimes go in and visit them after work.

I left the caterpillar where it was and slowly made my way over in the direction of their camp, my head pounding. Ania and Kasia were out working with their father, but their mother was there, looking after the youngest child. She let me stay there in bed until the afternoon, and I fell asleep, dreaming fitfully about caterpillars and sledges and Soviet guards and, through it all, always the face of Vassili, leering at me out of the dark. But little did I know that this would not be the last that I would see of him.

* * *

Around May and June, the weather started to get slightly warmer. When the snow and ice started thawing, we would cover our boots with galoshes that came to the ankle. There were so many logs on the river in spring time that some people used to try to run across the river on the floating tree trunks.

Alexei, the NKVD guard, came up to our dormitory and started asking around for people who could do other jobs – he wanted people who could work in a blacksmiths to make bolts. Back in Poland my father could make anything, he used to make screws, hoops, wagon wheels and so on, so he volunteered and Billy and I went along to help.

The blacksmiths was down in Noshul and Alexei travelled with us. On the way, he bragged about how the war was going. The Soviet Union had taken over the Baltic states of Estonia, Latvia and Lithuania, as well as parts of Romania, in June 1940. They had also made some gains in Finland, following the Winter War there, although I heard from others that the Soviet army had not found it as easy as they might have liked. Much of this was territory which the Russians had controlled in the past before the First World War and they were eager to try to take it back. In the west, the Nazis had invaded Denmark, Norway, the Netherlands, Belgium and France, and had been parading through the streets of Paris by the summer of 1940. The future seemed bleak.

The blacksmith crew was a mixture of Poles and Russians. There were five men and five boys around the age of Billy and me. Billy helped our father and I was told that I would work with another man, one of the Russians. I had to look twice when he walked into the blacksmiths. Surely it's not him I thought to myself. But it was, it was Vassili who had been brought to work in the blacksmiths too.

In the blacksmiths I pumped the bellows and helped others to beat out the metal with a second hammer. We made lots of things – horseshoes, steel chains, bolts. Vassili hadn't changed. 'Pick up and hand me that bolt, Staszek,' he called out, when he dropped a bolt that he had been hammering. I bent down and almost picked it up, before I felt the heat coming off it. 'It's still burning hot, Vassili!'

'Haha!' he laughed. 'Yes, my clever Polish friend. Haha! Now you can be sure you'll never try to do that again,' he added, indicating to me to use the tongs. The other Russians joined in laughing with him. 'Stupid Polak bastards! No wonder the Germans walked all over you! The Russians would never have let that happen to us. You don't mess with the Russian people; the Russki Narod!'

* * *

After we started working in the blacksmiths, my father, Billy and I left the dormitory in the forest, and went to live in another house about ten kilometres away, just on the outskirts of Noshul. There were ten of us in the house. We slept in wooden beds, which were high off the ground, and had bed covers made of wool. We had to share our beds and I normally shared with Billy. I sometimes shared with my father, but no-one really wanted to share with him as he snored. You could hear him on the other side of the room, snoring like a train.

All the houses were made of wood and the Russians used moss to insulate the gaps. There was also a steel fire in the room, but we were always worried about the house catching fire. We had a stove in the room, with four rings on it for cooking, heated by burning wood underneath. There was also a diesel generator for the lights in the houses, but it didn't work well – it was always breaking down and the lights were really dim.

Every house had a speaker inside which broadcasted the radio, but only Soviet propaganda. Billy and I were always trying to find ways to stop it working as we were fed up listening to it.

After we moved away from the forest dormitory we weren't able to clean our clothes as much, as my mother had always helped with this; we didn't have the time after work to do it ourselves and it was difficult to get hold of soap. We often slept in our clothes, as it was cold, and we ended up getting lice which got into our beds too. The lice were in our clothes and in our hair. We used to hit our clothes with a hammer to try to get rid of the lice. It might help a bit, but they were always there.

The lice were so itchy, we used to scratch all the time – you'd try to scratch your back against anything. My father eventually managed to get hold of some soap from a camp guard when he said that he needed to boil the clothes and sheets. The three of us took all the clothes and blankets to a big boiler in a building nearby to boil them clean and kill the lice. We cut our hair right back to the scalp in uneven clumps, using an old pair of scissors and checked each other to try to make sure that there were no lice left.

The blacksmith work was paid in cash, in roubles and kopeyki. It was better to be paid in cash as you could buy some things in the shops in town. There was a restaurant provided for the workers in the blacksmiths where we could get things like fish soup, bread, potato scones, or potato soup. Sometimes we could get sweets, margarine or sugar and sometimes they gave us half a kilo of potatoes, or maybe tea. The tea was brown and solid and looked like a stock cube. We could sometimes buy eggs, bread, milk and margarine from local Russian farmers or the shops in Noshul, and we would take what we could back up to my mother, Mietek and Rozia, who had even less than us.

It was a bit more food than it had been in the forest, but still not nearly enough and we were hungry all the time. But it was more than just being hungry, it was an overwhelming lack of energy from months of little food, and it was a lack of hope too about how we were ever going to get out of there, when it seemed like the Soviets and the Nazis were taking over all of Europe. I felt like death warmed up some days with barely enough energy to get out of bed and make it to the blacksmiths. I was shuffling around like a skeleton dressed in rags, suffering with a cough that never seemed to fully go away, walking round in a daze, like I was never fully awake.

In order to survive, we had to try to find food from other sources. As the weather got warmer and summer approached, those of us who came from farming backgrounds managed slightly better than those who came from towns, as we knew more about which foods could be gathered and collected in the forests and countryside. Some families supplemented their rations by bartering – they would try to trade some of their belongings with the Russians for food.

There were only about two or three months of summer. The weather could be warmer, maybe 20 degrees Celsius, and some people would go into the forest to look for wild blackcurrants and mushrooms, to try to get more food, but you had to make sure that the Russians didn't catch you as they would take it from you, or make you pay for it.

Potatoes were the main crop in Russia and we used to dig them up and steal them from the collective farms nearby. These farms didn't even bother harvesting properly as they received the same from the Soviet government whatever they did. The farmers would just let lots of the potatoes rot over the winter, and they didn't care if you stole one row or six rows of them. After we stole them we hid the potatoes under our beds. The guards would have found them if they lifted the sheets, but they never did.

Chapter 12

Russki Narod

My mother, Rozia and Mietek continued to stay in the big dormitory in the forest, which was about ten kilometres away from the blacksmiths. They all slept together in the same bed and I used to visit them every second weekend and shared the bed with them.

'Did you see any bears on the way over?' Mietek would always ask, but I never did. I would buy eggs or milk from some of the local Russian farmers and bring them to my mother. I carried the food in a rucksack that I made out of an old potato sack. They were still given hardly any food, as they were not working for the Soviets, and she would cook the eggs on a basic cooker that was in the shared kitchen beside the dormitory.

They were getting skinnier, like all of us. My mother had developed a wheeze when she talked. Lots of people were getting ill. 'Old Mr Wozniak died last week,' my mother told me, lifting an emaciated arm in the direction of the far corner of the dormitory, the ragged sleeves of her clothes falling back towards her elbow. She spoke in short, staccato phrases as if it was an effort.

I had known Mr Wozniak. He hadn't been well for a while, struggling with his breathing. They thought it was maybe tuberculosis. He had died in his sleep; maybe it was for the best. He was from Lviv originally and used to be a policeman. His wife had died a few weeks before him and he seemed to give up the fight after that. Mietek and the youngest Lewandowski boy scavenged some wood to build the coffin. We had known the Lewandowskis from Poland, they lived in the next village and their youngest boy had been a friend of Mietek at school. Mr Wozniak had been buried in the forest. The guards had said we could have the funeral if it didn't affect the work quotas.

Then the Lewandowski boy died himself a few days later. They said he caught tuberculosis from Mr Wozniak when he had been helping to look after him. He had been scavenging wood for a coffin last week then he was getting buried in one a week later. It was such a small one, such a small coffin. His mother had taken it very badly. She had stopped eating entirely. We were the only family in the dormitory that was all still there, all still alive.

'God help us all,' my mother said so softly that it was a struggle to hear her. She looked around, and crossed herself, then started coughing uncontrollably, bending over double and bringing up a lot of phlegm with a rasping breath. 'Do you know they want Mietek and Rozia to go to school here? They say that there is a school for the children. I heard that in the schools here they teach them that there is no God. They teach them to believe only in Stalin. They teach them to betray their parents if they criticise Stalin. In the Soviet Union the parents can't even trust their own children! I'm never going to send them there. Never! I will teach them myself what I can each day.'

I wondered if any of us would be left in the end, if we would ever get out of this place, if anybody would help us. In Siberia, I prayed to God. I prayed every day. I prayed as I thought I'd die. I prayed for food, for warmth, for clean clothes, for rest, for freedom.

* * *

My younger brother, Mietek, died very quickly. It was in September 1940, after we had been in Siberia for about seven months. He had been walking barefoot, as his shoes had worn out, hungry and trying to find some berries in the forest to eat, when he had stood on a piece of wood which had broken off and gone into his foot. My mother had taken the splinter out when he got back to the dormitory, but his foot never seemed to heal. The wood must have been rotten somehow. The cut became infected and began to swell up; it turned red, oozing yellow-green pus. Mietek became weak and feverish, lying sweating on the wooden bed in the dormitory.

My mother and father rushed to bring him by cart to Noshul where there was a hospital, but they couldn't save him. I saw him lying rigid in the hospital, staring up at the hospital ceiling with lifeless blue eyes. His once round face had become hollowed out over the time we had spent in Siberia, cheekbones protruding prominently over sunken cheeks; his brown hair plastered to his sallow forehead in cold sweat.

My mother sat beside him holding his hand in her two hands, her head bowed, tears falling onto the floor, and whispering to herself over and over: 'Oh Jesus, Mary, give me my son back. Don't take away my little boy. Don't take away my little boy!' And I remembered how back in Poland Mietek and I had used to take fruit from our neighbour's tree, and then run away when he chased us and how I had always made him clean out the horses, his nose wrinkled up with the smell. It was only a few years ago, but it seemed like another world and as I looked at his dead body, I wondered whether that would be the fate of all of us; whether we were destined never to get out of this damn prison camp, and to be worked until it was our turn to die too.

My father and some other men made a coffin for him and carried it to the grave. Then they were told to get back to work. In the Soviet Union, if you killed an animal, you were taken to court. If you killed a person, you were told that it didn't matter, there were plenty of them.

* * *

Nobody told me when my mother died.

I don't know why. Maybe they were trying to protect me. Maybe they were too emotional themselves. Too many maybes. I don't know if they even knew themselves really why they did that. It was in the winter of 1940, a month or two after Mietek had died. I only found out later after my brother and father had already buried her. It must have happened quickly, as I had just visited her a week or two before, and she had seemed fine; as fine as anybody could be in that place. I only found out because Vassili asked me one day why I was in the blacksmiths and if I wasn't going to the funeral. By that time it was too late to go, as it was a good distance away.

I had stared at Vassili in disbelief. 'Aren't you going to the funeral?' he had asked, looking at me with surprise. I was taken aback. What on earth was he talking about. Who did we know that had died? There had been plenty, but none in the past few days. I tried to think of some friend, or colleague that had passed away, but none came to mind. 'What funeral?' I asked him. Then a cold wave of shock and fear started to come over me. What was going on? I stared at him. I wanted him to tell me, but I also didn't want him to tell me. And I just wanted to get out of here; this blacksmiths, this town, Russia, the whole rotten lot of it.

'Your mother...' he had finally choked out. 'Your mother's funeral.'

I felt faint. My mind was numb, my legs felt weak. Dizzy. I wished that he was making some kind of sick joke, but I could tell that he wasn't. I hoped that he was mistaken, that he had got information mixed up or been told the wrong thing, but deep down I knew that wasn't the case. I just stood there, frozen. I said nothing. What could I say. I couldn't think. There were no words that could express how I was feeling. All I could feel was this crushing weight on me, this blurry overwhelming numbness of shock and of disbelief that was spreading through my mind and my body. A heavy pain that was in my chest. A lack of energy to do anything, to go anywhere; even to turn my head or sit down. I just stood there. But no tears, not then. At that moment there was only shock.

I can't even tell you what I did the rest of that day. I know I left the blacksmiths, blankly staring, without a word, and I walked into the forest, but I have no memory or recollection of it after that at all.

The tears would come later; along with the anger. 'Damn all of you!' I shouted, day after day, shouted into the empty Russian forest, up to the uncaring sky, to the indifferent wilderness. Shouted out to all the bears and tigers and prisoners and guards that were out there, and the whole Russki Narod, all the Russian people that couldn't hear me. 'Damn the Soviets, this camp! Damn you for not telling me what was happening! Go to hell the whole damn lot of you!'

But then I tried to fight those thoughts, as that way only lay despair and defeat. It was another sure way to the Siberian grave. You just had to focus on getting through one more day, one more task, and try not to think about next week, next month. Or if you did, you had to have faith. Faith that something, anything, somehow would come to save you.

I found out later that there had been a typhoid epidemic in the camps. My mother was buried in an unmarked grave like all the others, in the middle of the woods, with a simple wooden cross. They had struggled to dig the grave in the frozen ground. Buried in a landscape of forests, snow and rivers. And in a landscape of graves. I promised that, after this was all over, if I could ever find it, I would bring her bones back to Poland.

Chapter 13

Roubles and Kopeyki

After my mother died, Rozia came to stay in the house with my father, Billy and me. Through the winter, she just stayed in the house during the day when we went out to work. During the winter of 1940 and into the start of 1941, I feared more and more that we wouldn't ever manage to leave Siberia. The Soviets had taken over the Baltic states and Eastern Poland; the Germans had taken western Poland and had quickly defeated France and other West European countries. The British were coming under intense bombing from the Nazis in the blitz. The United States was staying neutral. Who on earth could come to help us?

Some of the boys at the blacksmiths got to talking with Billy and me about escaping to Finland. They had already stolen a compass and a map. But one of their fathers, who was an old Polish veteran of the First World War told us not to do it. He said that it was too cold in winter time for the journey, and we would need about one month's supply of food – how could we carry it? And how could we get the food anyway without arousing the Soviets' suspicions? The Soviets might then send us to the white bears, and then we'd never get away; and don't forget that the Soviets had invaded Finland before, so why do you think you would be safe there?

When the spring of 1941 came we would sometimes take Rozia down to the river with us. Once she almost fell in amongst the logs that were floating by and my father only just managed to get her out in time. Rozia was only eight years old and the only girl, and everyone tried to look after her. As the spring weather gradually got warmer we decided that we would treat her to some new clothes with the money that we had earned at the blacksmiths. We stood from morning till night, taking turns to wait in line at a shop in Noshul to get her a new frock and clothes. She looked great in them. But in order to help pay for the dress, I had to get my money back from Vassili. I had stupidly lent money to him a few weeks before, when he said he needed help, and now he wasn't paying it back.

He had told me that he would pay me back the next pay day, but he didn't. Nor did he pay me back the one after that.

And I thought back to when I had been left alone with Vassili in the blacksmiths; just me and him and he had put his hands on my shoulders and pushed me back into the corner, and shoved his red face with his squashed nose up close, so that his alcoholic breath made my eyes water. 'Staszek, can you lend me some money? It's just a small amount Staszek. A small insignificant number of roubles and kopeyki. I just need to pay a guard for something he got me. I need it Staszek, just give me it. Give me it!' And his grip on my shoulders had got tighter and tighter.

I confronted him one day in the restaurant, demanding my money back. 'I'll pay you back when I'm good and ready, Polak,' he replied with a snarl, suddenly unfriendly. I lost my cool and hit him in the face with my fist, drawing blood from his nose. All of a sudden, the room fell silent. I could feel everyone looking at me and him. Then my father and Billy were beside me, rushing over and pushing me back, standing between us and I knew that there were going to be problems, because Alexei and the NKVD blue tops had seen us, and were running over.

Alexei stared at Vassili, pointing his finger at his chest. 'Yes, I recognise you. I recognise you. You're the one who has been fighting over the vodka and not meeting the quotas. And if you don't meet the quotas, then I don't meet my quotas either! What the hell are you doing, disturbing our Polish friends?'

Polish friends? I looked at him in confusion. What was going on? He had never called us that before. Why was he being nice? Was it some kind of trick?

But Alexei continued to Vassili. 'You idiot, the Poles fought bravely against the Nazis and now you treat them like this! You were taking money for the vodka I suppose. I know what you get up to – smuggling alcohol into the camp! This is it for you now – I'm going to send you to the white bears!' He shouted to one of the other guards: 'Take him away!' as Vassili was dragged screaming out of the canteen.

* * *

The next day Alexei came round to fix the radio in our house. Tired of the Soviet propaganda, Billy had finally found a way to disable it. Alexei was still being friendly; suspiciously so. 'Comrades, how are you today? You've been working very well, my friends. You must be hungry – just let me know if I can get you more meat?'

He adjusted some of the connections to the speaker and the radio kicked into life again, with the familiar voice coming from the speaker. Then Alexei shook my hand before leaving the house. I sat on the bed still trying to work out why the guards were being nice to us. Offering us extra food? They had never treated us well before. I didn't trust what they might be up to. There had to be something going on. But what?

Then I suddenly heard something on the radio that froze me in shock.

The German pigs have no shame, blared the voice from the radio. *The German pigs and devils have broken their peace treaty with the Soviet Union.*

Then the voice on the radio changed, as the Soviet Foreign Minister Molotov spoke:

Without a declaration of war, German forces fell on our country, attacked our frontiers in many places ... The Red Army and the whole nation will wage a victorious Patriotic War for our beloved country, for honour, for liberty ... Our cause is just. The enemy will be beaten. Victory will be ours!

The Germans had invaded the Soviet Union!

* * *

The Nazis were advancing quickly. By June 1941 they had taken Lviv and Ternopol and all the area where we used to live. They were up in the Baltic States too and almost at Kiev. The Soviets were being pushed back everywhere!

Despite their peace treaty the Nazis and Soviets had never trusted each other. The difficulties of the Soviet army in Finland had emboldened the Nazis, and they had invaded seeking raw materials, living space for Germans and the elimination or enslavement of the Soviets.

As the news spread, the Russians who were working in the blacksmiths beside us became more and more miserable and anxious. We found it hard to sympathise with them after the way that they had treated us. 'You don't understand!' they cried out. 'We'll be drafted into the army or into tank crews to die like cattle! The Soviet army doesn't care about casualties, it just keeps throwing more and more men into the battle! And if we don't fight, then the Germans will come and deport all our families to Siberia.'

'Well, doesn't that sound like what the Soviets did to us,' I replied to them. 'I thought you said the Soviets would never be beaten like that by the Germans! I thought you said that us Poles are stupid bastards and dogs!'

A rumour started to make its way around the camp, a rumour that made my heart leap and that I wanted desperately to believe more than anything, but that I didn't dare to believe. It was a rumour about the possible release of the Poles from the camps! It was said that there had been an agreement between Stalin and the Polish leader, General Sikorski. The Poles would be allowed to form some kind of Polish army to help fight the Germans!

We bombarded Alexei with questions when he came to check that his radio speaker was still working properly, but he wasn't keen to reveal anything. 'Ah, well... you see... I mean, it would be a very dangerous journey to meet up with that army. And of course, not everyone would be able to attempt that journey... we will look after you all very well here... And we can all work well together to meet all of our quotas.'

Well now we know why he's being so nice, I thought to myself. They don't want us to leave and join the Polish army, as then they can't meet their quotas.

I was seventeen and again I was torn between leaving and staying, just like I had been on the train from Poland to Siberia when I hadn't known whether to try to escape or not. On that occasion I had decided to stay. On this occasion I knew that I had to leave; but not everyone could leave. Some were too young, too old, too sick, too weak. My younger sister Rozia was one of these. She was only aged eight and my father needed to stay to look after her.

So, in August 1941 Billy and I decided that we would have to leave without them. There was no definite destination or plan in mind, as no one knew exactly where to meet the Polish army, but the rumours were that everyone was going south to Kazakhstan so we decided to do the same. I had never heard of Kazakhstan, let alone knew where it was or how to get there. But everyone said to go south.

I didn't know what the future would hold, I didn't know where to go, but I knew I couldn't stay like this in Siberia always hungry, always cold, working to exhaustion and always wondering if this day would be my last. I knew that I had to try to help end this war, to help us get back to Poland. But I was torn, I felt like I was abandoning Rozia and my father and I was going to miss them so much.

And they were going to miss us too. As Billy and I were leaving, Rozia ran after us, her brown hair flying behind her in the wind. Down the track from the house she came, crying and shouting 'Staszek, don't go!' She stopped a couple of metres away, and I could see the tears on her face, and her lip trembling as she looked up at us. It was quite a warm summer day and her face was flushed and her large brown eyes anxious.

'Everything is going to be OK. Go to Dad. I'll see you after', I said to her gently. She walked slowly back and stood there beside my father, holding his hand and crying, wearing the new frock, decorated with flowers, that we had stood all day to buy for her. 'Don't worry,' I called out, 'I'll see you soon.' But I knew that wasn't true. I didn't know if I would ever see them again. I had to quickly turn away. I only looked back again when I was far away. I gave a final wave before we turned the corner and then they were lost from view behind the trees.

Chapter 14

Freedom

Billy and I had to walk to the nearest train station in Murashi. It was a long way, almost 100km. It took us about a week to make the journey, but at least it was during the brief Siberian summer so the weather was reasonably comfortable. We didn't have much to carry with us, not much food and just the clothes that we were wearing, but it seemed that the Russians had been told to help the Poles as we found it relatively easy to get help, food and shelter on the way.

At Murashi station we got on a steam train which they said would take us down to Kazakhstan. The train was like the one that had taken us to Siberia from Poland – a cattle truck. Again, there was no toilet and no seats or beds in the carriage. But there was a stove, with a chimney that went out the roof of the wagon. The Soviet soldiers told us that we could collect coal for it at the stations.

There were lots of other Poles on this train too who had left the gulag camps on their own, or in small groups of threes or fours or fives, all talking with each other in hopeful and excited tones about the Polish army, but also uncertain and anxious about where we were going and if we had made the right decision to leave the camps.

I felt a crazy mixture of exhilaration to be leaving Siberia and to be doing something, maybe even helping to free Poland; but sadness at leaving behind my father and Rozia, and anxiety that we might never find the army and even end up in a worse situation than Siberia.

The journey seemed never-ending. As with the train to Siberia, the Soviets always said that they would stop at a nearby station for food but they rarely did. But we did stop often, randomly and for hours at a time, in the middle of nowhere. Stalin wasn't bothered about our time, not while there was a war on. He wasn't bothered about our stomachs either. I was just as damn hungry here as I was in Siberia.

Whenever we stopped we would clamber off the train and go to the nearby fields to see if we could find anything to eat or drink. We would gather water from streams or get cabbages and sugar beet from the fields. When we could, we would cook it on the stove in the train, but we couldn't always get the coal that we needed to boil the water, and then we had to eat the cabbage and sugar beet raw, wiping of the dirt and earth that was still sticking to them. The sugar beet tasted great, but the raw cabbage tasted pretty awful, and they were both terrible for your stomach, and led to really bad diarrhoea which would then get sprayed over the outside of the wagon carriages.

For days after days the train travelled through the endless Russian countryside, past towns and cities that I had never heard of before. We travelled east initially, passing through a city called Perm, winding through the Ural mountains, then turned south at Sverdlovsk, which had formerly been called Yekaterinburg. This was where the Romanovs were executed by the Bolsheviks during the Russian Revolution in 1918, when the communists took over the country from the Tsars.

Then, continuing south, the weather gradually getting warmer, we passed a city called Chkalov and we entered Kazakhstan. We passed into the Kazakh steppes, huge areas of flat, open grasslands, stretching as far as the horizon in every direction. The appearance of the people whom we saw as we passed also began to change as we travelled further east and south. People's complexions became darker, with darker hair and eyes. Some people looked more Asian like the pictures that I had seen in school of Mongolian or Chinese people. Sometimes you could see them in the countryside herding camels, huge animals with two humps, across the plains. The camels were used for transport, for milk, or just as a way to show wealth. When not working, the people clustered around their wood and mudbrick houses or in tents called yurts. The yurts were circular wooden-framed tents, covered with a light brown felt which was decorated with colourful patterns or designs.

Some other Poles joined us on the train along the way. They told us stories of Poles who had been travelling on trains which just had open platforms rather than covered carriages and who, weak from Siberia, had frozen or died from exposure on those open trains, or had died from disease or malnutrition. They didn't know where the Polish army was either, but just told us to keep going south.

During the journey we would play cards or sing songs. We passed other trains heading in the opposite direction, which were carrying Soviet troops going west from Manchuria. The word went round that the Soviet soldiers had been fighting the Japanese in border skirmishes around the far east of the Soviet Union, but were being moved to the west to fight the Germans after Stalin signed a non-aggression pact with Japan in 1941.

In the next wagon to us were Soviet officers who were terrified as they were going to the front. The more terrified they got, the more they would drink vodka. One of the Soviet officers came in drunk to our Polish wagon and started shouting and swearing at us. 'Hey, you Polish dogs, shut up with the singing! You're bloody Polish pigs!'

'I had enough of this Soviet bullshit back in Siberia,' said one of the Poles in our wagon, who was sitting on the floor beside the stove. We had all had enough of it, and when the Soviet officer was going back to his wagon, still shouting and swearing as he staggered along the rocking carriage, we grabbed his arms and legs, opened the door and threw him, yelling, off the train. We all changed wagon at the next station so that we wouldn't get caught.

* * *

On a few occasions the train would stop at stations to change engines. When this happened, we tried to get hold of any food that we could. At the first station we stopped at we tried to get bread. I waited in one queue while Billy and the others from our wagon went to find bread elsewhere. But everyone was desperate for food and, as I was queuing alone, some of the other Poles and Russians waiting behind me started pushing me, trying to bully me and kick me out of the queue.

Fortunately, Billy came back just in time but he hadn't been able to find any bread yet either. He joined me in the queue to help out, but the moment we got to the shop window the Kazakh shopkeeper shouted 'no bread' and slammed the window closed in our faces. We were even more hungry at the next station where we stopped, which was down around the area of the Aral Sea. We couldn't leave empty-handed again; we had to get some food, as my stomach couldn't handle any more raw sugar beet and cabbage.

We decided that we would have to try to play a trick with some sugar that Billy had managed to buy at the station from some locals. We got an empty food tin and filled it up with sand almost to the top but not quite. Then we topped up the last part with the sugar that we had, so that it looked like the whole food tin was full of sugar.

We went over to a Kazakh merchant who was selling some scones; they looked delicious and I was so hungry. We started trying to barter with him – our sugar for some of his scones. We tried to draw out the negotiations for as long as possible. We kept haggling until the train started hooting. We knew that on the third hoot it always started moving, so on the second hoot, we made a quick swap with the merchant and ran onto the train, just as it started to move.

We divided the scones between us, and started to eat; my mouth watering with the smell of the freshly baked scones. 'Hey! Hey!' came the shouts from the platform, as I took my first bite from the scone, which tasted like heaven. I looked out of the wagon door to see the Kazakh running along the platform, shouting at us and waving a knife! He had found out that we had tricked him and he was furious. Billy and I watched him run along the platform, holding his knife up in the air and yelling. For a moment I wondered whether he might catch the train, but he never did.

* * *

At the final station in Kazakhstan we met some other Poles, who said that we should go on to Uzbekistan as the Polish army was now assembling there. We got on the train bound for there, clambering onto another wagon. We didn't bother with train tickets, nobody ever really checked, and if they did we just told them that we were on the way to join the Polish army.

After we got on the train, I wasn't feeling so good. So while we were waiting on the train to leave, I ran to the woods to go to the toilet. I hadn't been feeling well for a few days, due to eating almost nothing but raw sugar beet and cabbage for a while. I had just pulled my trousers down when I heard the train hoot that it was leaving, so I desperately started to run back with my trousers not even belted up, holding them up with one hand. I managed to reach the train just as it was leaving, climbing onto the last carriage as it pulled out of the station.

There was a family in the carriage, sitting in the shadows in the corner; two adults, and an indeterminate number of children. Not moving. In a bundle of rags and blankets. 'Is this the train to Uzbekistan?' I asked them after a few seconds when I caught my breath, 'where the Polish army is assembling?'

The woman answered slowly, in Polish, with a voice that cracked as she spoke. She sat on the floor wearing a headscarf, which framed a thin and lined face, dirty from the days of travel. Her clothes were filthy. She looked up at me with tired eyes. 'No,' she said listlessly, 'we're not going to Uzbekistan.' She looked down again. Nobody else in the carriage said anything.

I started to panic – I was on the wrong train! In my rush to get back from the trees, I must have boarded another train that had been at the station! I had to get off quickly before it picked up too much speed and I was stuck on it until who knows what destination! The train was still picking up speed, but I felt like I could still make it off if I was quick. I went to the door, and climbed down the rungs of the ladder until I was only a couple of feet off the ground. The closer I got to the ground, the faster the train seemed to be moving. If I got injured, I didn't know if I would be able to get any help, but I knew that I had to take the risk.

I spotted a point ahead that looked fairly flat and smooth, so I aimed for that, took a deep breath and jumped. I tried to adjust my fall for the movement of the train, to move my body to compensate for the speed of my movement. When I hit the ground it took my legs away and I fell forwards, rolling over and over in the dirt for a few metres.

I was bumped and bruised after the fall, but fortunately I hadn't hurt myself in any serious way. I got up quickly and started to run back to the station, to get onto the correct train before it left. The station was only about 200 metres away and I could see it in the distance. But when I looked up I couldn't see any train there! Where had it gone? I was confused. Had it left already when I was in the woods? But how had there been time for that?

I turned back again, towards the train that I had just got off, now maybe 100 metres away, the front of the train starting to turn a corner to the right behind a copse of trees. I could see someone leaning out of the train about three carriages from the back. Suddenly I realised that it was Billy! They were on the train. I had been on the right train all along! I shouted after him, but he didn't hear or see me. I started to frantically sprint after the train as fast as I could, but it was picking up too much speed and I didn't have enough energy or strength after Siberia. I held my distance to the train constant, agonisingly, for a couple of hundred metres, but then I started to tire and the train inexorably eased away.

I was alone and lost in Kazakhstan.

Chapter 15

Uzbekistan

I felt a cold sweat wash over me; I was in an unknown country; I didn't know where to go; I didn't have anyone who could help me. Billy was the one who was holding on to most of our money for us! Was I ever going to see him again? Or any of my family? Would I ever be able to find the Polish army? Was I going to be stuck wandering the Soviet Union? For a moment I couldn't think clearly, as my mind started to reel off all the terrible things that could happen.

I stood still, beside the railway tracks, then sank down to my haunches, sitting on the railway line with my head in my hands. *Calm down, Staszek. Calm down!* I told myself, over and over again. Until, eventually I felt my mind start to clear, my heart rate start to lower and my breathing start to calm.

The only thing I could try to do was to travel to Uzbekistan. That was where my brother and the other Poles were heading and where we had last heard that the Polish army was assembling. OK, that's your plan, Staszek. Just keep calm and focus on that, I told myself. Maybe you'll find Billy on the way, or maybe he'll be waiting for you at one of the stations. Just don't give up.

I walked back to the station and managed to get another train about half an hour later that went to Uzbekistan. I didn't know where in Uzbekistan I should go, but the train was travelling to the capital, Tashkent, so I decided that I should go there. This train was better than the ones we had been using before. It was a proper train with beds and seats, and it stopped at proper stations. You could get water at the stations from water pipes.

The train was very busy with people standing and sitting everywhere. Sitting opposite me there was a girl from the Soviet army. She had dark hair and wore a Soviet army uniform of a khaki tunic and skirt with black leather boots. Her tunic was held in place by a brown leather belt with a metallic buckle on which was a star, the symbol of communism. Her tunic buttons displayed the same star.

She was a girl of about my age, her hair was slightly curled and she looked more European, rather than Asian like many of the people in Kazakhstan and Uzbekistan. She smiled at me: 'Would you like to share some of my bread and tomatoes?' Until that point I had never liked tomatoes, but I was so hungry that I ate them all up and even asked for more. The girl was friendly and she told me about Uzbekistan as we travelled; how it had changed so much in the previous fifteen years since the Soviets had taken over. How women used to have to wear long robes that covered their head and body, and a heavy horsehair veil that covered their face when they left the house, but the Soviets had banned that and encouraged women to burn their veils.

I told her that I was travelling to Tashkent. I told her how the Polish army was supposed to be forming in Uzbekistan, but nobody exactly knew where it was and how I was looking for Billy. I wanted so badly to tell her all about my story, just to talk to someone, to make a friend, to tell her how we had been taken from Poland in the middle of the night and sent on a train to Siberia. How we had been forced to work for food, to work to survive. How my brother and mother had become weak and ill and died. How we had been allowed to leave after the Germans invaded, and how I had journeyed with my brother to find the Polish army. But then how I had lost him and now I was here, on my own, and didn't know where to go.

But I was worried about telling her too much. My head told me that it wasn't safe to trust anyone – even a friendly face might have been in the NKVD secret police. I knew that not every Soviet person was bad; some were in similar situations to the Poles, families arrested or separated by the NKVD or losing their homes due to the Nazi invasion or just trying to survive the war, but my experiences had made me distrustful.

'The city of bread. That's what they call Tashkent,' she told me. 'It started when there was a famine in the 1920s after the end of the Russian civil war – people went there to get food. Now they're going again from places like Ukraine after the Nazis invaded,' she added, pointing out all the people on the busy train.

She said that you could buy whatever you wanted in Tashkent and that there were all kinds of food available: shish kebabs; rice *pilaf*, cooked over an open fire and made with pieces of meat, grated carrots and thinly sliced onions; a soup made with mutton and vegetables called *shurpa*;

stuffed dumplings and buns; or *dimlama* stew; as well as raisins and nuts, and colourful spices, laid out in open wicker baskets: yellow saffron, red paprika, brown nutmeg, ginger, black pepper, green dill, rose hips. She said that there were many tea-houses, serving green tea and black tea, or a chilled yoghurt drink mixed with salt, called *ayran*, which was drunk in hot weather.

For centuries Uzbekistan had been at the heart of the Silk Road, a series of trade routes across thousands of miles, along which merchants had carried their goods with horses and camels between China and Europe. The way she described Tashkent, I began to imagine being in an exotic city of plenty, filled with all manner of food, goods and produce, surrounded by people, colours, smells and noises that were all new to me.

We sat together, talking for an hour or two, as the sun gradually set outside. When her station arrived, she gathered her bag onto her lap, and stood up. 'I really hope you find your brother,' she told me. Then added, 'You should arrive in Tashkent in the morning.'

* * *

Tashkent was not what I had expected. It was the biggest city I had ever seen in my life. There were more than one million people living there in 1941 and about half of them were refugees like me.

As the west of the Soviet Union had been invaded by the Nazis, so evacuees from the war zones travelled east to places like Tashkent. Stalin also stripped down factories and relocated them from Russia and Ukraine to Tashkent, in order to keep them safe from the Germans. Tashkent was thousands of kilometres further east and far enough away to be safe from any German air raids. The city was overcrowded, it was incessantly busy and bustling, with people, machinery and equipment constantly arriving on loaded trucks and trains, throughout the day and night. All of the Soviet Union was on the move making its desperate way east. The Soviets had also evacuated thousands of children to Tashkent without their parents. They thought they would be safe there.

I went to the bazaar in the centre of the city, but it wasn't how I had imagined it. There were hundreds of people, waiting in long lines for hours for bread or for fruit and vegetables. They were sold from baskets by women with long dresses and headscarves, with dark eyes, dark hair and sun-tanned round faces; or by men wearing a long shirt, or padded jacket, tied with a sash round their waist and a traditional embroidered cap. It was a daily battle for food and for shelter, and I had little money as Billy had most of it when I lost him in Kazakhstan.

You could see every type of person, from women of Iranian background who might have blue or green eyes, to Russians with blond hair, to children who looked like they came from China, or darker complexioned Tatar or Uzbek men.

Tashkent was a city of small one and two storey houses and tall poplar trees. It was a city of contrasts, of dirt lanes, and steep and narrow alleys, but also canals and bridges and wide streets and squares. On the streets, trams ran alongside donkeys and camels. The climate was dry and sunny. When it was hot, everything was covered in dust, centimetres thick, and it would blow around in the wind and get into your hair and eyes and clothes. But when it rained the dust would turn into a thick mud that would suck in your boots.

There was a huge mosque there called the Tillya Sheikh Mosque. It was a sand-coloured brick building, topped by minarets and turquoise blue domes and made from brightly coloured tiles. According to legend, a lock of hair from the Prophet Muhammad was kept there. People had traditionally gone there to pray on Fridays, but the mosques had been closed by the communist Soviet government, just like they had closed all the Christian Orthodox churches, and they stood silent and empty.

And there was no sign of Billy and no sign of the Polish army. My heart sank. The trail had gone cold; I had no idea where he could be, or where the Polish army could be. I had no idea where to go and Tashkent was not the exotic paradise that I had hoped for. It was a city of hungry refugees, without enough food or places to stay, bursting at the seams, like a leech that had sucked up so much blood it was ready to burst.

* * *

At first I slept in a dump where people threw out the ashes from their fires, as that provided some warmth. When I woke up, my hair and clothes were all black. It was late September 1941 by the time that I arrived in Tashkent. Autumn was beginning and the weather was starting to turn colder. Even though I was further south than Siberia, Tashkent was in the middle of Asia so it would get cold at nights.

At other times, I would sleep at the railway station. I slept below the chairs in the station or hid in the toilets. When the station master came round to lock up at the end of the evening, I would stand on the toilet, so that he wouldn't see me when he looked under the toilet doors. I would then be safely locked in overnight and it was much warmer like this. Every night I prayed to God that He would keep me safe, that He would help me to find some food and help me to keep warm, that He would help me to find Billy and the Polish army.

I tried different ways of hiding each night so that I wouldn't get caught by the station master. The station master would see me again every morning, but I always made up some story for why I was on the platform so early. I never slept in, as some of the train horns were so loud that they would have woken the dead. I wandered around, trying to find out what to do and where to go next. I listened out for any news about my brother, or about where the Polish army was being assembled. But the days passed, and no news came.

I sold my boots for one kilogram of bread. I was so hungry. But it was so cold too and I could hardly feel my feet. I knew I couldn't go barefoot for long, or in my socks, which were full of holes so I went looking for blankets that had been hung out by the local women. I planned to steal them when it was a dark night, and then wrap them round my feet to keep them warm, but in the end I stole the boots of someone who had left them outside on the street.

Then, one day I met another Polish man and his daughter on the platform at the train station. They had also come down from Siberia. He told me that they were heading to a farm just outside Tashkent. They invited me to come with them and I agreed. It was a big collective cotton farm, called a *kolkhoz*. They had been told that they could pick up work at the farm and that there would be accommodation and food.

In those days, there was no private ownership of land in the Soviet Union, just collective farms. Stalin had taken control of all the land in the 1930s to weaken any opposition to him. 'He's a paranoid bugger,' the Polish man told me. The Soviet government decided how much produce would get sold and what the farm workers would get paid for it.

The cotton plants grew in vast fields and were about three feet high. The Uzbeks called the cotton *white gold*, and it was the main crop in Uzbekistan. You had to pick each cotton bud by hand one by one, using your fingers to pull open the hard shell surrounding the cotton, gradually collecting larger handfuls of them and then stuffing them into large white burlap sacks which we hung from our waists. The sharp ends of the hard shell sometimes made your fingers bleed, but you weren't allowed to stain the cotton. It was back-breaking work. You had to stay bent over all day, as the plants were so small, or crawl along on your knees if you got tired. You had to drag the sack behind you, which gradually became heavier and heavier, and might weigh 60 or 70 pounds by the time it was full.

We had an assigned quota of cotton that we had to pick each day, maybe 300 pounds of cotton. We had to empty out our burlap sacks a few times during the day, and all the cotton then got piled up into huge mounds maybe five or six metres high and ten metres wide, which you had to use ladders to climb to the top of. Besides us, there were many other people in the fields, picking the cotton: farm workers, teachers, nurses, children. At times it seemed as if the entire country had been conscripted to help with the cotton harvest.

We picked the cotton from morning to night. When we finished work exhausted in the evening, we stayed in a barn on the farm and were fed on bread and on food that was like canary seed which we boiled. We would eat every single seed that we were given and pick it up from the floor if it fell. We went to bed hungry and tired and woke up hungry and tired; it was barely enough food to survive.

Desperately I began to wonder whether I should have stayed in Siberia with my father and Rozia and whether the Soviets really would have treated us better there.

Chapter 16

The Polish Army

But then news started to spread around the farm that the Polish army was assembling to the west and I decided to leave the farm and try to find them.

The others didn't want to leave the farm as winter was coming, so I travelled on alone. I took the train west, travelling past a city called Samarkand in the direction of a city called Bukhara. The next station where I got off was in a small town of maybe a few hundred people. There, the local police told me that I should wait at this town for further news. They gave me directions to some local people, whom they said would host me while I waited.

I was taken to another barn on another farm. There were two other Poles already there, a husband and wife, and the three of us stayed there while I waited for news. The other two Poles were from Ternopol, the big city near where I was brought up. They told me that they used to be university lecturers, and taught science there before the war.

'So you're looking for the Anders' Army?' the woman asked me. The Anders' Army was the nickname for the Polish army, called after its leader, General Anders. Some people even called him the uncrowned King of Poland in exile.

But the trail had gone cold again. It was hard to get any information about what was happening, and it was hard to get anywhere too. There were not enough trains and too many people travelling – Soviet refugees, Polish refugees, and the Soviet army too. The Soviet army was being moved west, the Poles moving south, and the Soviet factories and millions of Soviet people moving east to escape the Nazis. People sometimes had to stand in line and wait for days for tickets or trains with space, and then the trains went so slowly that it took days to get anywhere.

To pass the time, we used to walk through the town. There was a bazaar in the main square and I was so hungry that I always thought about stealing some food from there and running away, but in the end I thought better of it. If the police had caught me it would be a really bad situation and I might never get to the Polish army.

There was a restaurant in the town staffed by the local Uzbek people. I got bread and tea from them, but I didn't have any money to pay them. I told them that they could claim back the cost from the Polish army, and they told me that I was a damn Pole and not to come back again. When I got back to the barn the two Polish lecturers told me that all the travelling Poles were supposed to get five roubles each day from the government to help support us, but we never did.

On one occasion, I managed to get hold of some vodka from a trader. I carefully took off the seal and the cork and then exchanged the vodka with water. I then managed to sell it on and got some money that way. But it wasn't enough, I was soon out of money again and there wasn't anywhere left that we could get food. I was so hungry and I knew that I couldn't take much more of this. I couldn't even remember anymore how it felt to eat properly, or to feel strong or healthy.

I had been hungry ever since I arrived in bloody Siberia and it hadn't got any better since I left. Jesus, that had been almost two years! Almost two years since we were taken from Poland! Two years of shit! Two years of hunger, illness and no energy and seeing people die. I could just about see all the bones in my body… I prayed to Jesus and Mary and God every day. Why have they done this to us? What did we do to deserve it?

And so, in desperation and hopelessness one day, the three of us killed, cooked and ate a dog, as we were so hungry. It was a dog that we saw on the street; I told myself it was a stray dog. A local man saw what we were doing. He started angrily shouting at us as he came over. 'You bloody Poles, you killed a fucking dog! You're like animals!'

'You never give us any damn food!' I shouted back. 'If you fed us properly, then we wouldn't have to!'

I cried after that; after eating the dog. What are we turning into… it's true what he said, they're turning us into animals… eating dogs… What next…

I was losing hope that I would ever find Billy and the Polish army. I need to find them soon, I thought to myself or I'm going to go crazy or die from hunger, or both. I've been travelling for months since Siberia. My mum and younger brother died there, for fuck's sake! Then I had to leave behind my dad and sister and then I lost my older brother too, and for what? I'm 17 years old, with none of my family, starving and I'm eating fucking dogs. I can't find my brother and I still don't know where the Polish army is…

* * *

But then, just when I felt at my lowest ebb, and that all hope was gone, I heard that the Polish army was assembling nearby, beside a city called Kermine.

It wasn't a long journey on the train, only a few hours, but once I arrived at the station I was told by the police that I had to walk to reach the rendezvous point with the army. The army camp was near the mountains, outside the town. I walked uphill in the direction that I had been shown, but it was getting cold and dark and I was tired. Snow started to fall and as I walked further uphill, it began to lie more thickly on the ground. I saw a big haystack, and wondered whether I could make a hole and sleep in there. I thought it might be more insulated and warmer inside. You could see animal marks round the haystack where they came to eat and sleep.

No one seemed to be around, but when I started walking towards the haystack, someone suddenly appeared out of nowhere and tapped me on my shoulder.

'Where are you going?' he asked me. I explained that I was looking for the Polish army, but it was getting late so I was going to sleep in the haystack. The man shook his head and told me, 'don't sleep there, son; it's too cold, you'll never wake up… There's a village about 2km ahead,' he continued, pointing along the hillside. 'There is an army camp there where you can spend the night; they have a canteen there too.'

I don't know who that man was but maybe he saved my life. I carried on in the dark towards this village with the snow falling harder around me. There was a full moon rising over the hills, which helped to light the way and reflected off the snow. When I reached the village there was indeed a small army camp there and they gave me some bread, soup and Russian tea, as well as blankets to sleep on the floor. It wasn't the main camp and wasn't a place where I could join the army, but after months of searching it was the first sign that I was getting close to my goal. For the first time I felt that maybe I would make it after all; maybe I would be able to find my brother again; maybe I would be able to join the Polish army and get some food and some clothes and shelter and then somehow be able to go back home. Despite my tiredness, I was so excited that I could hardly sleep that night.

I was up early the next morning, my heart racing; could this be the day when I would finally join the Polish army? I didn't want to waste any more time. I got directions and set off as soon as the sun was up. My body was tingling with excitement and anticipation, but also anxiety and nerves; what if the Polish army camp wasn't here after all or what if they didn't want me? The adrenaline started pumping even harder when I saw an army camp come into view in the distance. As I got closer, I could see that the camp consisted of accommodation tents, as well as a kitchen and a store; square tents, maybe five metres on each side, with the roofs secured by ropes fixed into the ground. The camp was close to the mountains with high peaks behind.

When I arrived, I stopped at the edge of the camp, suddenly unsure what I should do or where I should go. There were soldiers moving about helping to set up more tents, and bustling about the camp. I could hear them speaking to each other, with the odd word coming across to me on the breeze; they were speaking in Polish. This must be it! This must be the Polish army camp! I just stood there and watched them for a few minutes, allowing myself for a moment to relax and realise that I had finally made it. I had found the Polish army.

Then, eventually, one of the soldiers saw me. He waved me over with a smile, and told me that he would take me to see the commanding officers in one of the tents. It felt so good to hear his Polish accent. The two officers were middle-aged and dressed smartly in uniforms with neatly trimmed moustaches. They looked me up and down; I was standing there in clothes which were like rags, falling off me as I was so skinny.

They asked me my name and how old I was. I told them, and then I told them that I wanted to join the army. The first officer looked at the other one, and shook his head. 'We'll never be able to get him into the army; he is too young!'

My heart suddenly sank as I stared in shock at this man with his smart moustache; could it really be that I had spent months travelling from Siberia, all around the Soviet Union, looking for the Polish army, and now they were not going to allow me to join because I was too young?! Were they going to send me away? Back to Siberia? I started to feel like I might even be sick; I couldn't stand being sent away! I had seen just a glimmer of hope; a ray of light at the end of the tunnel and now it was all going to be taken away again? Just like that!

No! I couldn't let that happen! I was about to start talking, to argue my case; I was not going to go without a fight – did they have any idea what I had been through, what I had seen? I had seen more by the age of 17 than some people had seen in their whole lives. Did they know what I had lost and risked to get here? That my mother and brother had died; that I had left my father and sister behind, and lost my older brother, all in the hope of finding the Polish army. And I had survived on my own, somehow surviving and making my way here. I know how to use a gun and live off the land from growing up in Poland and isn't that exactly the kind of skills that you want in the army? But now they are sitting there in their smart uniforms with me standing here starving in my rags, and they are saying that they don't want me because I am too young! I was about to open my mouth and start saying all these things, when the first officer began talking again.

'Look, this kid wants to join and we need soldiers. We could add a few years on to his age. Who would know? There is no birth certificate that could ever check it.'

So that's just what they did. When I went to bed that night, I just lay there for a time, staring up at the roof of the tent. I was filled with contented, shocked, disbelieving happiness. I couldn't believe that I had made it; part of me was worried that this was a ruse by the Soviets, that someone would come round at any moment and throw me out. But it was true, more than six months after leaving Siberia, after being lost and alone, hungry and hopeless, I had finally found the Polish army.

* * *

I stayed in the army camp for several months, through the winter of 1941 until spring 1942. I was given a khaki British army uniform made of wool and some supplies like a dixie, which was a metal pot that you could cook food or boil water in. At first they didn't have the right size boots for me. I needed a size 7, and the closest that the store had was size 9, so I was given plimsoll gym shoes instead. I had to take care that the plimsolls didn't get too wet or cold in the snow when I went out of the tent to eat or have a walk.

We were given food every day from the camp kitchen, dishes like stew, often using mutton. They only gave us a little food at first, then slightly more food each day in order to build us up gently. We had been underfed for so long that there was a risk we would get ill if we ate too much too quickly.

But we were so hungry that we couldn't resist; I and a couple of others used to sneak around to the back of the kitchen to gnaw on the bones that the cooks used to dump in barrels, as they still had some meat left on them. Then one day, the officers caught us, and lined us up beside the kitchen and shouted 'You're not animals! You're in the Polish army now! If you want to eat like dogs then we will send you back to Siberia!' The threat was more than enough to make us stop.

It took about two or three weeks for the right size boots to arrive for me. Until then, I was told to wait in my tent, rather than go to exercises with the other soldiers, as the plimsolls weren't suitable for the snow and if I wore boots that were too big for me then I would damage my feet. We were given gentle exercises to gradually build up our strength and stamina and to build discipline. They were exercises like marching, or fitness exercises like star jumps, but I couldn't do many before I became exhausted. We weren't given any rifles yet and I thought to myself that I would be too weak to carry one anyway.

We were given soap and we used it to wash in a nearby stream. When I looked down at myself, I could see all the bones in my body but the soldiers were good to each other as we all knew what we had been through.

I had still not seen Billy or heard any news about him. I asked the camp officer whether he had any records of my brother being in the camp. He came back to me a few days later and told me that he didn't, but that there were other camps and it was possible that Billy might have passed through them.

I stayed in the camp along with several hundred other new Polish recruits. Eventually, once spring had come, in late March 1942, we were told that we would be moving on. 'You'll maybe go by ship,' the officers with the neat moustaches told us, but they didn't tell us the destination. We all got on lorries, then onto a train that took us further west. The journey took us a few days, into another Soviet republic called Turkmenistan, before we arrived at a port on the Caspian Sea called Krasnovodsk.

Chapter 17

The Middle East

We arrived at Krasnovodsk around the end of March 1942. Krasnovodsk was a large fishing port on the eastern shores of the Caspian Sea, where huge cargo ships would dock and make their way across the sea, transporting materials. It was situated on a shoreline between the sea on one side and brown, craggy and treeless hills on the other. Railway lines ran into the port area to help with loading and unloading the ships. There were a mixture of small and large ships, sailing ships and industrial steam ships in the harbour and many refugee camps had sprung up around the port area as people waited to be transported by ship.

About thirty of us were put on a small Soviet steam ship and told that we were to go over the Caspian Sea from the Soviet Union to Persia. The boat was small, packed and overcrowded with people so that it sat very low in the water. I worried whether the ship would even manage to make the journey, or if it would capsize with all the people on it. On the boat we were given some salt herring from a barrel but it made us all so thirsty. Beside the barrel there was a pipe with fresh water, which you could collect with your dixie, but the water ran out before I could get to the front of the queue. I was so thirsty that I even tried to drink the water in the Caspian Sea in the hope that it might not be salty. I attached an army drinking bottle to a rope and lowered it down to the sea. It bounced along on the water as I tried to fill it, but when I tasted it I realised that I couldn't drink it.

It was only an overnight journey and we spent the night on the decks where there was barely enough room to lie down, but it felt so good to know that I was leaving the Soviet Union, to see it disappearing across the sea. 'Good bye Russia!' I shouted towards the disappearing shoreline, 'I hope I never see your Soviet paradise again!' Then I sat down on the deck with my head in my hands and cried with happiness.

The next day we arrived in spring sunshine to the port of Pahlevi on the southern shores of the Caspian Sea. When we arrived at the port, I could see Polish soldiers who were marching properly, three abreast. When the soldiers saw us they threw chocolates to us, shouting 'you don't need to starve anymore!' I broke down again and cried at the soldiers being so kind to us. I sat down on the portside and prayed and I thanked God for bringing me here.

Along the shoreline, I could see many tents, like the ones where I had stayed in the army camp in Uzbekistan. There were scores of them, like a tented city all along the side of the Caspian Sea, made up of medical facilities, toilets, accommodation, kitchens and laundries. But despite all the tents there was still not enough room there for all the refugees. It seemed like there were thousands of refugees in the port, or along the shoreline, or arriving on various boats and ships, so a Polish officer marched the thirty of us through the port to the beach and told us that we would stay there. We didn't have any tents and just slept there with blankets. 'Summertime is coming,' he said, 'so the weather is quite warm, but just be careful where you sleep because of the tide coming in!'

We were fed rice and mince at most of the meals and yet more mutton. The kitchen was next to the beach and had big boilers for cooking the rice and potatoes. The cooks were Indian, and there was a Polish officer beside the kitchen at mealtimes to make sure that there weren't any problems and to help translate. We kept asking for more food, but still weren't allowed. 'Your stomachs are very small after having been underfed for so long,' we were told again and again. 'Look at how thin you are; we can see all your bones. Your stomachs will burst if you eat too much too quickly.' The thirty of us stayed there on the beach for about two or three weeks; we would continue to do some easy gymnastics exercises each day to build up our fitness, but I was still very weak.

One day a captain in the Polish army came to see us. He was around fifty years old, slim and wiry, with blue eyes and light brown hair. He walked with a limp as he had been wounded in the leg in 1939 by the Germans. He lined us up and called out with a gravelly voice, 'Come forward if I call your name.' He called out the names of all the younger ones. About half of the thirty of us were called forward, including me. 'You'll be moving out with me soon,' the captain announced, 'we're going to Iraq.'

In a few days the fifteen of us were loaded onto a lorry and driven by Indian drivers all the way through Persia to Iraq. It was a long journey, almost 1,000km, and the captain had given us some basic supplies of dry biscuits and water to eat and drink. It took a long time, travelling all day and through the night.

It was a spectacular route winding its way up from the Caspian Sea, through valleys, along hillsides, with steep drops below and cliffs rising above, and then through the high Zagros Mountains. The landscape started off green and fertile, but gradually became more desolate as we climbed higher until there was almost nothing growing. The mountains still had snow on the top and it was beautiful when the setting sun shone and reflected off these peaks.

* * *

'We are going to be based at this army camp,' the captain told us when we arrived and got down from the lorry. It was about 6km outside a city called Habbaniyah and about 100km from Baghdad, the capital of Iraq. It was a big camp; the tents were large and had been laid out in rows by Indians. They were all a kind of camouflaged colour – khaki, beige or brown. The Indian army was there too, and there were Indian and Polish cooks and food. It was really like a desert round there, although there were a few palm trees and some scrubby bushes.

The captain, whose name was Kosendiak, explained that our job would be to help process all the Polish refugees coming from Siberia out of the gulags. I had seen hundreds or even thousands of refugees waiting beside the sea at Krasnovodsk, or at Pahlevi, but we expected even more. It had initially been expected that around 40,000 Polish men would come to join the Polish army, but it looked like far more were coming – and not just men, but women and children too.

We had to divide the refugees out amongst the tents, assigning about fifteen or sixteen people to each tent. We first allocated them to the tents at the top of the camp, then worked our way down. The refugees stayed for a maximum of two or three days, and then they would be taken away to other countries in the British Empire, countries like Palestine, India, Uganda, Kenya, or South Africa.

When they arrived, the Polish refugees looked terrible. They were hungry, skinny, dirty and wore poor ragged clothing. They would be taken to an area enclosed by a reed fence, which held about eight showers. There was a large tank which held the water for the shower, which the sun would heat up so the water wasn't too cold. We put a powder disinfectant into the water tank so that when the refugees had a shower, it would kill any lice. Afterwards, we would give them new clothes that we kept in big jute bags; people weren't fussy about fashion or getting the exact fit or length of clothes. Their old clothes were then burnt with diesel.

I always looked out for my brother in case he passed through, but I never saw him and there was no sign of his name in the camp records either. One day, I saw a woman who had been in the same dormitory as my mother and Mietek in Siberia. I didn't go to speak to her initially, as I thought that she might be embarrassed at the way she looked. After she had showered and been given new clothes, she looked so much better that it brought tears to my eyes. I went to talk to her then and asked her about my father and sister, but she hadn't heard anything. She stayed for a few days before she was moved on.

As the days passed, I got healthier and stronger and I started to feel more positive and optimistic about the future. We were given new army clothes – shorts and trousers, underwear, two pairs of shirts – and an army rifle.

As spring turned into summer 1942 the heat in Iraq grew and grew. The sun blazed down every day. I had never experienced heat like it; it was around 45 degrees Celsius or more every day as we sweated our way through all the sweltering summer and it felt like you were standing in front of an open oven door. It could literally take your breath away. We would wear shorts and shirt sleeves, rolled up at the elbow and during the day you would try to stay in the shade as much as possible. It only started to cool down from about 7pm in the evening, and even then only a bit.

A laundry van came around regularly to take away dirty clothes and to give out clean ones. You put your name on your clothes with a special dye so that you would get the right clothes back afterwards. The clothes were taken to Habbaniyah, the main town nearby, to get washed. But if you couldn't wait you could wash your clothes with soap in a nearby ditch that had a stream running through it. You could even make a small pool by blocking the stream a bit, and let your clothes soak overnight if they were really dirty. This water wasn't for drinking though.

The water for drinking, and for the shower, had to be transported from the next village. I went there with an Indian soldier with a wide handlebar moustache, by lorry that had a big tank on the back. There was a pump with a hose at the next village which you used to fill up the tank. The pressure of the water coming out of this hose was so strong that you needed to work in pairs in order to hold it in position. The pump was on a small hill and you could see over the surrounding countryside, over the houses in the village and into their gardens and courtyards. In one of the courtyards I could see a small group of women working, about three or four of them in long robes, tending to the plants. I stood and watched for a while, taking a break after having filled up the water tank.

The next moment I heard a commotion starting down at the house. There was a man down there, screaming and shouting, pointing and gesticulating in my direction. Then, the same man started running out of his house and up the hill towards me, still shouting. What on earth was going on? I looked around but there was nothing and nobody else up on the hill, except me. The man continued running up the hill, he was wearing a long white robe, with sandals, and a red and white checked scarf which covered his head; and as he got closer I could see that he was carrying a knife in his hands.

I had begun to pick up some English from the Indians living in our camp, and I could pick out some of the words which he was shouting. 'I'll kill you!' he screamed. 'I'll kill you for looking at my women!' He waved his knife towards me; his dark eyes were wide, and as he shouted wildly, spittles of saliva came out of his mouth, some of them collecting in his black beard and moustache. I stared back at him, not backing down but keeping a safe distance in case he did anything crazy.

By now my Indian colleague was beside me, talking quickly, remonstrating with the man and trying to calm him down, apologising, telling him that there had been a big mistake; that I was new to Iraq, that I didn't understand the local customs and that I had meant no offence. The man continued shouting for a few minutes then gradually started to calm down. The Indian soldier, still apologising, thanked him for being so understanding about the situation and then led me away by my arm.

Most of the local Arabs were generally pretty friendly though. Sometimes they gave pomegranates to the soldiers for free. There were also Arab shepherds who used to graze their sheep in the countryside near our camp. They sat beside the road smoking tobacco water pipes called hookahs. You could hear the water bubbling as the shepherds took deep inhalations of the smoke, passing the hose around from one to another. Once they offered me a try, but to me it tasted horrible – it was so strong!

I bought lots of sardines and biscuits from the NAAFI which was a shop where you could buy supplies. The NAAFI also sold cigarettes for half price, and I got tins of ham there too which came from Australia; but you had to eat these quickly, as they went off in the heat. To make them last longer, I would put them in the used biscuit or potato tins, surround them with ice which I took from the kitchen, and then bury them in a hole to keep them cooler. It was best to bury them beside the stream as the earth was damp there, or bury them inside the tent where it was shaded.

Sometimes I helped out in the kitchens. Our diet continued to be still more mutton and rice, and we used to stir the mutton mince in the boilers with a shovel as the boilers were so big! We occasionally got dried potatoes in tins. You had to put these into water overnight and they would then suck up all the water and soften up a little. These potatoes were really popular as everyone was getting a bit fed up with rice at every meal.

Whenever potatoes were on the menu the cook kept guard in the kitchen, as some people would try to sneak back for seconds before others had been given anything. At night, we would take it in turns to sleep in the kitchen in order to guard it from animals. You could hear wild dogs howling outside the camp and there were monkeys there too.

Chapter 18

Billy

Ever since I had been given my uniform I always took pride in how I looked. I washed regularly in the stream and made sure I got my laundry done once a week when the truck came. One day, Captain Kosendiak came up to me: 'I've noticed that you are a tidy soldier, Staszek. Would you like to be my batman?'

Being a batman was like being the captain's assistant. It was a good job as you got treated better and could also sometimes be excused from things like exercising, so I accepted enthusiastically. I got paid sixpence extra a day for being the captain's batman. I used to do things like cleaning his shoes, bringing him water, making his bed and laying out his clothes. The batmen would often be around when the officers were talking about important things and we had to make sure that this information remained secret.

I really enjoyed working for Kosendiak. He was well-mannered and educated, and he was kind. As his batman I looked after him but he looked after me too. When he went away to Habbaniyah on business, he would let me sleep in his bed. He used to share out his beer with me too, and would only say 'just leave some for me'. *He's even better to me than my own father,* I thought to myself one day.

Kosendiak had a motorbike which he let me use. It was a big Norton 250cc motorbike. I was crazy about motorbikes in those days and loved to take it out for rides. It got up to a good speed and the dust was really flying behind me when I drove over the sandy desert roads.

Kosendiak said that he wanted to promote me and make me a lance corporal, but I refused. He tried to convince me but I wouldn't change my mind and I even told him that I would leave the army if he tried to force me. I told him that I didn't want others getting jealous and thinking I was getting preferential treatment, and being made a lance corporal only because I was his batman. But the truth was that I was too embarrassed to take the job. You needed to be able to read and write to be a lance corporal in order to write up things like the duty list, but I was worried that I couldn't read and write well enough. I had spent more time on the farm than in the school back in Poland and I had never learnt properly.

All the officers, even majors and generals, used to come for their meals to the restaurant tent in my camp. An older soldier and I would set the table, lay down the paper tablecloth and serve the food. The officers sat on benches at long wooden tables, and each server took one side of the table. The officers would often talk about how the war was going, and about the evacuation of the Polish refugees.

I learned that the Soviets had taken an immense number of Poles to Siberia; it was estimated around one and a half million people! Then, after the Nazi invasion of the Soviet Union, Stalin had agreed with the Polish leader Sikorski that a Polish army could be formed on Soviet soil. General Anders had been released from a Moscow prison and would command the army. The first Polish army camps had been set up to the east of Moscow at Totskoye and Buzuluk. Temperatures there got down to minus 50 degrees Celsius in winter. Some of the men froze to death in their tents.

Other Polish Anders' Army recruitment camps were set up further south in the Soviet Union. The climate was warmer but the diseases were terrible: typhus, cholera, measles, scarlet fever, malaria. There were burial sites of Poles all over Uzbekistan.

The Polish soldiers were poorly equipped; they had to train with wooden rifles, and only got a few ancient uniforms from the Soviets which had belonged originally to the old Imperial Russian or Austrian armies. Other equipment had been promised from the Soviets: trucks, rifles, artillery guns, boots, coats, but it never arrived. Stalin had been pushing for the Poles to join the Soviet war effort against the Nazis, but General Anders resisted. None of the Poles wanted to fight for a country that had invaded Poland and sent us to the gulag in Siberia!

When the Poles refused to fight for the Soviets, Stalin had announced that rations in the Polish army recruitment camps would be cut, and that the numbers of the Polish army would have to be reduced. Many of the Poles used to survive by helping out in the towns and villages; fixing ploughs or axes, building sheds or houses, mending tools. In return, they were paid with food. Then, in March 1942 the British made an agreement with the Soviets that saved the Polish army. The agreement allowed the

My only picture of my mother. This would have been taken when she was still living near Krakow, as evidenced by the expensive clothes.

Habbaniyah, Iraq. I was aged 17 when I arrived at the refugee camp.

Habbaniyah, Iraq. A lot of the refugees, both men and women, signed up for the Polish army, which was nicknamed the Anders' Army. I am at the front left of this picture.

Habbaniyah, Iraq. October 1942, aged 18. Our job in the camp was to help all the Polish refugees who were coming from the Soviet Union. I am at the back left of the group.

Habbaniyah, Iraq. November 1942. The Polish women and girls used to work as nurses or secretaries, or some of them drove trucks. My colleague in the camp really fancied one of them and wanted to take a picture with them.

Scotland, October 1943, aged 19. I had recently qualified as a paratrooper. You can see that I have not yet been in battle from my eagle badge – there is no wreath in the eagle's beak.

1943. Paratrooper training. Around one in ten paratroopers would break an arm or leg when landing.

1943. With one of my friends in the First Polish Independent Parachute Brigade.

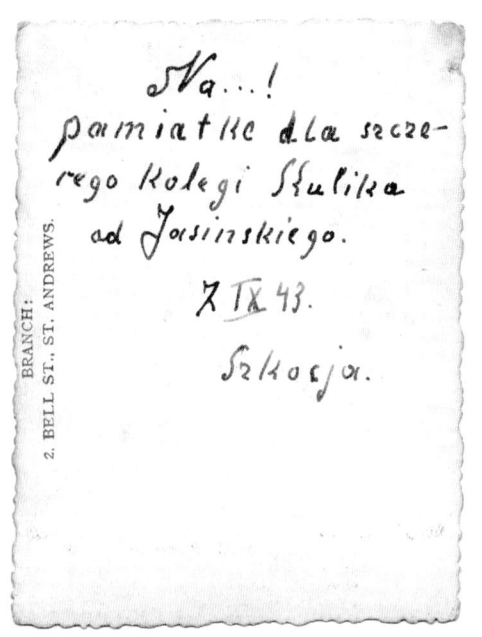

September 1943. 'For the memories, for a dear friend.' In those days it had been a tradition in the brigade to give photos of ourselves to close colleagues and friends as a memento and to write a few words on the back. Bartek had given me such a gift before he was shot.

1943. Seen here at the back right, I was one of the youngest paratroopers in the brigade.

Isa, my future wife.

Isa and I getting a formal photograph together in 1944. I'm not sure why we look so serious!

Granny and Fe, Isa's parents.

A picture of the brigade. Can you find me? I'm on the right side, second row from the front.

Rifle practice. I was a pretty good shot in those days. As well as the rifle, I shot the Bren gun too, and we were also given grenades and a Sten gun.

Recreation. In our free time we played games like volleyball. Often this was section versus section.

I also enjoyed boxing, although my nose never looked quite the same after one sparring session with Bartek!

I always enjoyed riding motorbikes, with and without passengers!

This was the picture which Willem from the Dutch underground gave me of himself and his music group. Willem is in women's clothes, sitting and holding the guitar at the front! Looking at this picture helped lift my mood when I was stuck alone behind enemy lines for weeks.

After returning from Arnhem. There is now a wreath in the beak of the eagle on my badge, which shows that I have taken part in Operation Market Garden.

Isa and I with our first child, Stanley, who was born in 1945.

After the war, I was sent to help occupy Germany as part of the British Army of the Rhine (BAOR). This picture is from 1945. I'm in the middle at the back, in short sleeves. Some of the others used to play the violin or the banjo.

In uniform, in 1946.

1946. BAOR. We were based in a place called Bramsche which was near Osnabruck, beside the Dutch border.

1946. BAOR. My group stayed in dorms in what had been a German army camp. There were thousands of refugees there.

1946. BAOR.

1946. BAOR. Suntanning during some free time in the summer. I was very slim in those days!

There were refugees from Poland, Yugoslavia, Czechoslovakia, and Russia. We helped keep them under control, like the police. There was lots of fighting between different nationalities.

1946. When the weather was nice in the summer we would all go down to one of the local lakes.

Summertime.

BAOR. I'm second from the right, at the back. I was trying to grow a moustache, but it didn't last long as Isa did not like it!

1946. BAOR.

With my suit from Germany, which was made by the tailor in his secret room, in exchange for cigarettes and coffee beans.

My brother Billy, taken in 1947.

With my two children. On the left is Isobel, my daughter, who was born in 1947. On the right is Stanley.

At Boarhills beach, in Scotland.

With Isobel and Stanley again, now a bit older. After settling in Scotland I really enjoyed keeping pigeons and racing them in competitions. I won a number of trophies and medals!

After the war, my father (on the right) remarried. Rozia, my younger sister, is second from the left. They both went back to Poland and lived in a town called Jelenia Gora. This picture is from 1949.

1977. Isa and I are now grandparents. The baby is the author!

1995. Isa and I celebrate our 50th wedding anniversary. It was a wonderful evening with family and friends.

Driel, Netherlands. 2014. Attending the 70th anniversary of Operation Market Garden with the other Polish paratrooper veterans. Isa also attended, and is in the second row.

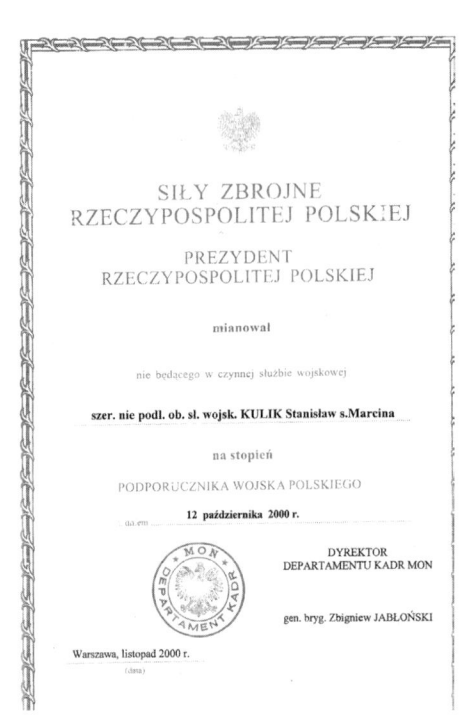

In 2000 I received an honorary promotion to the rank of Second Lieutenant from the Polish Government.

In 2006 the First Polish Independent Parachute Brigade was awarded the Military Order of William. It is the oldest and highest honour of the Netherlands.

I attended the ceremony in The Hague. The award was made by Queen Beatrix of the Netherlands.

Anders' Army and other Polish refugees from the gulags to cross the Caspian Sea and enter British-controlled territory in the Middle East. The Anders' Army would become part of the British Army and would be used to help guard the oil fields in the Middle East.

The Poles came across from the Soviet Union to Persia in two main waves, in March 1942 and August 1942. Not all of them survived the evacuation though; they were just too weak. A few thousand of the refugees died from disease, even after making it over to Persia.

A lot of the evacuees that made it signed up for the Anders' Army. Both men and women and even some children as young as 14. So many Polish children had come, often just on their own, that the younger ones were brought to a city in Persia called Isfahan. It was called the 'City of Polish Children' as so many passed through there. When I heard about all the children coming out of Siberia, it reminded me of Rozia and my father. If other children were making it out then maybe they could too! I decided I would need to add their names to the enquiries in the camp that I regularly made about whether there was any sign of my brother.

One other mystery that remained was where all the Polish officers were. There were far fewer officers joining the Anders' Army than had been expected. Stalin said that they had all gone to China, but it seemed unlikely that this would be the case. Nobody knew the answer, but we would all find out later what had happened to the Polish officers.

* * *

Some of the officers who came for meals in the restaurant tent came from the Polish 5th Division of the Anders' Army, which was a couple of kilometres away from us over the river. The 5th Division was made up of Poles that had come out of Russia. You could hear them training and firing guns from where I stayed. There were both men and women that had enlisted. The Polish women and girls used to work as nurses or secretaries, or some of them drove trucks delivering supplies such as ammunition, petrol and food. We used to serve food to them too and the other server fancied one of them.

I warned him not to get too involved, as we didn't know how long we would be staying in Iraq, and would likely be off somewhere else before long; but he had somehow got hold of a camera, and after work he got me to come with him down to the river to take a photo with some of the army girls that he knew. After we had finished, I looked out across the river towards where the 5th Division were, and then stopped short in surprise at what I saw in the river, my heart in my mouth. There was a person in the river, washing and splashing about who looked very familiar. Could it be? Was that my brother in the river?! It looked just like Billy! I couldn't believe it, not yet. I didn't want to let myself believe it yet, and then be disappointed. *Keep calm* I told myself, but my heart started racing. I excitedly walked closer and yes, I was sure it was him! Sitting down in the river, up to his waist, washing himself, with his clothes in a pile on the river bank!

He hadn't seen me yet, so I decided that I would hide behind one of the bushes nearby and play a joke on him. I crouched down and shouted out 'You better give those balls a good wash!' He looked up, shocked. He looked all around but he couldn't see me, and he couldn't tell where the voice was coming from. He quickly rinsed himself down and started to move towards the bank to pick up his clothes.

I shouted out again: 'Give me all your money!' A look of confusion, then of disbelief started to spread across his face, as he recognised my voice. 'Staszek?' he called out. 'Is that you?'

I stood up from behind the bushes, waving and laughing. His disbelief turned into a smile and then a big grin and then he too started laughing. He pulled his clothes on quickly, and I ran down to meet him at the side of the river. We gave each other huge bear hugs; scarcely able to believe that we had found each other, telling each other that it was a miracle. Yes, it must be a miracle. And then I tried to fight it, but I could feel the tears coming, first gently and then uncontrollably, my body shaking, as I remembered everything that we had been through and how I had spent months searching for him on my own through Kazakhstan and Uzbekistan, and never knowing if I would see him again.

'I thought I might never see you again after the train!' he exclaimed, echoing my thoughts. 'When the train started to move, I didn't know whether you had managed to get on or not, so I didn't know whether I should stay on or get off! I was at the carriage doors, looking out for you, but I couldn't see you!'

He told me how he had gone to Uzbekistan and joined the army there. He had been assigned to the Polish 5th Division. He said that the Polish army even had a bear! Some of the Polish soldiers had found an orphaned bear cub in Persia, named him Wojtek and brought him with them all the way to Iraq. Wojtek was enlisted into the Polish army as a private, but was then promoted to corporal! He got double rations, enjoyed boxing and wrestling with the soldiers and was also rather keen on smoking and drinking!

The British and Polish armies had been stationed in the Middle East to help defend the oil fields in Iraq and Persia from the advancing German forces, and to secure the Allied supply lines up to the Soviet Union. There was a lot of oil in Iraq and beside the river were many oil derricks, although these weren't working at the time. Whoever controlled the oil fields was going to have a big advantage in winning the war.

I asked Billy about our father and Rozia, but he hadn't heard anything about them either; it was impossible to get any news from Siberia. We stayed there for a good few hours, talking about the war and catching up with what had happened to us both. I was so happy to have found Billy again, to have my brother in this strange land. We made sure to meet up whenever we could and we would talk with each other about how we were getting on, what was happening with the war, and what we might do in Poland after the war was all finished.

* * *

I stayed in Iraq for about a year. We helped and assisted thousands of Polish refugees as they made their way out of the Soviet Union. In total, more than 100,000 Polish people had managed to leave the Soviet Union. About one third of them were civilians and the remainder soldiers. I hoped that my father and Rozia might manage to leave too. I looked out for them every day in case they arrived, and checked the camp records for any trace of them whenever I could, but there had been no sign of them.

I also closely followed the news about how the war was going. The Nazis had appeared unbeatable at first. They had invaded North Africa and were pushing further east into the Soviet Union, getting close to the oil fields in Azerbaijan and the Caucasus. But then the tide started turning. The British defeated the Nazis at El Alamein in Egypt in November 1942, and the Nazis became bogged down at Stalingrad, a city in the south of Russia which was turning into a key battleground in the war.

The Nazi air force (Luftwaffe) had reduced most of Stalingrad to rubble but the Soviets still hadn't surrendered. The city was named after Stalin and the Soviets did not want to lose it. They threw everyone they could into the battle, anyone who could carry a rifle, and if they didn't have a rifle they just had to pick up the gun from their dead colleague. They were fighting the Nazis house by house and there were hundreds of thousands dying on both sides. I wondered if any of the Russians from Siberia ended up being taken there; they had been terrified about being drafted into the army.

Then, around January 1943, Kosendiak told us about bad news that had come through from the Soviet Union. Stalin had announced that he was cancelling the agreement with the Poles and the British. Although there were still a lot of Poles left in the Soviet Union, all the remaining Poles would now be considered citizens of the Soviet Union and would not be permitted to leave. I heard the news in shock. What about my father and Rozia?! They hadn't come out of the Soviet Union yet! Did that mean that they would never be allowed to leave?!

Chapter 19

The Mariposa

The closing of the border to refugees meant that there wasn't any more work for us to do in the camp. One day soon after the news, Kosendiak called out the names of the younger soldiers, including me. There were about nine or ten of us. 'I've been given an appointment to the 5th Division, so I will be moving across the river. You're going to be going away. The Allies need people for the air force and navy.'

I had always suspected that I would need to leave Iraq sooner or later, but I was sad to have to go. It had felt good to look after the refugees coming through, and to be looked after myself after my horrible experiences in the Soviet Union. And I was really sorry to be leaving Kosendiak too; he had been so good to me. I would have joined him in the 5th Division if I could have. I didn't know what would lie ahead for me after this.

We had to get a medical where they checked things like our hearing and eyesight, to ensure that we were fit enough to go. I passed. The next morning Kosendiak told us that we would be going to India. It all happened so fast that I realised that I didn't even have time to tell Billy, but I asked Kosendiak if he could try to find Billy and tell him what had happened.

We were first taken by lorry to the nearby village where we used to collect the water, and where the Arab had chased me with the knife. Then we got a train that took us through the Iraqi desert, to a port called Bandar-Shahpur in Persia. We didn't hang about there. From the train we were put straight onto a boat. I wondered what we would be going to do in India, or whether India would just be a short stop before we moved on to somewhere else.

It was quite a small steel steamboat which was manned by a crew of Arab seamen. There were about twenty of us in total on the boat and we slept in bunks that were four-high, from the floor to the ceiling. The only food we got was bread, cheese and jam, as there was no kitchen on board. When I looked over the side of the boat, I could sometimes see fish jumping out of the water alongside. I asked one of the crew what they could be and he told me that they were called flying fish; that they lived in warm waters and that he had even seen them jump into small boats sometimes.

The journey took about five or six days then one morning we saw land on the horizon. We headed towards it, and as we drew closer the details of the shoreline became larger and clearer. It was a big city; there was a large port area, with many ships and buildings clustered at the edge of the sea, and more buildings which stretched back inland behind. There were huge steam ships, as well as small wooden sailboats called dhows that had braved the waters of the Indian Ocean from the Arabian peninsula. As we drew closer still, I could see people bustling around, as well as vehicles, animals and wagons moving back and forth.

A few hundred metres away, at the edge of the water, there was a grand light-brown stone gateway consisting of three sections, each with a small archway in it. The middle section was larger and higher than the others and was topped with four small turrets. Behind and to the left was a wide five-storey building which looked like a palace. It was fronted with rows and rows of windows and was topped with a massive red dome. We were told that these buildings were the Gateway of India, which had been built to commemorate the landing of King George V in India, and the famous and exclusive Taj hotel. We had arrived in Bombay.

* * *

As we got off the ship, we were met by an Indian army officer who led us along the quay towards the port and the city. My senses were hit by an explosion of sound, colour and smells; it was an extreme contrast to the week of quiet that we had had on the ship and was rather disconcerting at first.

There were people everywhere; there were skinny, but deceptively strong men carrying baskets of goods on their heads, or sacks of grain on their shoulders, or pulling by hand huge two-wheeled carts loaded with tins, boxes of food or vegetables. There were carts pulled by oxen, or other cows just wandering around doing as they pleased, wandering in and out of traffic, or eating any food which they found. 'The cows are allowed to do what they like,' the officer explained with a smile, 'as they are considered to be sacred animals by the Indians.'

There were dark-haired Indian women, wearing long, brightly coloured saris: reds, blues, greens. There were homeless people sitting at the side of the road, wearing little but rags, holding out their hands for money or food. There were the smells of petrol fumes, food, animals, dirt and grime. There were the sounds of people shouting, the hum of machinery, the loading and unloading of ships of all different sizes, scores of which waited at anchor in the harbour, or glided in and out, transferring supplies to and from India and around the British Empire.

The army officer brought us to a train which was waiting for us and we were taken out to a British army camp located about 200km northeast of the city. We had to walk the last bit from the train station to the camp. It was a large camp and had facilities for thousands of people to stay there, but at the time we arrived it was quite empty. There were only about twenty of us there.

'A British camp has been here for almost one hundred years, to support the British Empire in India,' the Indian officer explained. He was a Sikh officer; he wore a turban, and had a moustache and long neatly-trimmed beard. The camp was used both as a training camp for new soldiers, and as a transit camp where soldiers who had finished their tour of duty waited for their ship home to arrive. These ships only sailed in winter or spring, so sometimes the soldiers had to wait months and months for the ships, through the summer heat and the monsoon, with little or nothing to do.

'The camp is called Deolali,' the officer continued, 'but many people pronounce it Doolally. You are lucky that the camp is quiet now, but when there are lots of soldiers here it gets very overcrowded. They have to sleep on the ground, and they get bitten by sand fleas. Then you have to be careful for malaria too – it can lead to fevers, sickness and serious illness. The soldiers call it going "doolally" if it all gets too much for them!'

A crew of Indian soldiers ran the camp. They were all Sikhs, and many were called Singh, which meant 'lion' in their language. The Sikhs were a religious group in India, who originally came from a place called the Punjab in the northwest of the country. The Sikhs always carried a curved iron sword or knife called a kirpan, and they also never cut their hair, but instead tied it up under their turban, which was made each morning by wrapping metres and metres of cloth around their head in complex layers.

The Sikh officer showed us to our accommodation, which was in proper huts rather than the tents that we had got used to in Iraq. Inside, all the beds had nets hanging over them, and one of the Indian soldiers told me that it was to keep the mosquitoes away when we were sleeping, that there were lots of mosquitoes in this part of India and it was very important to use the net so that they did not bite you, as then they could give you malaria.

I was exhausted after our long journey and I went to bed early, throwing my clothes in a pile beside my bed, and telling myself that I would sort it all out in the morning. I fell asleep immediately and slept soundly through the night, waking up feeling refreshed in the morning. I awoke to find my clothes folded neatly beside my bed. I was told that an Indian soldier did it and that they also cleaned your boots and made your bed. You had to give them sixpence a week, or two shillings a month in return. It was a new experience for me, in Iraq I had been the one helping out the officers and I had never had anyone help me out like this before.

The chefs were also Indian, and it was the first time that I had tasted Indian food. They made curries, dishes like butter chicken with the meat still on the bone; or biryani, which was a rice dish with vegetables or lamb. There were various kinds of flatbreads, like naan or chapatti. We were never given beef, as that would be offensive to the Hindus, or pork, as that would be offensive to the Muslims. Many Indians were vegetarian and we were also served dishes such as daal, which was made from lentils in a sauce, and which you could mop up with pieces of the flatbread.

There wasn't much to do in the camp. We did some exercises but generally just had leisure time. We never went to Bombay, but I occasionally went for walks around the camp. We were in the country, so there were only some small villages round there. You could see the local people working in the fields, dark-skinned from working in the sun all day. They would use oxen to pull single ploughs through the earth, or would be bent double all day planting or harvesting crops such as rice or wheat.

The villagers made use of everything. The women used to collect the cow and buffalo dung and mould it by hand into pancake shapes, about the size of a large dinner plate. They would then lay these out in the sun to dry, in neatly organised mounds. Once dry, they could burn these as fuel for heat or for cooking.

I never went too far from the camp, as it was a foreign country and I didn't know if it would be safe. All the Indians were friendly, but I had had too many bad experiences in the past few years, and was worried that maybe the locals would think I was a 'rich' soldier and try to rob me. Not that I had much money. I and the other soldiers never got paid while we were in India. We had managed to save some money in Iraq, as there hadn't been much to spend it on, but now our savings went down to nothing.

On one occasion, I went to a nearby town called Nashik, which was one of the holiest places for Hindus in India. Hinduism was the main religion in India and in Nashik there were temples lining the banks of the river; brightly-coloured shrines to different Hindu gods and goddesses that I had never seen or heard of before. The temples were tended by bare-chested Hindu priests wearing flowing robes around their waist which came up to cover their left shoulder.

Hindu worshippers would come to lay garlands of bright orange marigold flowers around the statues of the gods, or to bring offerings such as fruit or incense. There were statues of Krishna, represented as a blue-skinned boy playing the flute; or Ganesh, with a human body and elephant head; or the monkey God, Hanuman, wearing an ornate golden necklace and headdress, with his tail rising up behind him.

Hindu pilgrims would come to bathe in the waters of the Godavari river, which was said to be holy and could help to wash away bad karma. There were holy men, called sadhus, who would walk about naked beside the river, and rub ash over their bodies to symbolise dedicating themselves to the spiritual world. They would survive on donations of food and drink from others and meditate beside the river.

But Nashik was also home to other distractions, such as gambling, gin parlours and brothels. It was said that the reason we didn't receive any wages in India was because the major, who was Polish, gambled away all our wages on roulette.

* * *

After about a month in the camp, we were taken back to Bombay and put on a massive US ship called the SS *Mariposa*. The *Mariposa* had originally been built as a luxury cruise liner back in 1931 and had carried passengers between places like New York City and Cuba, or through the Panama Canal to the Pacific Ocean where it would sail between Los Angeles, Hawaii, Australia and New Zealand. It was famous for being one of the fastest ships in the Pacific.

After the attack on Pearl Harbor by the Japanese in December 1941, the USA had entered the war, and the ship had been requisitioned by the US government, fitted with guns and converted for use as a troop ship. It transported supplies and troop forces around the world, and since its last visit to India six months previously, it had already been to New York City, Rio de Janeiro and the port of Aden in Yemen. It had originally been designed to hold about 700 passengers in its luxury cruise days, but since being used for war transport, this capacity had been increased to over 4,000 troops. There were thousands of people already on the ship when we embarked. On board there were US soldiers, members of the French and British armies, as well as civilians.

The ship was huge and it didn't feel much like a luxury cruise liner by the time we got on. It was almost 200 metres long, with two massive chimneys each four or five metres across, rising high out of the top of the ship. There were about twenty small wooden lifeboats arranged on the top deck, ten on each side. Then below this were three or four floors of cabins, which ran the length of the ship with hundreds of little portholes in the hull.

We left Bombay on 27 February 1943 and were on the ship for weeks. We got a meal once a day. If you got breakfast one day, then the next day you wouldn't get a meal until about 1pm. The meals consisted of bread, a small amount of meat and sometimes egg or bacon. The kitchen and restaurant were in the bottom of the ship which sometimes rocked so much that you had to hold on to your dixie, or it would skid off the table and onto the floor with all your food! Some of the waves in the open sea were massive. I couldn't believe that the ship would get through them – its nose would go right down and be covered by the water.

The soldiers slept separately from the women and the civilians, and just like on the steamboat which had brought us to India, we slept in bunks that were four-high. Every night there was a American guy on the bottom bunk who used to amuse himself by shouting 'don't crap on me!' to another American guy on the top. There were a lot of American soldiers on the ship and I sometimes played dice with them to help pass the time.

Some of the US sailors on the ship could talk perfect Polish as they had Polish parents, and they could also help to translate if we needed to talk with the others.

We played by wagering on the number that you thought would come up on the dice. Some of the soldiers became so desperate that if they ran out of money, they would put in possessions, like their watch, to bet. I managed to win a fair amount of money at this game; maybe $30 or $40. It was like a fortune as I had only earned about £1 per month as Kosendiak's batman! To keep it safe, I wrapped it in my uniform and hid it under my pillow when I went to bed at night. But when I woke in the morning, I was shocked to find that it was gone. During the night someone had cut a hole through my mattress and stolen all the money, just leaving my uniform on the floor. I had never heard or felt anything!

At night I sometimes walked around the deck to get some fresh air. You weren't allowed to light up a cigarette there in case the Japanese saw you; there were said to be Japanese submarines everywhere. We couldn't drop paper, matches or anything into the sea that might give away our position. If you were caught you were court-martialled. The ship had been torpedoed three times before, but had survived – its hull had three steel walls for protection. The torpedoes had got through the outer two layers, but never the third.

We sailed without any escort protection. The *Mariposa* was called one of the 'monsters' – ships so fast that it was thought they could outrun most enemy ships and submarines and therefore needed fewer naval escorts as they sailed around the world. But when I went to bed at night, I still worried we wouldn't survive to the next morning because of all the Japanese submarines. At night, the captain put on all his three engines, and the ship would go fast – the water behind would be frothed up white, and the ship would shake with the speed and the power.

The stern of the ship would snake behind us as we powered through the water, moving from side to side. I asked one of the American soldiers why the captain steered like this and he told me that it was to avoid torpedoes. During the day the captain slowed down to one engine so that they could watch out for submarines. It might have been my imagination, but I felt like we even went in circles sometimes to confuse the Japanese and German submarines, and this contributed to making the journey still longer. During the day, the crew also practised firing all their guns in case of an attack. They had shells and heavy machine guns, and it made an incredible noise when they fired; fortunately, we never had to use the guns for real.

The ship took us first of all to Cape Town in South Africa. It was on the south-west coast of South Africa and over the city towered a strangely shaped mountain called Table Mountain, the top of which was completely flat. We were given a three day pass to visit the city while the ship was being loaded up with food and fuel, although we always had to be back by 7pm. I went into the city with three of the American soldiers that could speak Polish. We spotted a hotel that looked nice and went in, but there was a sign that said that only officers could enter. I turned to leave, but one of the Americans said 'screw them, how will they know we're not officers. We'll just speak Polish and pretend we don't understand them if there's a problem!' So we sat down, brass-necked it and got served food and drink. *These guys don't lack any confidence – are all Americans like this?* I laughed to myself, as the Americans ate and drank, and then proceeded to try to chat up the WREN female navy officers at the next table.

Chapter 20

Scotland

It was raining when we arrived at Liverpool on the west coast of England in the spring of 1943. After our three days of leave in Cape Town, we had set sail again and made our way up the west coast of Africa. The weather had gradually turned cooler as we travelled north, away from the Equator and the tropics, then past North Africa, Portugal and eventually to Britain.

Liverpool was the main link for the UK to Canada and the USA and had been heavily bombed by the Germans a few years before in 1941. You could still see many bombed and burned-out buildings around the city. In those days, Liverpool was the most important port in the UK, and there were miles and miles of quays spreading along the waterfront of the river Mersey. Almost 90 per cent of the materials and equipment that the UK needed for the war came through that port.

Nobody checked passports in those days. We didn't even own passports or any kind of identification. There were no security checks, no immigration officers, we were just taken off the ship and put on a steam train.

As well as me there were about fifteen other Poles travelling on the train. It was an overnight train that took us up to a place called Kinghorn in Scotland, a seaside fishing town on the east coast in a region of the country called Fife. When we arrived at Kinghorn we were taken to the local church where we stayed for a few days. We slept on blankets on the floor, and were brought food. We got soup, a little bit of meat, potatoes, cabbage and one loaf between three men. There was always lots of discussion between us about how to divide the bread equally: 'move the knife a bit to the left…no, my bit's too small…move it more to the right…'

On the third day, a captain came and told us that we were going to join the paratroopers. His name was Kobak. I wasn't keen to be a paratrooper at first – I had always wanted to be an air gunner and I told him so. I wanted to fire the machine guns that would defend the bomber from enemy aircraft. Three others then joined in that they wanted to be air gunners too and not paratroopers. Captain Kobak turned to us and frowned. He was a middle-aged man with sharp blue eyes. He said: 'Look, a Messerschmitt doesn't worry about the pilot, he wants to knock out the air gunners first. Just look at the statistics for air gunner fatalities!'

This captain really tried to convince us to join the paratroopers and not the air force. He took us outside to try on a parachute. We all assembled beside him on a grassy open space which overlooked the sea, which stretched out below us from the base of a small cliff around 20 metres away. I could tell he was trying to make being a paratrooper seem like fun, but we were all dubious. We knew that it was just for show and the reality wasn't like that. 'No, no,' said Kobak, with a nervous smile, 'I'm not trying to convince you,' as the next person was harnessed into the parachute. Then the wind got up and just about blew the man with the parachute out over the cliff. The rest of us had to quickly pull the parachute down, stifling our laughter.

Polish troops had started arriving in Scotland back in 1940. After fighting against the Nazis, they had escaped from Poland when it was invaded by the Soviets and it had become clear there was no longer any chance of victory. They had escaped via Hungary or Romania, or the Baltic states; many initially went to France, but then were brought to the UK after the evacuation from Dunkirk. By the time of my arrival there were around 20,000 Polish soldiers in the UK, and about 3,000 civilians led by the Polish government-in-exile, which had been set up in London, under the leadership of the Polish Prime Minister, General Sikorski.

Some Poles had been put to work protecting Fife and the east coast of Scotland from the threat of Nazi invasion. Fife was important as there was a major airbase at Leuchars and a naval base at Rosyth. They had created a network of beach defences: mines and barbed wire; huge concrete blocks called the 'dragon's teeth', designed to stop German landing craft and tanks; machine gun emplacements and observation posts along the Fife coastline. They even used sandbags to build defensive mounds over the famous Old Course golf course in St Andrews.

Polish pilots had fought alongside the RAF to win the Battle of Britain, an air force battle to control the skies over London and the south of England. Other Poles had fought to try to liberate Norway alongside the British, French and Norwegians.

The paratroopers were officially known as the 1st Independent Polish Parachute Brigade. It was based in a town called Leven just a few miles away, and in the surrounding areas on the east coast of Scotland. It had been formed back in 1941 after the threat of Nazi invasion from Norway receded. Initially there had only been about 500 in the brigade, but the numbers had been increasing as evacuees from the Soviet gulags arrived in the UK and joined up.

Kobak really wanted us to join the paratroopers. He told us that the commanding officer was Polish, Colonel Stanisław Sosabowski, who was very experienced and had fought the Russians in the First World War. He told us that the brigade was independent of British command and answered only to the Polish government-in-exile, and the brigade was going to liberate Poland by parachuting into Warsaw when the time was right to support an uprising of the Polish underground army against the Germans.

When the captain finished speaking to us, we told him we would think about it and would wait to hear what the air force said. But nobody from the air force came to visit us, and overnight we all spoke about what we should do. The next day we decided to change our minds. We all joined the paratroopers.

* * *

We were then taken by train to Leven. We were split up on arrival and some of us were taken to the brigade commander's office. There we were given a jute fibre bag which had a second uniform and some dixies in it. The uniform was a standard British one – khaki-coloured, with rimless parachute helmets onto which we drew our own Polish eagle insignia in yellow. On our jacket lapels we had silver-coloured diamonds, outlined in yellow trim with silver parachutes. Our beret was grey, which was in contrast to the maroon colour of the British paratroopers.

The commander's office then gave us tickets for the bus to Elie which was about ten miles further round the coast, in an area that they called the East Neuk. The East Neuk was home to a number of traditional fishing villages that stretched along the coast from Elie and Earlsferry in the south, up through St Monans, Pittenweem, Anstruther, to Crail in the north. The road wound its way over an undulating landscape, past farms and fields, green crops just starting to poke their heads out of the dark earth as spring progressed. There were small copses of trees, beech hedges and dry stone walls running alongside the road.

When we got to Elie, we went to the brigade office and I was assigned to the 9th Company, 3rd Battalion. The brigade had been divided into three different battalions, each of which was then further divided into three companies, so that there were nine companies in total, each under the command of a captain. There were even smaller groups within the companies, which were called sections and as well as the paratroopers there were also engineers, artillery batteries and medical companies within the brigade.

A sergeant soon came up to me: 'One of the captains has asked you to help him and be his batman.' But I told him that I had just arrived and didn't know anyone, and didn't want to be batman to someone that I had never met. The sergeant went away, but then came back a second time a few minutes later. 'Don't you understand that this is an honour?!' he said to me in exasperation. But I still refused and so the captain then moved me to the 10th Company, 3rd Battalion. The rumour was that the 10th Company was a smaller company where soldiers were sent for disciplinary reasons.

The 9th Company was moved away from Elie, but the 10th Company stayed in the town. We were billeted in various places around Elie and Earlsferry, two small towns that were so close together that they ran into each other, and you couldn't really tell where one ended and the other began. Some of us were billeted in Earlsferry House, others at Rockliffe House or Earlsknowe and still others at the Beach, Queen's and Golf Hotels. Some also found accommodation in the homes of local people and, when extra accommodation was needed, additional wooden buildings were built on the golf course behind the Golf Hotel. My section was billeted in a large house called The Marne.

The Marne was one of the 'mansion' houses in Earlsferry. It was an imposing grey-stone building with high ceilings and bay windows which had tape criss-crossed over them to prevent people being hurt by shards of broken glass, in the event of the Germans dropping bombs. It stood in a large garden on a high elevation looking over the water of the Firth of Forth. Being so close to the water, there were always lots of seagulls, and they used to wake me up early in the morning with their calling as they circled in the air or sat on the chimneys of the houses.

* * *

There were about twenty-five of us in the 10th Company. Most of the others had come through the camps in Siberia, just like me. The officers had come to Britain in different ways. The others in my section were a nice crowd. I shared a room in the Marne with three others – Yitzhak, Jurek and Mietek. Yitzhak used to sleep above me in the bunk. We called Mietek 'Big Mietek' as he was about six feet tall, which was tall for a Polish man in those days, and broad. In the other room was Andrzej and a lance corporal called Bartek.

Big Mietek became my best friend in the brigade. He was from the east of Poland and also from near Ternopol. Like me he was from a big family and was the oldest of nine children. At first, I found it difficult that he had the same name as my brother who had died in Siberia, as it brought back a lot of memories, but over time I became glad that if anybody was to share his name it would be my best friend in the brigade.

Big Mietek had been taken to a different camp in Siberia in February 1940. His mother and father had both died there as well as his two sisters. But despite all these experiences he was still a gentle giant; he could have crushed you with his size, and he was a tough paratrooper when he needed to be, but he was a big softie really. I liked his company. He was a good-natured man with a deep rolling laugh and as happy as could be with just a fish supper and a beer.

One of the officers in our battalion was called Richard Tice. He was from the USA but had volunteered to join our brigade to help with the war effort. He couldn't speak Polish when he first joined, but he was learning. He used to say that Poles like Tadeusz Kosciuszko had helped the Americans in their war of independence so now he wanted to return the favour. He was made a lieutenant.

The kitchen was at the back of the house and breakfast was at 7:30am. We generally had white bread, jam and cheese. We sometimes had an egg, which was always boiled, as that was easier to cook for larger numbers of people. We also had a blue cheese, a bit like a Stilton. Hardly anybody ever ate it as we had never seen anything like that before!

The kitchen would deliver food to us if we were out exercising. For dinner we often had soup, then meat which would be mince or in a stew. Sometimes there was bacon, boiled ham, corned beef or a dried biscuit. 'That bloody biscuit is hard enough to break your teeth!' Yitzhak exclaimed, biting into one. 'Hey Staszek, do you want my boiled ham? I'm not very fond of it.'

Yitzhak had been taken with his family by the Soviets in 1940 from Poland to Kazakhstan, where they had shared a mud hut with two Kazakh families and had been forced to work on a collective farm. Both Yitzhak's parents had died from typhus before he had managed to make his way out via Persia and Iraq. Yitzhak never ate any of the ham or the bacon, as he was Jewish, although he never spoke about it and tried to keep it secret. 'Just don't tell anyone, OK Staszek?' he told me one day.

Don't get me wrong, there were plenty of good men in the brigade; everyone in our section was fine, but I had heard rumours about some of the men in the other sections. When we heard on the radio about how the Nazis were trying to exterminate the Jews, I was told that some of the men in another section had been saying that they would like to finish the job after the war.

We were given three meals a day, but they weren't big meals and we were often still hungry after all the exercise, so we would go and buy other food from some of the local stores. There was a nice bakery in Elie, called Boullet's Bakery, which was situated in a small cottage around the corner. We quite often got bread from there – we would all give some money to one person from the section, who would then go along with a big jute sack and collect loaves for us all. When we put the fresh bread into the sack it used to scrunch up like a concertina. A lady called Minnie worked in this bakery and was very good to the Polish soldiers. She was one of the local people who lived along the coast in the area around the East Neuk, who were called Coasters. She was good-looking and married and we always used to have a joke with her and tease her.

It was the same arrangement at the chippie – one person would gather all the money together, then go in and get six fish suppers for all our section. There was always a long line outside the chippie, as it was one of the foods that wasn't rationed. The cook used to just put all the six fish and chips together in one big piece of paper. When we got it back to the house we would open it up on the table and share it between us.

Soon after my arrival, in April 1943, news swept through the brigade that had everyone talking angrily. The Nazis said that they had found mass graves in a place called Katyn, when they invaded the Soviet Union.

They said that they had found the bodies of 20,000 people there – bodies of Polish officers!

'It's bloody Stalin!' big Mietek told me, and he was right. Stalin was scared of anybody who might be a threat. He wanted to bring the Polish army to its knees and make sure that there was nobody to lead it. That explained why there had been so few Polish officers joining the army when we were in the Middle East. And every time that he had been asked where all the Polish officers were, Stalin had said that they were all safe and had gone to Manchuria in China when all the while he knew that he had executed them.

And now we're supposed to be allies with the Soviets?! I thought to myself.

* * *

I used to go to the church in Elie on Sundays for the services. I went with Jurek, a French-Polish paratrooper in my section. He had been born and lived in France but had Polish parents. When France was invaded, he first went to join the French army, then transferred to the Polish army.

The church was sparsely decorated inside, in contrast to the Catholic and Orthodox churches that I had been used to. The minister of the church told me that it was an old church from the seventeenth century, and was a Protestant church, which was the main religion in Scotland. Scotland had used to be Catholic, like Poland, but hundreds of years ago there had been the Protestant Reformation. Things had turned violent and there had been battles between armies supporting the Catholic church and forces supporting the Protestants.

'But I don't mind that you're Catholic, and I'm Protestant,' the minister added, after one of the services. 'There is just one God, and more than one route up the hill to meet him. Here, I've got something for you,' and he gave me a picture of Our Lady of Czestochowa, one of the most holy Polish religious icons. It was a picture of a dark-skinned Virgin Mary, holding the baby Jesus, both wearing ornate robes and surrounded by golden haloes. I stuck the picture on card so that it was stronger and I carried it with me during all of the war in my pocket. I told my comrades that if I kicked the bucket, they should bury it with me. Maybe it brought me good luck, but I don't know about God and I don't know if God looked out for me; whether he was Catholic, Protestant or whatever.

Chapter 21

Paratrooper Training

We had our first paratrooper training in Upper Largo which was a town near Elie about five miles along the coast. The parachute brigade had taken over a grand house there, called Largo House, as its headquarters. It almost looked like a stately home or a palace and an assault course had been set up in its large grounds. The assault course was nicknamed the Monkey Grove because the training involved us swinging, climbing or jumping between the trees, just like monkeys. At the gates to the grounds, the gate pillars were each topped with a large sculpture of a Polish eagle, and there was a painted sign that said 'If you are looking for death you have come to the right place – abandon hope all you who enter here.'

The exercises were designed to build our strength, agility and the skills we would need to be a paratrooper. Kobak called out to us as we lined up in front of him in the grounds of Largo House: 'Our brigade leader Sosabowski himself trained to be a paratrooper at fifty years of age, and he said that within two weeks of this training his stomach got smaller and his lungs got bigger!'

There was one exercise on a swing where you swung back and forth, and then had to jump off when Kobak yelled. You always had to time it correctly and manage to land softly on your feet. Another exercise involved being sent up on a kind of trapeze to a height of about five metres, and then being suddenly dropped without warning; you never knew if you were going to be dropped forwards or backwards. Or we would have to climb ropes or pull ourselves across on two parallel ropes, suspended high up between trees, or cross balance beams, or run and sprint against each other, or swing ourselves across gullies on ropes.

We would also practise how to land from height by jumping from gradually higher platforms, as well as doing forward rolls over obstacles, and vaulting or somersaulting over pommel horses, or over high wooden walls. The only protection that we had were some mattresses or blankets.

At the end of the day, I didn't know if my stomach was any smaller, but I could hardly stand!

Some days we were taken by lorry to another town called Leslie where we trained inside what looked like an old factory. We had to walk along a narrow ledge against the wall, about five metres high, from one side of the building to the other. We also had to walk along a thick plank that was only about six inches wide, but was four metres high and ten metres long. It wasn't against the wall, but was in the middle of the building. We all looked up apprehensively. Kobak said: 'I'll do it first. If I'm not afraid, there's no reason for you to be afraid. You'll do it without kit, but you won't be tied onto anything. If you fall, it's your neck. We'll train you to do it because you might have to do it for real later.'

We had to walk along the ledge with our backs to the wall and our feet slightly angled, slowly edging our way along with palms sweating and every part of our body pressed back against the wall as much as we could. We always had to look up, never down, as that could make us lose our balance. After the first attempt my hands were shaking, but Kobak made us do it again and again and each time it got easier and faster.

Within a week or so, we were taken to the next stage of training which was the parachute tower. It was located about a mile away in Lundin Links and we were taken there about twice a week. It was a huge tower made from scaffolding about thirty metres high. You had to climb a long ladder to the top, which snaked back and forth, gradually getting higher and higher. We were all scared when we got to the top. 'It's normal to be afraid!' Kobak called out. 'Sosabowski only wants men who can master their fear! Some of you may find that you can't handle the height and can't jump. There is no shame in that – we will send you on to another unit.'

One at a time we were then put into a parachute harness, with the parachute above us, already opened. But the parachute was just a dummy, for show, as it couldn't slow you down much over a distance of 100 feet. The top of the parachute was attached to a cable which Kobak could release when he wanted, and which would then cause you to drop down.

Captain Kobak would shout 'attention!', so you knew to get ready and then he would drop you down. He dropped us slowly at first, maybe half speed, then faster the next time, and after two or three weeks at full speed. The instructor could stop the cable halfway, or whenever he pleased, in order to correct any mistakes that we might have been making. There was sand at the bottom which cushioned the drop somewhat. You had to keep your feet and arms together and then roll on landing to reduce the impact forces. When you went down at full speed, you went like a bullet. It was like jumping from a lorry at thirty miles per hour.

After a few weeks we were assessed by our instructors. If we received any negative scores then we had to repeat the whole training, but if you passed then you would be sent to Ringway aerodrome in Manchester to complete your training.

* * *

Ringway had been the centre for RAF training of paratroopers since 1940. The training there lasted for about four weeks. When we arrived, in May 1943, we were first taken on a tour of the hangars where most of the training on the ground would take place. A young officer took us to one of the packing halls and introduced us to one of the ladies from the women's auxiliary air force who packed the parachutes. She stood under a sign that said 'remember every man's life depends upon every parachute you pack.'

'The parachute is very safe and therefore doesn't need a reserve chute,' the officer continued. I looked at Big Mietek, standing beside me and raised my eyebrows. He gave a slight smile and shrugged.

When the parachute was deployed, it would be over 7 metres across. It would slow us down a good bit, but we would still be going fast, so we had to learn how to use it properly and how to land properly. 'Almost every tenth jumper breaks an arm or a leg,' the officer told us.

At first our training was on the ground and we continued training to jump from the scaffold. The instructors told us that you had to start easy like this, as when you are up in a plane, the space and distance beneath you is so frightening that you just wouldn't do it. The next stage of the training was at nearby Tatton Park, where we were told that we would use a parachute for the first time and would drop from a balloon.

'You'll get your parachutes anonymously', the instructor told us, as we waited anxiously outside the packing room. He pointed over towards the wall, 'they'll come out the chute over there from the packing room. It's done anonymously so that the packer has no idea who is receiving a particular chute, and the paratrooper has no idea who has packed it.

Just in case there are any problems…' There was a nervous silence. My stomach was churning inside me. *In case there are problems…?* I repeated to myself.

At Tatton Park we put on our parachutes and harnesses, supervised by the instructor. The balloon was an old white barrage balloon, shaped a bit like a small airship. Hanging underneath the balloon was a steel and canvas basket which could hold four or five men. We were divided into small groups and stood about apprehensively, waiting our turn and watching the others ahead of us. The balloon was attached to a lorry by a pulley which would control the rise and fall of the balloon. Once the balloon got to a certain height, the men would jump out of the basket, one at a time, feet first down through a hole in the bottom of the basket.

My heart was in my mouth when I watched them. For the first thirty metres or so the men would just fall; they fell so fast and their parachute didn't open and you even began to wonder if it ever would, but then, just when you thought that they were going to freefall all the way to the ground, and to their death, the parachute suddenly billowed out above them catching their fall and they would float towards the ground, swinging and moving in the wind. Meanwhile, there was an officer on the ground shouting instructions, like 'feet together,' through a loud hailer.

Then it was my turn and my group got into the basket. I was incredibly nervous, my knees felt weak and shaking like they might give way and my hands were trembling, but I was determined not to show it, or to give in to it.

The instructor in the basket showed us how to attach our parachute cord to a bar in the basket. 'These X-type parachutes use a static line opening,' he explained. 'You attach your parachute cord to the basket or the aeroplane, and the parachute then opens automatically once you have fallen a certain distance, rather than you having to open it manually.'

Once we were all in the basket we were told to sit round the sides, and the winch on the lorry slowly began to turn and let us up. We gradually rose into the air, higher and higher; 300 feet, 400 feet, 500 feet; we could see the ground falling away below us through the hole in the bottom of the cage. The people below us became smaller and smaller and my stomach started to turn somersaults inside me – 600 feet, 700 feet, then the target height, 800 feet.

Now I just wanted to get it over with. I wanted to be the first one to do it. Maybe he sensed my nerves but the instructor looked at me first. He pointed towards me, 'move forwards and get ready to jump.' I crawled my way along the floor, until I was sitting on the edge of the hole. The circular hole was about three feet deep, and four feet in diameter, and had been designed to replicate the same size and shape as the hole in the floor of the Whitley bomber that the paratroopers jumped from. Between my feet I could see the ground far below, small figures moving about, and the army lorry to which we were tethered, which now looked like a toy truck.

'Remember the right way to go through the hole,' the instructor reminded me. You needed to push yourself slightly upwards and outwards, so that you got your body in a position that almost looked like you were standing to attention; but you had to be careful not to push too far forward and to always keep upright as otherwise you might bang your head on the opposite side of the hole. That was called ringing the bell! There were a lot of men who got bruised, broken noses, black eyes or concussion.

It was all I could do to control my emotions; not to think about how high we were, the huge fall in front of me, or what could go wrong. I still wondered whether I would be able to jump or not when the moment came. 'Ready number 1,' the instructor called out. Then a sudden calmness and resolution came over me. I remembered everything that I had been through, about Siberia and my mother and brother and how we now had a brigade that was fighting for Poland, and how this was the way that we could get our homes and families back. I was still scared, but now I knew that I could jump.

The instructor swung his arm downwards, gave a loud shout of 'go!' and I pushed myself off from the edge. I fell through the hole, freefalling down and down, faster and faster, my stomach feeling like it was up in my throat. All I remember thinking was 'open… open!', willing the parachute to open. I seemed to freefall forever but then there was a big jolt, and I could look upwards and see the parachute open above me and I had such a feeling of relief.

* * *

We made about two or three jumps in total from this balloon. Each time it got easier and each time you could focus more on improving your technique, helped by the officer on the ground shouting out instructions.

Paratrooper Training 109

Next was the real thing – we were taken to jump from a plane. 'In order to get qualified as a paratrooper, you're going to make four jumps,' the instructor told us. 'The first two times you'll jump from the flying barn door.' The flying barn door was the nickname for the Whitley bomber. It was a twin-engine British bomber that had been developed in the 1930s. It was one of our older aircraft and a bit slow and vulnerable for frontline missions, but was used for paratrooper training.

I hated that aeroplane, crouching in the dark, windowless fuselage, groping to find a place to sit. It was so small and cramped. It was supposed to hold ten men, but it struggled to hold more than about six or seven. It felt very different to going up in the balloon. There were no seats and we had to sit sideways on the hard floor, across the inside of the fuselage, facing alternate directions. It was so narrow that you could only just straighten out your legs.

The aircraft took off, juddering into the air with a low rumble. In order that everyone left the aircraft in an orderly way, we had each been assigned numbers, depending on where we were sitting. As we approached the drop zone over Tatton Park, the instructor folded back the hinged doors over the exit hole, and I could feel the blast of cold air coming into the aeroplane. 'Get ready!' the instructor shouted, over the noise of the aeroplane. The first man came to sit over the edge of the hole. The next man sat opposite, ready to swing his legs into the hole. Then the green light came on, and the officer shouted '1 go, 2, 3', to get us to jump when our number came up.

I was towards the back of the line. In front of me was Bartek, the lance corporal, and then behind me was Captain Kobak. The men in front dropped through the hole one by one, from alternate sides; it was getting closer and closer to my turn. Soon it was Bartek's turn, and I was the one after.

'Go!' shouted the instructor to Bartek and I got ready to swing my legs over. 'Go!' but Bartek didn't move. He was frozen there looking out down through the hole. 'Action stations, go!' the instructor shouted again; but still no movement, as the instructor's shouting echoed around the plane. 'Lance Corporal Bartek, jump out of this plane right now!' shouted out Captain Kobak from behind me. Then, when there was still no movement, Kobak came around and, with a great push from his boot, kicked Bartek forwards out of the plane!

Then it was my turn. When I came out through the hole, the speed of the aircraft and the air rushing past pulled me backwards away from the plane, and I felt myself dropping quickly before the parachute deployed.

When we landed, Bartek came up to me with a big grin on his face. 'That was great!'

'I didn't think you were going to do it,' I laughed, 'when Kobak had to push you out.'

'What are you talking about, Staszek. Nobody pushed me out!'

I was going to answer him, but then I saw blood on my jacket and when I bent over to look more closely, I suddenly saw more blood dripping from my head; all over my clothes and onto the ground. With all the nerves and adrenaline, I hadn't felt anything.

'Ah shit, Staszek, you rang the bell.'

* * *

For the next two jumps we used a Dakota which held about twenty men. The Dakota was a newly developed aircraft from the USA. It was twin-engined like the Whitley, but was a much better aircraft. There were metal seats facing each other along each side of the cabin and you could stand up properly in a Dakota. Instead of jumping through a hole in the floor, we jumped out of a side door located at the rear of the aircraft.

A red light signalled action stations. We had to stand up from our seat and make a queue, all facing the rear. We lined up in the order that we were sitting, and our parachute cord was chained onto a rail on the wall. Each man was to check the equipment of the man in front of him, to make sure that he hadn't got anything twisted through his harness. Then the first man stood in the doorway, holding on to each side of the doorway, ready to go.

My position was second from the door. Everyone would stand, watching the light, which was on the right side of the doorway. When we were over the drop zone the pilot would put on the green light and we had to jump, one by one, in the order that we were lined up; moving quickly forward as the man in front stepped out of the doorway, and was pulled backwards and away by the slipstream of the aircraft.

With more experience we gradually learned how to control the parachute better on our descent. Our X type parachutes had four controls, two on each side, which allowed you to steer and control your flight. You could 'slope' the parachute by pulling the front down and make it fall faster. Once you landed, you could quickly release the harness cables from the 'box' on your chest, so that you could rapidly get rid of the parachute.

Two of our jumps were at night. One night there was a half moon, but the other time it was really dark. After seven jumps – three from the balloon and four from a plane – you were a qualified paratrooper. Once fully qualified, our pay went up from 2 shillings per day to 8 shillings a day, but it was conditional upon always being fit and combat ready. Every month we had a full assessment of our physical condition, such as running while carrying all our kit, as well as our parachuting skills.

If you wanted to give up, you could still go and join the infantry. But nobody did, because being a paratrooper was something special and it paid more.

I became a fully qualified paratrooper on 19 June 1943, aged 19. Kobak awarded me my qualification badge which he pinned on to my chest. It was a silver eagle, attacking and diving with its talons outstretched and its wings stretched out behind.

On the reverse was written 'Tobie Ojczyzno', which means 'For You My Country.' We used to call this badge our 'donkeys ears' badge, as the stretched back wings of the eagle looked a bit like the ears of a donkey.

If we saw action, a wreath would be put into the eagle's beak.

Chapter 22

The Coasters

In total, we had about four weeks at Ringway in Manchester, before we got fully qualified and came back up to Elie in June 1943. After we had been back up in Elie for a few weeks, Big Mietek from my section started going out with a girl from Methil, a town near Leven. She was called Elsie, but we all called her Helena for some reason!

She was a big, solid girl! 'But I'm a big, solid guy too,' said Mietek, 'so what's the problem?' She was with the Land Army, so she had her own uniform and used to work the land to help the farmers.

Big Mietek invited me to the dances with him and Helena one day. Helena would be bringing one of her friends too, so there would be four of us. They had the dances over at the town hall in Colinsburgh every Friday evening – it was mainly Poles there, and the Land Army girls from Colinsburgh.

'We're really popular with the local girls!' Mietek called out happily. 'Just click your heels together and kiss their hands, just like some of the men did back in Poland; watch how Kobak and the other officers do it. The Scottish guys here don't do it, so the girls love it! Plus, some of the local guys are away, due to the war, so there is a shortage of men!'

Maybe we were too popular sometimes. I had heard that Sosabowski was having to go to visit local church ministers, to get them to warn their congregations after some of the local girls got pregnant. There had been quite a few marriages already! Not all the locals were so keen on us though. Some of the men were jealous and some of the more religious families, in the Church of Scotland, didn't look so kindly on Catholics. Some of them thought that you were mad if you went out with a Pole!

There was also a lot of communism in the area with the men in the factories. They never believed us when we told them what had happened to us in Poland and Siberia, or that we were treated badly by the Soviets. A few weeks before, Mietek and I had gone along to a dance that they had organised and when they spotted us, they had closed the door on us.

* * *

It was easy for Big Mietek and I to get a pass to go to the Colinsburgh dance. It was only a couple of miles away so we just walked there. We didn't have a car, and petrol and diesel was rationed anyway. One of the ladies, who lived near the hall, prepared tea and cakes for us all. 'This is great!' Mietek said happily, and introduced me to Helena's friend, called Isa. 'We don't get any food or drinks at the dances in any of the other towns!'

There was a Scottish band there with four musicians playing the drums, accordion, fiddle and piano. They had Scottish country dancing, like the Dashing White Sergeant, where you had to link arms and spin the girl around, as well as other dances like the foxtrot, quickstep or tango. Some of the guys drank too much and thought it would be fun to just let the girl go when they were spinning her round. The girls would then fall on the floor and burst into tears. There was no beer at the dancing, but some of the men had been in the pub beforehand. As Polish paratroopers we wore our army uniform with big army boots, and the Land Army girls had breeches to their knees, then thick wool socks, green v-neck jumpers and big brogue shoes. We made so much noise we sounded like horses dancing!

Isa's full name was Isabella, but everyone called her Isa. She was sixteen and pretty, with jet black wavy hair. She was wearing a kilt with a cockerel foot on it, along with a blouse with a nice jacket, and the sturdy working shoes that everyone had in those days. Isa wasn't in the Land Army, but worked on a local farm called the Stenton. She had gone to school at the Wade Academy in Anstruther but had to leave at fourteen. 'Even though I wanted to stay longer and study,' she told me. 'I was told that I would go and work like all the others.'

She was the youngest of eight, with two older sisters and five older brothers. Most of them worked on the farm, but one of her brothers had joined the RAF. 'Another is a right boozer,' she added after a pause. 'I've always disliked too much alcohol…'

Her father had been the foreman at the Stenton for twenty-six years. Isa worked in the house, keeping it neat and tidy, cooking for all the family on the coal fire, or preparing jam sandwiches for the men working in the fields. 'I have to go out and hunt around the fields to deliver it to them,' she said. 'We fill lemonade bottles with tea, and then put a sock round it to keep it warm! Some of the workers cook up lots of porridge in an iron pot and then store it in drawers – then they just cut out slices to eat in the morning! Everyone starts at 7am. Then when I get back, I have to peel tatties to fill the pot. I'm always peeling tatties! I'm never going to forget that pot!' she told me.

Chapter 23

1943

You are my sunshine, my only sunshine; you make me happy when skies are grey. 'Hey sunshine!', that's what they used to call me – sunshine – as I sang that song so much, or played it on the harmonica. *You'll never know, dear, how much I love you, please don't take my sunshine away.*

The brigade would sing Polish songs too, like our national anthem, when we were marching, or on the way to training down at Shell Bay in Elie, or at Largo House.

Poland has not yet died;
As long as we survive!

Some of the local boys would run up alongside, and start marching beside us enthusiastically, trying to sing along, although they couldn't pronounce the Polish words properly.

What the enemy has taken from us;
We will take back with our swords.

We had been given our first gun, a Lee-Enfield rifle, when we arrived in Elie, and we were taken regularly to shooting practice throughout our time in the paratroopers.

The storeman would only give us four bullets each, as we didn't have many to spare. But I would always try to wait for when the storeman was talking to someone else and would then quickly take a handful of extra bullets from the box, which I would use for extra practice. We felt we were not being as well equipped as the British paratroopers, and many of us thought that this was because our brigade commander, Sosabowski, wanted us to remain independent and not come under British command.

We used to shoot at 'bullseye' type targets, made up of concentric circles of different sizes, the circles gradually getting smaller until you got to the bullseye which was the smallest of all. You got 1 to 10 points depending on how close you got to the centre. We started shooting from 100 yards, then 150, 200, and up to 400 yards. At 400 yards you had to keep your rifle bloody still or you would completely miss the target! The targets were raised up by soldiers who hid in a trench underneath, and they also signalled the score, as we were too far away to see how we had done. They signalled with a long stick that had a round bit at the top. They waved it from side to side if you missed the target and got zero, and moved it up and down three times if you got a bullseye.

As well as the rifle, we were given grenades and had a Sten gun, which was like a small machine gun. It was light and portable, but its range was only about 100 metres, much shorter than the rifles. We were also taken to practise shooting with the Bren gun. This was another machine gun, but much more powerful than the Sten gun and much larger too. The Sten gun could be carried and fired by one man when standing, but the Bren gun was so heavy and large that to fire it you normally had to place it on a two-legged stand on the ground and then lie down on your stomach to fire it. The Bren gun had a selector switch that enabled you to choose whether you wanted it to just shoot a single shot at a time, or whether you wanted it to fire multiple rounds, one after another, if you kept your finger on the trigger.

When training, we always had to make sure that it was just on the single shot mode. But when it was my turn to shoot, I made a mistake and it went off like a machine gun when I pressed the trigger. *Brrrrrr*, the gun roared, as it fired off twenty or more shots, ripping through the air towards the target.

'Bloody hell, what is wrong with you, I said just a single shot!' Kobak shouted at me angrily, coming over and standing over me, his face turning red. 'You're wasting all of our bullets!'

Just then the soldier by the target moved his stick up and down three times. *Bullseye.*

'Hmm,' said Kobak, looking over at the signaller. 'Just make sure it doesn't happen again. Come to see me in my office afterwards.' I nervously arrived in his office later, expecting the worst. 'I could give you a punishment for machine gunning,' he eventually said. 'But I was told that you put 36 rounds spot on into the bullseye; ripped it to shreds.'

After that, they wanted me to shoot the Bren gun for our section! The gun was very heavy and weighed about 35 pounds in total, including an extra barrel that had to be carried too, because if you fired a lot, the barrel got red-hot and the bullets began to stick. It was taken apart for transportation, and I shared carrying it with our lance corporal, Bartek. Every man in the section also carried some back-up ammunition for the Bren gun: two magazines per man, each with 30 rounds of .303 cartridge.

Bartek had been one of the first Poles to arrive in the UK. He was from Warsaw and had fought in the army when Poland was invaded in 1939. He had then managed to escape, before being evacuated at Dunkirk. He had left all his family behind in Poland and he didn't know what had happened to them. He anxiously wrote letter after letter, but never received any replies. He was a bit older than us and had a wife and daughter in Poland whom he missed dreadfully. He used to show us photos of his daughter, Basia, whom he said would be six years old now, and should have been getting ready for her first day of school. 'Train hard, boys,' he would always say, 'we're going back to Poland soon.'

Bartek was very fit. In Elie, we used to have races for the whole battalion, over about two miles. Bartek and I used to leave the others well behind, but I could never beat him; he never seemed to get tired. We used to do wrestling, or boxing sometimes too. We borrowed equipment from the store and we made a boxing ring from ropes. Bartek was taller than I was and had a longer reach; you always need to be careful when you are boxing someone with a longer reach than you. He caught me clean on the nose and there was lots of blood, so I was sent to the doctor. 'Hmm, your nose does look a little squint now,' the doctor said, but he was a young doctor and didn't bother doing anything about it.

* * *

In July 1943, sudden news came through that General Sikorski, the commander-in-chief of the Polish Army and Prime Minister of our Polish government-in-exile, had been killed in a plane crash. He had been on the way back from inspecting Polish troops in the Middle East.

His plane crashed into the sea soon after taking off from Gibraltar on the way back to the UK.

Sikorski had been our strongest voice with the British and the Americans, and we worried that Poland would lose a lot of influence now. It was officially listed as an accident, due to cargo in the plane shifting to the back, or jamming the controls, during take-off, but all sorts of theories started to circle about what had really happened. Some of the paratroopers even thought that the Soviets might have been involved in sabotaging the plane.

A few days after Sikorski's death I began to feel really ill. I felt very cold and my whole body was aching; my head was pounding, and I really felt like throwing up. I had no energy at all, so Big Mietek took me immediately to the army doctor, who told me that I had malaria. He said that it was likely that I had picked it up in the Middle East, or India, where there were lots of mosquitoes about and the mosquito nets maybe couldn't keep them all out.

The doctor gave me some quinine tablets and sent me to hospital for a few days. Isa came to visit me every day and always brought food with her: 'That will fill a corner, and keep the wolves from the door,' she told me. I felt good with Isa. For the first time in a long time, I felt like I belonged somewhere; almost like I had found a home. I hadn't experienced that for a long time.

But whenever I started to feel too comfortable, overhanging it all was still this damn war, and the fact that I might be called into action at any time. The fact that Poland was still occupied, that my brother could also be called into battle, that my father and sister were in Siberia or God knows where. Five years of war and the shadow of Hitler and Stalin hanging over us for even longer; for more than a decade and for as long as I could remember.

Isa told me that she was going to be moving house. Fe, her father, had given up his job, so that meant that they lost their house on the farm; you only got the house if you worked on the farm. Fe had always hoped that one of Isa's brothers would take over from him, but her brother had decided to join the travelling mills instead and was going around the local farms, threshing the grain, and getting paid with beer and bread. Fe was so disappointed that he gave up the job.

Isa said that twice a year all the farm workers who wanted to change farm went to Cupar, which was one of the bigger towns in the area. It happened in November and May, but mainly November – if it happened in May, it meant something was seriously wrong. It was only the men that went; the women and children were left at home and they wouldn't know where they would be going until the men came back.

Some of the places the workers ended up going to were like bothies; just basic huts or slums. Then the men would say: 'don't even bother unpacking the boxes,' as they had no intention of staying for long in a place like that, and would move again the next year. Isa told me she would go to Pittenweem for a bit to stay with her married brother. She had got a job in an oilskin factory there which made coats for fishermen and for the navy. 'The smell there is terrible though!' she said.

Fe was hoping to get a job on Clephanton farm near Anstruther. When that job started, Isa would move back in with them, and go into service to help the farmer's wife in the farmhouse, scrubbing the floors, doing the laundry, those kinds of things. She would start at 8am and finish at 5pm; six days a week Monday to Saturday and would get paid just £1 per week for her troubles.

Chapter 24

The First Polish Independent Parachute Brigade

When I was allowed out of hospital, I was told not to exercise for a while. The doctor said to be careful, as malaria could come back. It took over a month until I felt totally better. I still used to get cold sometimes, especially at night, and I was sent back from exercise if I started feeling bad.

As the year progressed, summer gradually turned into autumn; the days became shorter, the sun lower in the sky, the mornings cooler and crisper and the leaves changed colour on the trees. In autumn 1943 all the paratrooper brigade were taken up to a place called Huntly in the north of Scotland. We were to get survival training in how to live off the land: four weeks living outside in the woods in the countryside, learning how to find food and make shelters.

We were shown how to use signs like the moss on the trees to help navigate if you were lost, as it tended to grow more on the north side of the trees; or how to make a tent from raincoats, which were called 'pelerynas' in Polish – they were like a big cape with no sleeves. If you got three pelerynas together, you had a nice roomy tent. The American, Lieutenant Tice, used to come and join in with us, as you couldn't make a tent from just one coat. You hammered wood into the ground and hung the pelerynas over it – two to give the width of the tent and the third to cover any gaps. Then you tied it down with ropes and put down bracken on the floor so you wouldn't sleep on the bare earth.

The kitchen was supposed to come to us with food, but it hardly ever did – maybe only once a week. So we would go out onto the hills and shoot animals like rabbits for food. We would take out the guts and then roast them on a fire, with their skins still on. Sometimes we tried to shoot hare, but this was difficult as it had a white coat over winter and was hard to see against the snow on the hills. Other times we used to steal potatoes and chickens from local farms to help feed ourselves. We would eat the food with our dixie mess tins, spoons and knives. We didn't bother with forks; our fork was our fingers!

After Huntly we were taken to Stirling for a fortnight of exercises against the British infantry. The British were inside Stirling pretending to be Germans, and the Poles were stationed outside the town, attacking.

Although we were on the same side against the Nazis, we all wanted to beat the British. Once the Poles caught some British machine gunners sitting around drinking tea and 'took them prisoner'. Another time, three of the Poles went into town at night to spy on the British. The Poles carried firecrackers and crept into the British base in Stirling. The British were all in bed and the Poles threw the firecrackers inside, meaning that all those inside were 'dead'. Then they went back to the Polish trenches where we were holed up outside the town.

Things escalated from there. The next night, three British soldiers came and hit one of the Polish paratroopers on the head with a pick-axe shaft. There was no reason for it other than revenge for being caught out the previous night – they just picked on the Pole who was closest to the main road. 'He was bleeding like a pig,' Bartek told me angrily, after he got back from the incident. Some of the other Poles had come over when they heard him shouting out, and the British soldiers had run away. But the Poles were so bloody angry that someone put up a flare, and some of them even shot live bullets at the British as they ran into the distance. None of the shots hit though. The next morning Kobak told us that the whole exercise was cancelled – they feared there would be revenge from the Polish paratroopers.

* * *

After Stirling, we were taken to Cupar towards the end of 1943. Everyone in the brigade was wondering when or where we might be called into action, but there had been no news.

Our section stayed in a house behind the church on the main road. The locals welcomed us, and they even organised to have a Polish bugle call, the Hejnal Mariacki, played every day at noon, from the Corn Exchange tower in the centre of the town. It was a tune that made many of us feel at home. The Hejnal Mariacki had been played back in Krakow in Poland every day in the main square, by a bugler high up in the church tower, and the bugler always stopped in the middle of a note before the tune could finish. It came from a legend hundreds of years ago about a sentry in the city of Krakow, who warned the city about an attack from the Mongols. They were able to shut the city gates in time, thanks to him, but he was shot by an arrow before he could finish the tune.

To pass the time we played football and volleyball with the other boys from the brigade. It would be section versus section. We were in pretty good shape in those days; sometimes just Bartek and I managed to beat five people at volleyball.

When we played football, Kobak always joined on our side, which was fortunate for us, as he hated losing and he was also the referee. The other side had Lieutenant Tice, who played as their centre forward. Once I tripped him when I couldn't catch up with him, before he could score. He fell to the ground with a clatter, sliding in the mud, before jumping up angrily and ordering me off the field. I started walking towards the edge of the pitch, but Kobak stopped me. 'Where do you think you're going? Tice, next time I'll send you off instead!'

Chapter 25

1944

By the start of 1944, some of the brigade were starting to become impatient about liberating Poland. The Nazis were still occupying Poland, but ever since Stalingrad the Soviets had been pushing the Nazis back and by January 1944 had pushed them back to the pre-war Polish-Soviet border. We all remembered the previous Soviet invasion of Poland in 1939, the Siberian gulags and what the Soviets had done to our officers at Katyn, so we didn't trust what they would do this time if they got to Poland.

Every day I worried about what was happening to my father and sister back in Siberia. I asked everyone I could, but nobody knew anything. I hadn't heard anything from my brother Billy either, since leaving Iraq. Many of us had left behind family in Poland or in Siberia. Bartek was desperate to get back to Poland and was anxious about what had happened to his wife and daughter there. We all wondered if we would be dropped into Poland, but as the days continued to pass no order came.

I got a shock when I woke up one morning in early 1944. The bed of Yitzhak, from my section, was empty and hadn't been slept in. All Yitzhak's belongings, like his uniform and gun, were in neat piles on the bed, but there was no Yitzhak. None of us in our section could find him anywhere. When we went to exercises later, we discovered that he wasn't the only one to disappear. Some of the other Jewish paratroopers had also left.

'They've gone to join the British Army,' one of the men in another section called out.

'Sneaked off to join the Jewish army, more like,' someone else shouted back sarcastically. 'That's your Polish patriots right there! I heard plenty of them deserted before, when our Anders' Army passed through Palestine after leaving Russia.'

'Well, maybe they didn't feel welcome, if that's the way you spoke to them.'

I wasn't sure what to think. I hoped that Yitzhak would be OK, but I felt let down that he hadn't told any of us what he was planning to do after everything that we had done together.

* * *

Then in May 1944 things started to develop. First, Kobak told my section and about twenty other paratroopers that we were going to be flown down from the airbase at Leuchars in Fife to Ely in England. It was near Cambridge and near to an airfield there called RAF Witchford. The rest of the paratrooper brigade was to remain up in Scotland.

We waited in Ely for a couple of weeks for further instructions. It was a small town with a big cathedral and sat in the middle of miles and miles of flat countryside called the fens. It was a land of black earth, farmland, marshes, rivers and canals. Dotted about the countryside were wooden windmills, which were used to help drain the fields.

There had been a rumour going round that we could be going to Norway with British paratroopers to hit a German heavy water plant. Both the Americans and the Nazis had been trying to develop a new weapon, the atomic bomb, which they said would end the war, and which needed a special kind of water, called heavy water.

Or there were other rumours about a big German factory in France, where the Nazis were supposed to be making batteries for machines; or about Sosabowski agreeing that we would help with the invasion of Western Europe. We had all heard that there was a plan for the allies to start liberating France, but nobody knew when or where it would be.

The command never told you what would happen until the last moment in case the information got out to the Germans. After a couple of weeks nervously waiting for whatever it was, it seemed to have been cancelled, and we were flown back up to Leuchars and then taken back to Cupar. I felt a mixture of relief, but also somehow anti-climax, after having been on edge for so long, and having got my mind and emotions into a state where I was ready to see action.

Back in Fife I went to the cinema in Leven with Isa. It was a Western film, called *In Old Oklahoma*, with John Wayne. I always liked Westerns and John Wayne, but before the film, there was a Pathé news clip, all about a battle at Monte Cassino in Italy, near Rome.

It showed the Polish Second Corps, battling the Nazis over the ruins of an old hilltop abbey. The Polish Second Corps had been formed from various Polish units, including the Anders' Army, and they had sailed from Egypt to Southern Italy in December 1943. My heart skipped a beat when I realised which army it was. 'That's my brother Billy's army!' I whispered to Isa, shocked. 'I hope he's OK...'

I hadn't heard from him for a long time; ever since I had left Iraq. I hung on every word of the newsreel, trying to work out what had happened. It sounded like a tough battle, with lots of casualties. Advancing through Italy was not turning out to be as easy as Churchill had said it would be, but in the end the Poles and the Allies had won the battle, with Wojtek the bear, by now almost two metres tall and 200kg, helping to carry the shells. A bugler had played out the Hejnal Mariacki over the ruins; the same tune that they played for us in Cupar.

* * *

But I only stayed in Fife for a couple of weeks before the whole brigade was taken down to the south east of England at the beginning of June 1944. We were taken to the area around Peterborough which was about thirty miles north-west of Ely, where we had been before in the fens. There were many airbases and airfields around there, due to the flat landscape. Isa and I promised that we would write to each other regularly while I was away. I had been trying to learn how to read and write some English, but I knew that I would need some help.

My section was taken to a place called Easton-on-the-Hill. It was a beautiful little village made of honey-coloured limestone buildings. The other sections were billeted in surrounding villages, such as Wansford, Stamford, Blatherwycke, or in Peterborough itself.

By this time, our brigade numbers were up to their highest – around 3,100 men including all the support staff. We were also presented with our regimental colours in a ceremony. It was a red cross on a white background, with four gold eagles in each corner diving in attack, just like the eagles on our badges. It had been made in secret by women in Warsaw and was consecrated in a church there in 1942 before being smuggled out to the UK.

In Easton-on-the-Hill you could really see that the country was building for an invasion of Europe. There were shells and tanks hidden up just about every side street, and covered with camouflage so that enemy planes couldn't spot them. By then, there were lots of Americans also arriving in the area. They received much higher salaries than us and lived like kings. The Americans had all sorts of supplies and food; they brought candy, Coca-Cola, chewing gum for the children and nylons for the ladies.

On 6 June 1944, soon after we arrived in Easton-on-the-Hill, we heard that the Normandy landings had started, as the Allies tried to take back France, and then the rest of Europe, from the Nazis. The airborne troops had landed first in Normandy – 24,000 of them. There were paratroopers making night jumps and other troops brought in via glider. Their aim was to destroy the German communications and guns and to secure the bridges and the sides of the invasion area.

'That was almost us,' I said to the others. 'But they dropped the 6th Airborne instead. I wonder what they have in store for us.'

One thing that was in store for us was that our brigade would be reorganised to come under British command. We would come under the command of the British Major General Roy Urquhart, as part of the British First Airborne Division.

It had been agreed that our brigade would take part in one Allied operation after the Normandy landings, somewhere in Western Europe, and after that the brigade would be free to go to Poland whenever an appropriate moment arrived. After we heard the news, there was a lot of growing speculation, doubt and even anger, by many in the brigade about whether that appropriate moment might ever arrive.

Later on, I would wonder whether it might have been better for us to have been dropped at Normandy after all.

Chapter 26

The British First Airborne Division

After our brigade joined the British First Airborne Division we gradually got better equipped, until we were equipped to the same level as the British paratroopers. We were given more ammunition – bullets on a belt instead of a few individual ones, Sten guns and PIAT anti-tank weapons.

The training also intensified. At Easton-on-the-Hill we continued to do shooting, exercises and map work at night. We did two or three jumps from aeroplanes, which we hadn't been able to do when we were up in Scotland. We took off from the airfield at RAF Spanhoe which had the longest runway in the area. The olive green Dakotas would quickly gain height and then we would practise our jumps over the nearby RAF Wittering.

After Easton-on-the-Hill, my section was taken a few miles along the road to stay in Stamford which was the town where our brigade leader Sosabowski had his headquarters at Rock House. Stamford was another picturesque English town, full of quaint old-fashioned buildings. Some of the Poles were billeted in Stamford School, some in Barn Hill, but most of the paratroopers stayed in half-moon shaped huts made of corrugated iron, called Nissen huts. They had a door and a couple of windows at each end, and in the middle of the hut was a little coal-burning stove and chimney for cold weather.

Our brigade acquired a mascot – Smokey the sheepdog – who had been found on a bomb site in London by one of the brigade. He wore our emblem and had his own parachute – he even accompanied us on all our flights, although he stopped short of jumping out of the plane! In Stamford, it really felt that we were preparing for the front. We had more night and day jumps from RAF Spanhoe; I had about twenty-one jumps in total. We would practise jumps with more and more planes and men, to get ready for a real battle situation, where we would need to drop large numbers of paratroopers in a co-ordinated way. Eventually, the entire brigade of 1,700 paratroopers jumped together on Salisbury Plain.

On one night exercise which took us out over Salisbury Plain, one of the aircraft let its paratroopers out too low. The absolute minimum height had to be at least 300 feet so that the parachutes could deploy properly. It was a disaster. I could hear the paratroopers screaming on the ground when I passed them for my landing. I heard later that there were many broken legs and twenty dead. I knew one of the boys that died. He was due to be married to one of the girls up in Scotland.

But that accident wouldn't be the only misfortune that we would encounter. Operation Burden was an exercise in July 1944 which had involved 369 Polish paratroopers from some of the other companies in our brigade. Two of the aircraft carrying them had made a mistake – they had drifted towards each other too close and touched wings, becoming locked together and losing control, and had tumbled to the ground, near a village called Tinwell. Some of the paratroopers in the planes tried to jump, but it was too late, and their parachutes failed to open in time. There were twenty-six Polish paratrooper fatalities, all from the 8th Company, 3rd Battalion, as well as eight of the American plane crew. Only one man had managed to survive from the two planes, an American corporal who had jumped early. They said that they could only identify some of the casualties by the colour of boots that they found on limbs that had been separated from bodies; Americans wore brown, Polish paratroopers wore black.

It was a big blow to us, especially to those of us who were friends with the paratroopers that died. We hadn't even entered battle yet, but we were already losing people.

* * *

In those days people married young, generally in their early twenties, or even younger. Things had been getting serious between Isa and me, and I would go back up to visit her in Scotland whenever I had the opportunity. We had spoken with each other about marriage, but our brigade wouldn't give me permission. They said that I needed their permission before I could marry and they would not permit me to marry a Protestant!

'Why doesn't she convert to Catholicism?' the priest asked me, apparently baffled that someone would choose not to be Catholic. 'It would make things so much easier,' and he handed me forms to give to Isa to convert her religion.

'No chance!' exclaimed Isa indignantly, when I explained what the priest had said and showed her the forms. 'You go back to the priest and tell him that!'

I went back to the priest and explained the situation; that Isa was a Protestant and that she didn't want to change; that she had always been a Protestant, and that her whole family was Protestant; that it was quite a complicated situation in Scotland with the whole Catholic and Protestant thing, but did it really matter anyway, as aren't we all Christian?

'Which way will you bring your children up?' the priest asked. 'Catholic or Protestant?'

'Well that would be up to my wife.'

He gave a deep sigh, and started going on about Protestants and how they didn't have respect for the Pope, or for Rome, and that they fought Catholics before, and burned down the Catholic churches, like the cathedral nearby in St Andrews.

He was making me mad. 'Are you going to marry her or am I?' I asked him angrily. 'I know her best!' The priest sent me out and refused permission.

* * *

By August 1944, emotions in the brigade were running high too. As the Allied armies continued their fight out of Normandy towards Berlin, there were further rumours about the actions that our brigade could be involved in. We were almost always on high alert; there must have been at least fifteen warnings to prepare for action. There was one drop rumoured to be near Paris, another in the north of France, another in Belgium, but these were always postponed at the last moment.

And as the Soviets continued pushing the Nazis back and began to advance into pre-war Polish territory, we learned about Operation Tempest. It was a series of uprisings by the Polish underground army, called the AK, against the occupying Nazis. The AK would come out of hiding when the Soviets approached and it had been decided that they would try to work with the Soviets against the Nazis.

However, as the weeks passed it gradually became clear that the Poles were being double-crossed. The Soviets only worked with the AK until they had taken the towns and cities that they wanted, like Vilnius or Lviv, then they captured the Polish soldiers and either forced them to join the Red Army or sent them to the Siberian gulag.

The final straw came with the Warsaw uprising. The Polish underground army came out of hiding but the Soviets did nothing and let them be massacred by the Nazis. The Soviets didn't want a Polish military or political presence in the country, in order to make it easier for them to take over the country.

Some of the paratroopers, like Bartek, wanted us to be dropped into Warsaw to support the uprising before it was too late, and felt let down that the British and Americans were not supporting this. 'They only care about Western Europe! They only care if we can fire a rifle, that's all we are to them. They don't understand the Soviets! They only care about the Nazis! Ever since we came under British command we have lost our ability to liberate Poland.'

Others argued back that we needed British and American support anyway, and that the Allies had said it was too difficult logistically to support a drop into Warsaw; that our aircraft didn't have enough fuel to reach Warsaw and that the request to use Soviet airfields had been denied. They said that it would be suicidal if we went to Warsaw, a massacre, and that maybe we should be thankful that it was not going to happen.

One day, at lunch, a scuffle broke out about this. One man pushed another, who then hit him back with his dixie, breaking his thumb. As he stood there, holding his hand gingerly, a third man clobbered the second in the chops, spraying the bread, cheese and jam that he had been eating all over the table. They had to be pulled apart by the others.

It felt like there could almost be a mutiny by some in the brigade and for a few days we weren't sure which way things would go. Then, in September 1944, another rumour started circulating about our brigade being dropped into the Netherlands. The situation this time seemed different; the days went by, and there was no sign of any cancellation. We were briefed by our officers about an action called Operation Market Garden. I wrote to Isa. I didn't tell her where we might be going, but I told her that I might not see her for a long time, and that she might hear about it on the news.

Chapter 27

Operation Market Garden

Operation Market Garden was designed to shorten the war by six months and get us to Berlin before the Soviets. Some of us hoped it might even get us to Poland by Christmas, before the Soviets could occupy the whole country.

The Allies had been pushing back the Nazis towards Germany, but it was hard going, and there was a big obstacle coming up – the River Rhine. If the Nazis dug in there, or blew up the bridges, it could take us a long time to get past it.

We were told that we would be going to the Netherlands. Our First British Airborne Division would work together with the Americans – the 101st and 82nd US Airborne Divisions. The plan was that 35,000 troops would land behind enemy lines by parachute and glider, and attempt to seize a number of bridges nearly simultaneously – there were six major canals and rivers where we needed to seize bridges, but the key bridges, the largest ones, were over two arms of the Rhine at Nijmegen and at Arnhem. Controlling these crossings would then allow the land troops of the British Second Army, led by the tanks and the armoured brigades of XXX Corps, to cross the Rhine straight into Germany and bypass the main German defences to the south at the Siegfried Line.

The 101st was going to land at Eindhoven, the 82nd would be dropped at Nijmegen, and our First British Airborne Division was going for Arnhem. It was the most difficult task. Arnhem was the furthest away from our front line, which meant we would have to hold it for the longest time before we could get any reinforcements. It was expected that XXX Corps would only reach us after four days.

We were told that most of the German army was already retreating, and that there were no tanks or motorised forces in that area – no Panzers. But, even if this was true, four days was a long time for an airborne force to fight unsupported. We don't carry the same level of supplies or heavy weapons that a regular army unit would.

To make things more difficult, because there were so many troops, we didn't have enough Dakotas to carry all the paratroopers and tow all the gliders, so we would have to split our drop into Arnhem over three days. The British 1st Parachute Brigade would be dropped on the first day on 17 September; then the other British parachute brigade on 18 September. Our Polish paratrooper brigade would be dropped on the third day, 19 September.

Furthermore, we couldn't be dropped too close to Arnhem, as there weren't many safe areas for the gliders to land there, and we couldn't risk the Dakotas running into flak after the drop, from the anti-aircraft guns the Nazis had stationed at a nearby airfield. Some of our division would therefore be dropped up to eight miles from Arnhem. Then, in order to secure the bridges, towns and drop zones for subsequent supply drops, we would need to defend a perimeter of 18 miles.

The Polish brigade would be dropped just south of the river, at an area called drop zone 'K', about a mile or two south of Arnhem road bridge. Our job was to reinforce the perimeter east of Arnhem, linking up with the artillery which would be flown in by glider. The whole operation would be an incredibly challenging task for everyone involved.

* * *

We were woken at 5am on 19 September. I didn't sleep much that night. I don't think any of us did. We were taken over to the aerodrome at RAF Spanhoe by lorries, and they issued each of us with a parachute and food, although nobody felt like eating. I took one bar of chocolate from the NAAFI, but the lady working there pushed a second bar into my jacket, saying 'take another one, dear, you might need it.' She was trying to smile, but I could tell that she was worried.

At the airfield the weather was poor. It was so foggy that our flights couldn't take off. We sat around, waiting to see if the weather would clear, but it didn't. Our drop was postponed. We were taken back to our barracks again. The worst thing was the waiting. The tension was unrelenting. We just wanted to get going. We could hardly sleep or eat.

Some of the Dakotas carrying the Polish troops in gliders had taken off from another location, but the Germans had been waiting for them in

Arnhem: it was a massacre. Some never even managed to get out of the gliders.

The next day we were taken back to the aerodrome again, but the weather was still the same. We were told to keep our parachute and equipment beside us as we could get the call to go at any time. But still the fog wouldn't lift; more waiting; more tension; we tried to distract ourselves in any way we could. Some men smoked non-stop, some tried to play cards; some prayed, talking quietly to themselves under their breath, and crossing themselves; some men talked about what might be happening in Arnhem, how our delay might be affecting things, how we would finally get revenge on the Nazis for invading Poland back in 1939, or about when the weather might change. Some tried to make jokes, and some men tried to laugh but it was all forced. We all knew what was coming, and we just wanted to get it over with. It was too much for some: one paratrooper put his gun to his head, pulled the trigger and blew his head off.

The fog didn't lift all day. Evening came, and again we were taken back to barracks.

On the third day of waiting, 21 September, the weather was clearer when we came to the airfield. But still we didn't go. We were taken back and forth to the take off point three or four times and each time the drop was postponed. Then, finally, we were to go in the afternoon.

* * *

I gathered my equipment together: rifle, Sten gun, part of the Bren gun, grenades strapped to my belt and ankle, ammunition, bayonet, mines, plastic explosives, dixies, inflatable lifebelt, spoon, knife, and water bottle. It could weigh up to 100 pounds, or more than 40kg. You would fall a lot faster when you jumped with all your kit.

We filled up our water bottles and if you needed new water after the drop, you would have to try to find running water and boil it. We had been given twenty-four hours of rations: a couple of corned beef rolls, extra cigarettes, biscuits and some beef mince – you could add the mince to water, put it in your dixie and then warm it up with a small heater which you put underneath.

We were taken out to the planes. I was in plane number 77. We lined up outside in our jumping order, then climbed aboard. The planes had been painted with alternating stripes of black and white paint, around part of the wings, and part of the tail of the aeroplane. This was so our planes could be distinguished from the German planes, so nobody would shoot at us by mistake. 'Only the right people will shoot at us,' Big Mietek told me, with a smile.

There were about eighteen paratroopers on each Dakota. On mine there was my section and one other section, along with a crew of about five. I sat down inside the aeroplane and took my place, second in from the door. Andrzej from my section was opposite me, Big Mietek was sitting next to me, and Bartek was diagonally across. Bartek sat expressionless, staring at the floor; I wondered what he was thinking about.

The pilot started the aircraft, shouting 'clear the prop' to make sure that nobody was near the propellers. The engines jumped into life with a roar. The aeroplane gave a shudder, and we started moving; first taxiing towards the runway, then as we turned onto it, we started accelerating. Faster and faster, until first the front of the plane started lifting into the air, then the rear wheels also came off the ground. We were off. We pulled up into the sky, following a route that over the next few hours would take us south-east across the fenlands of Suffolk, then out across the English Channel, continuing south-east until we met the Dutch coast around Rotterdam, then flying more directly east until we got to Arnhem.

We flew in formation and our Dakotas were escorted by three or four Spitfires from the RAF. I felt happier when I saw them, to know that we weren't entirely alone up there. Dakotas are good for transport, but they are easy targets. They are unarmed and they have to fly low and slow when they are dropping paratroopers. They have little or no armour plating and no self-sealing fuel tanks to stop the fuel leaking and igniting if you get hit.

I could see Andrzej across from me, looking rather pale and worried. Andrzej had been from the west of Poland. When the Nazis invaded, he had been made to serve with the German Wehrmacht armed forces in North Africa. He had then been captured by the British at the end of November 1941, but was allowed to join the Polish Army in Britain rather than become a prisoner of war. I shouted over to him, above the noise of the aeroplane, trying to reassure him as best I could: 'Would you like some chocolate?' and I pulled the chocolate bar from the NAAFI out of my pocket. He looked at me and said 'not awfully keen at the moment,

Staszek.' I could tell he was really stewed up, but he was trying his best to hide it.

Don't get me wrong, don't think I'm brave, but I never really got stewed up. Of course I was nervous, but it never took over me like it did with some of the others, I don't know why.

About halfway across the English Channel, the pilot shouted out something to us from the front of the plane, and motioned to come forward. Bartek, our lance corporal, went to see what it was all about, and came back a couple of minutes later. Standing at the front of the cabin, he shouted to us that there had been a last minute change of plans. I struggled to hear him over the noise of the aircraft, but he shouted that our drop zone was being changed; our original drop zone 'K' was no longer safe, so we were instead going to be dropped a few miles further away from Arnhem, to the west closer to a town called Driel.

As we came over the Dutch coast, we started drawing some fire from the German anti-aircraft guns on the ground. We were flying low, maybe at 600 or 800 feet, our speed maybe 150 miles an hour. The planes came in as low as possible, so that there would be less time for us to be shot when we jumped.

I could hear rounds of ammunition whizzing past the sides of the plane, and there was flak exploding all around us from the German artillery. The shells exploded in black puffs of smoke, which sent a blast wave and razor-sharp metal shrapnel flying out in all directions. The smaller rounds of ammunition couldn't be seen, but you knew that they were there because you could see the tracer rounds in the air; every fifth round or so would be a tracer round, so that the Germans could see how accurately they were firing. There were tracers all over the sky.

Suddenly, one plane ahead of us was hit; you could see its engine on fire. It released all the paras. The crew had fought to keep the plane straight and level, but then you saw it going down, down towards the ground, in a slow death spiral, smoke trailing back from its engine. I didn't see what happened to it after that.

Then we hit a massive air pocket; the plane gave a huge lurch downwards; I almost fell out of my seat and my stomach was up in my throat, as the pilot fought to control the plane. Then Andrzej opposite me, who was sitting closest to the door, suddenly jumped up, white-faced and panicking: 'we're hit, we're hit!' he screamed. 'We're going down! Get out the plane!' He looked wide-eyed at us all then, before anybody could stop him, he ran shouting to the back door of the plane and jumped out, disappearing out of the aircraft; his shouting growing fainter as he fell away from the plane, and I could see his parachute opening once he was far enough away, just leaving the end of his static line flapping around in the wind outside the door. Without a word, the crew chief walked to the door, and pulled the static line back in, so that it wouldn't damage the aircraft.

We all looked at each other in stunned silence. 'Well, I guess he's not going to the front!' I muttered to myself under my breath.

The German firing was non-stop; I wondered when our Dakota was going to be hit. As we approached the drop zone, we were flying low over the fields and the villages; so low that sometimes you could even see the Germans on the ground running around or firing their guns up towards us.

I took out my picture of Our Lady of Czestochowa and looked at the picture of this dark-skinned Mary, with two cuts on her face. I closed my eyes and prayed and hoped that I would get out of this safely. And I thought about Scotland, and about Isa, and about my family; and then the song *You Are My Sunshine* popped into my head, and I thought how ridiculous it was to be thinking about this song when I was about to be dropped into a hot drop zone with Germans firing at me. But doesn't the mind work in mysterious ways, especially when it is stressed.

Every second brought us closer still to the drop zone; the crew chief climbed a ladder into the 'astrodome', which was a transparent dome in the roof of the aeroplane, to watch for the signal from the lead aircraft, which had the master navigator. We all sat on edge, watching him, watching for any movement from him, any signal. We were on a hair-trigger to go, adrenaline pumping. My heart was beating hard in my chest like it was going to burst. Then, suddenly, he quickly came back down the ladder and walked to the back door of the aircraft. This was our signal to get ready to jump.

'I'll see you on the ground!' I called to Mietek, as we stood up and shuffled towards the back door. The jumpmaster was shouting 'jump!' and the first man went, then the second, then it was my turn. I was repeating in my head *don't think, just do it; don't think, just do it*; and then I was out of the door and falling, and I could see the flat Dutch landscape below me, with the tracer fire from the guns all around, and the sound of the German machine guns in my ears, going 'brrrr', sounding much faster than how our machine guns could fire.

And I was falling fast with all my kit, and I was praying as I fell 'Please God, let the parachute open… Please God, don't let me be hit… Please God, let me get back to Scotland, and see Isa again.' And then I heard my parachute open above me and felt the sudden tug upwards. But still I was falling fast, and the ground was coming up fast, but that was also OK, because it was a hot drop zone and the Germans were shooting at us and there were bullets all around.

And then, all of I sudden, I was on the ground and I rolled to cushion my fall, just as we had been trained. I had landed in the Netherlands.

Chapter 28

Driel

We landed around 5pm on Thursday 21 September. I unbuckled my parachute and looked around. We had landed on heathland, about a mile outside a small town. Up in the sky, there were hundreds of paratroopers floating down, swaying from side to side as they fell, with the tracer bullets from the machine guns all around them. But on the ground, no Germans seemed to be nearby; you could hear the sound of machine gun fire coming from the direction of Arnhem, but nobody was shooting at us once we landed.

I could see the Dakotas overhead, maybe fifty or sixty of them, but not as many as I was expecting. There should have been more than one hundred to carry the whole of our battalion. Had the other planes already left? Or had so many been shot down?!

Bartek gathered our section together and explained that we would go to Driel, the nearby town, and secure the area. 'Watch out for any Germans that are around, and clear out any that you find in the town. Make sure there are no snipers in any of the houses. Then find a secure area where we can dig in and take shelter and where we can take stock of the situation.' He told us that we were to take any Nazis that we captured to the town hall, where the Dutch underground would meet us.

Driel was about one mile away from us to the west, over the heathland and past a farm. Bartek was ahead of the group, leading us forward, and I was towards the back. It was tough going, carrying all of our heavy equipment over the uneven and boggy ground. I could still hear the sounds of the machine guns in the distance, coming from the other side of the River Rhine.

We reached a road and it led us past fields on both sides, the land pancake flat, with some trees, bushes and hedges dotting the landscape. We fixed our bayonets and cautiously walked along the road, but there was no sight of any Germans. As we got closer to Driel the road crossed over a railway line and the number of buildings around us started to increase. It was a small town of maybe a few thousand people; a cluster of low rise buildings, with a couple of tall church steeples which towered over the rest of the town. We headed towards the area around one of these churches, carefully looking down every street for Germans and at every window for possible snipers.

We didn't know who might be about, or how many Germans there might be, so we decided to take cover around the open area in front of the church. Big Mietek and I took shelter directly opposite the church, hidden behind a small hedge that was in front of a house. Bartek and Jurek also hid themselves and settled down to wait. There weren't many people about. Just some of the other paras that we could see in the distance, surveying some of the streets and houses in the town, or heading further north towards the river Rhine. Maybe all the residents were inside their houses; they must have seen the paratroopers drop and heard the guns, so were maybe staying inside for safety.

Then, after perhaps five or ten minutes, I thought I could hear something coming from the west, carried on the wind. It sounded like voices or even music; someone whistling. The voices and the whistling gradually grew louder then, around the corner of the building to our left, there appeared two men on bicycles. They were talking and whistling as they made their way down the road, with loaves of bread in the baskets at the front of their bikes. They were dressed in German army uniforms.

Mietek and I stood up quickly, shouting out 'hands up!' as we pointed our guns at them. The rest of our section came out of their hiding places too, rushing towards the two Nazis. The two German soldiers stopped their whistling and came to a sudden halt, throwing their arms up in the air with a look of shock on their faces. We surrounded them and checked them for weapons, taking away their guns and knives. We took them to the town hall, where the Dutch underground were waiting, and they told us that they would look after them.

Soon after, we heard another noise coming along the road. It was the sound of an engine; some kind of vehicle coming from the same direction that the two Germans had just come. We all quickly scattered to each side of the road, taking cover behind doorways as best we could, our rifles pointed in the direction of the approaching vehicle. As the vehicle got closer, I could see that it was some kind of armoured car, made of steel with a machine gun at the front, almost like a tank, but with large rubber tyres.

There was a crew of two men in the car. It stopped when it reached the area in front of the church, and I could see one of them stand up and look around. He appeared to be wearing a different uniform to what the German soldiers we had just met had been wearing.

It was the British! We stepped out into the street, waving in their direction. The two men told us that they were from the Second Army, XXX Corps. They had started out from Eindhoven, but had soon found out that the Germans had demolished the bridge over the canal at Son, so they had to wait for the engineers to make a replacement Bailey bridge. They had managed to make up time after that, and got to Nijmegen on schedule, on the morning of the 19th, but had then discovered another problem there.

XXX Corps had been supposed to just roll straight across the bridge at Nijmegen and up to Arnhem, but when they got there the bridge at Nijmegen had not yet been taken by the Allies. 'It was a huge bridge, almost 600 metres across,' one of them told us, 'and the river was too wide there for us to make any replacement bridges. It delayed us about thirty-six hours. We only managed to finally take the bridge yesterday evening, on the 20th.'

They had then been ordered to wait, as it was getting dark and their commander was worried about German counter-attacks on the bridge and to their supply lines to the rear. 'When we finally got the go ahead,' he said, 'we tried to make a dash up here to Driel. It's a narrow bugger of a road – Hell's Highway it's called – marshes on each side, so we had to travel in one long single file line. We were like sitting ducks, sitting in traffic jams. There were anti-tank weapons and a whole bloody bunch of Panzers.'

Panzers! I thought to myself in shock.

They had told us that there were no German tanks here!

* * *

We helped him camouflage his vehicle under some trees. I was glad he was staying, he had a bigger gun than we did!

As evening began to fall, we were joined by other Polish paras, as they made their way to Driel from the landing zone. We began to set up a defensive perimeter but soon realised that half our brigade was missing! After our take-off from England, the controllers had apparently recalled the planes due to the weather conditions, but only half our planes had received this message. We had also lost some planes to German attacks and had about forty paratroopers killed or injured. So we only had about 750 of our paratroopers. We didn't have any of the 1st Battalion and only half of our 3rd Battalion.

We could hear large amounts of heavy machine gun fire coming from the direction of the river and the darkening sky was being lit up by flares. It was hard to find out what the situation on the ground was. The radio communication was terrible, the trees were reducing the range of the wirelesses, so in the end our liaison officer had to swim the Rhine to try to get some information.

We learned that only a small number of the British paras, the 2nd Battalion, had reached Arnhem road bridge – they had taken it, or part of it, but weren't able to hold it. The railway bridge in Arnhem had been blown by the Germans, and the pontoon bridge was not useable. The remaining British paras were dug in across the river from us, in a small area around a village called Oosterbeek to the west of Arnhem. They were under attack from SS Panzer tanks and other German units; far heavier German forces than expected.

The situation across the river in Oosterbeek was desperate. The British paras only had a few anti-tank guns and howitzers and couldn't hold off the tanks much longer. The lack of radio communication and low clouds had also been affecting getting supplies and reinforcements out. The Germans had been using flares and markers to attract Allied aircraft to their positions so that they could shoot them down, or so that the resupply missions would drop the supplies there instead.

Added to that, the support from the British XXX Corps had been delayed. It looked like most of them were not going to arrive until the next day, the 22nd. XXX Corps were saying that they had had to stop to wait for infantry support and had been under attack on the road up to Arnhem, but the Americans said that after the US paratroopers crossed the river at Nijmegen in full daylight to help capture the bridge, XXX Corps had stopped to brew tea!

Our job would be to somehow get across the river and support the British paras.

Chapter 29

Crossing the Rhine

The next morning, 22 September, General Sosabowski came round to inspect us. He had set up his headquarters in an old farmhouse nearby, beside an apple orchard and had borrowed a local lady's bike to make his way over. We all cheered him and his bike when we saw him. 'Nice bike, General!'

Some of our brigade had tried to cross the Rhine the previous night, but had not been successful. The Heveadorp ferry, which they had hoped to use, was gone. Apparently, the ferryman had cast it adrift to prevent the Germans making use of it. So, instead, the paratroopers had tried to improvise rafts out of ammunition trailers, but they kept sinking and they were under too much fire from the Germans.

We continued to man our defensive perimeter during the day. There was mortar shelling from the Germans directed towards Driel; it damaged one of the churches and some of the buildings in Driel and resulted in some casualties on our side. One of the paratroopers who was in the defensive perimeter near us was hit in the stomach by a shell fragment; we could all hear him crying out for morphine before he died.

In return some of our XXX Corps artillery had managed to get a bit closer, and were sending shells over to the German positions across the river near Oosterbeek. There were also a couple of armoured cars from XXX Corps that had arrived in Driel. There were rumours of some Germans advancing towards Driel but that they had been beaten back by the armoured cars of XXX Corps that had joined us.

It was a few hours later in the day when I saw a group of men coming out of the trees over to our right, maybe a hundred metres away. A couple of them were wearing red berets, like the red berets that the British paratroopers wore. They were coming from the direction that some of the German mortar fire had come from earlier and were walking in our direction, with their hands up. There didn't seem to be anybody else with these British paratroopers. For a moment, I was going to get up and go out to meet them and welcome them, but something held me back;

something didn't feel right. Weren't the British paratroopers all over the other side of the river?

Then I saw movement out of the corner of my eye; somebody was going out from our lines towards them. It was Lieutenant Tice, the American in our brigade.

'Don't shoot!' we could hear the voices of the men in the red berets, carried to us on the wind. 'Don't shoot!' I watched Tice continuing to walk towards them. He put his hand up to welcome them as he got closer. Then, it all happened so quickly. Once the group got to within twenty metres of Tice they suddenly lowered their hands, pulled out weapons and began firing at him. A cold fear came over me, as I saw Tice's body crumple and fall to the ground. I tried to shoot back, but it was too quick; they were already running back to the safety of the trees. I stared in shock, as Tice lay motionless on the ground.

We were all furious about what had happened to Tice. The Germans had disguised themselves as British paratroopers, in order to trick us into coming out of cover. It was a dirty trick to kill a man like that; shameless.

* * *

Some more paras tried to get across the Rhine again that night of the 22nd, but only about fifty from our 8th Company were successful. Sherman tanks from XXX Corps had arrived to support but were too heavy to get down to the riverside. They just started sinking when they got close and the Germans had reinforced their positions on the north bank with more heavy machine guns.

A crossing had been improvised with six small rubber dinghies that we and the British had. The British engineers on the north bank, and the Polish engineers on the south linked the boats up to a cable which they ran across the river. But the cable kept breaking, so the paras had to row across instead. They could only get two men in each boat, and they had to row against the current, so it took a long time under heavy fire. After suffering casualties, a halt was called at 3am; there was just one boat left afloat by that point.

The next day, 23 September, Captain Kobak came to us. 'Our company is going to attempt the crossing tonight, along with the rest of the 3rd Battalion. We'll cross in the dark, when it's harder for the Germans to see us.'

* * *

It was our third day in Driel. Throughout the rest of the day, the sounds of artillery and machine gun fire continued from the direction of Oosterbeek across the river. The north bank of the river was under heavy German attack. The British paratroopers were resisting strongly but were suffering losses and were only in control of a small section of the other bank of the Rhine now; but they still controlled the landing area that we would need to get across.

We expected to go as soon as it was dark, in order to get support over to the British as soon as possible; but it was only at about 2am, that third night, when an English officer came to collect our section. 'It took a long time to get the boats from XXX Corps,' was all he said, his face lit up from overhead by the flares that the Germans were sending up.

My heart was racing and we could hear the sound of machine gun fire getting louder as we walked down to the Rhine. Captain Kobak was already there, rushing about, yelling and supervising the crossing. There were a number of boats in the river.

The Germans had put up parachute flares, so that the flares dropped down slowly and gave them more time to see where we were. You could hear the roaring machine guns from the German positions on the north bank, hear the bullets fizzing past you all around and see long lines of spray being brought up from the river as the bullets hit the water.

This must be what hell looks like, I thought to myself, my heart pounding as I fought to remain calm and not panic. The situation was desperate; the boats were under heavy fire. It looked like the Germans were firing on anything that was put into the water. There were wounded paratroopers who had fallen into the river, and were trying to swim but were dragged down by their heavy equipment, or swept away by the strong current. Wounded men were screaming; unmanned boats were drifting, circling or sinking.

On the mudflats beside the river there were a few small boats that looked of questionable quality. Our section was directed towards a nearby boat and we quickly ran over to it, and started dragging it down to the south bank of the river. We jumped inside, Big Mietek and I at the front, Jurek in the middle and Bartek pushing us off from the side, before he in turn climbed in. We grabbed what paddles there were and started rowing as fast as we could; but there weren't enough oars for all of us and those who didn't have a paddle rowed with the butts of their rifles. The boat was heavy and hard to control in the strong currents. The current pushed against us and we were making slow progress. Each paddle stroke hardly seemed to move us forward at all, fighting against the current, under the light of the flares above and the constant sound of the machine guns from the opposite bank.

We were sitting ducks! A bullet whizzed past my ear with a sudden high-pitched whine, and a round of bullets strafed a pattern in the water off to the left hand side of our boat. 'We're hardly moving!' I shouted to Mietek.

The boat offered no protection at all from the machine gun fire as we inched our way sluggishly across the river. As we approached the half way point of the river, there was suddenly the sound of a bullet hitting something next to me; a loud *ping* as it hit metal and Mietek was abruptly thrown backwards in the boat.

'Mietek!' I cried out, and turned to him. He was lying on his back against the side of the boat. He wasn't moving and his helmet had been knocked forward over his face. 'Mietek!' I called again. I stopped paddling and turned towards him, taking hold of the lapels of his army jacket. Then, slowly, he started moving. He raised his arms to his helmet, pushing it back from his face and then gently taking it off his head. He examined it closely, bringing it up to his eyes to see it better in the low light of the flares. Then, holding his helmet up towards me, he poked one of his fingers through a hole that had been shot in the top of his helmet, looking at me with a shocked expression. Then, he turned around and shouted 'Paddle!!' at the top of his voice to everyone in the boat and started paddling desperately with the butt of his rifle.

We all paddled. We paddled as hard as we damn well could and didn't stop, even when we were out of breath and our arms were aching, and the seconds seemed like minutes, and the other shore could never come quickly enough. 'Keep paddling!' shouted Mietek frantically again.

We gradually got closer towards the other shore and it became clearer that the landing zone was a short muddy area, with a fringe of trees about ten metres back. When we landed, we scrambled out of the boat as quickly as we could and ran up the mud on the riverside to the shelter of the forest which would offer some protection. There we sat and waited, breathing heavily. We watched, as the boats behind us tried to make their crossing. There weren't many boats after ours; I could only see two of them in the light of the flares. In the last one on the river I could see Kobak, at the back of his boat, shouting at his men to row as quickly as they could, as the bullets strafed through the water all around.

As I watched, the first boat was suddenly sent into chaos and confusion. A stream of bullets had ripped through the water towards it, then right through the middle of the boat, the men's bodies being sent into convulsions as the bullets hit them, then either slumping down in the boat, or being sent overboard into the river to sink under the water.

'*My God*,' I said to myself, as I watched the boat now start to drift and circle aimlessly down the river, taken by the current. I could see Kobak gesticulating, paddling wildly, and shouting at the top of his lungs to the other men in his boat although I couldn't hear what he was saying.

The men in Kobak's boat redoubled their efforts, paddling maniacally with their rifle butts and paddles, metre by metre, gradually getting closer to us, until we could see their faces and see their expressions of effort and fear; until they managed to reach the shore, their boat running up alongside ours and Kobak and the other men jumped out and came up to join us at the tree line.

There were no more boats after Kobak's. 'We're the last ones across,' he said, trying to catch his breath. 'Sosabowski has stopped the crossing; says it's too dangerous.' We had only managed to get about 150 paratroopers across, maybe a third of what we had hoped.

The landing zone was still controlled by the British, but the Germans were very near, so we needed to be careful. We had to get away from the river and find somewhere to rest. Kobak led the group of us through the forest. My ears and eyes were straining for any noise that might suggest danger. In our group there was my section and then the section that had come over in the boat with Kobak; about ten or fifteen of us in total.

It was hard going in the dark. We had to go carefully and quietly, crouching low and trying not to make too much noise as we walked through the undergrowth so that the Germans wouldn't see or hear us. I wondered where we could be headed and whether we were going to meet up with the other Polish paratroopers, or with the British. After some time, Kobak turned to us and said 'let's stop and have a rest here. We'll see better where we are in the morning.'

We were all exhausted after the past few days, so I put my rifle between my legs and my hands under my belt and fell asleep until morning.

Chapter 30

For the Memories

We got going again at dawn the next morning, Sunday 24th. There was a calmness in the air, a lull in the fighting after the incessant machine gun fire of last night. Maybe the Germans were taking a rest too, but I knew it was only temporary. We carried on through the trees and the undergrowth, going as quietly and as cautiously as we could so that the Germans didn't spot us. It was easier going than it had been in the dark the previous night. Eventually, through the trees we could spot the British paratroopers up ahead. They were digging into trenches amongst the trees for protection from the German fire.

There was one young paratrooper, sitting down beside a tree next to me; he wasn't digging. He looked up at me and we just stared at each other for a moment. He looked exhausted, his face was dirty and grimy from the digging and the soil and all the smoke and dust of the shooting and shelling and explosions.

'Have you got any food? I'm starving,' he said eventually, without much energy. No supplies had been getting through to them since they had landed almost a week earlier. Their radios weren't working well and they had even been trying to use carrier pigeons to communicate with the UK. I gave him one of my corned beef rolls and hoped that it wouldn't soon be my turn to be hungry.

'Do you know the Nazis have SS panzers here?' he looked up at me, eyes wide. 'The 9th and 10th Division Panzers; but it's the 9th Division you've got to worry about. They're the ones that execute their prisoners.'

He closed his eyes and stopped talking, and I took a moment to look around where we were. After the failure to take and keep the bridge at Arnhem, the British paratroopers had ended up having to retreat here, to the west of Oosterbeek and had been trying to defend it for about five days now; waiting until XXX Corps from the Second Army could get here. The Germans hadn't shifted them much, but they were running out of food and energy and ammunition now.

The river was their southern boundary and they were defending a perimeter around the west, north and east. At the centre was the Hotel Hartenstein, where Major General Urquhart was based. There were about three or four thousand British paratroopers still fighting there. They had started out with around ten thousand when they landed, but many had been killed, wounded or captured. Paratroopers aren't equipped to fight against heavily armed opposition like panzer tanks.

Only about 150 Polish paratroopers had managed to get across the river the previous night, added to the 50 from the night before that. We found ourselves in the eastern perimeter. The paratroopers were dug in amongst a few shallow trenches amongst the trees, and sheltering in a few houses around this area.

The British paratrooper opened his eyes again. 'There is a crossroads up the road, at the intersection of a couple of streets called Utrechtseweg and Stationsweg. It has been pretty heavy fighting up there,' he said. He paused, then suddenly continued. 'It's just luck! You think of all the training and so on, but at the end of the day it's just luck what happens to you. Pure luck!'

* * *

We all set to work helping the British paratroopers dig out the trenches, which were little more than small foxholes, dotted about amongst the trees. We dug in silence; there was no gunfire. There had been a temporary truce called to deal with the wounded. Over the previous days, first aid stations had been set up in homes around the area. They put the British and the German casualties all in there together, Dutch civilian casualties too. Sometimes it was the British in charge of a house, sometimes it was the Germans. It went back and forth, depending on how the fighting was going.

When we had finished digging, I settled down with Bartek in one of the small trenches, and we set up the Bren gun on its two-legged stand ready for use. The Bren was on machine gun mode and I got into position, with Bartek as my number two. He had the spare barrel and ammunition and would help me reload and change the barrel when it became overheated. I was about to say something to Bartek, but my words were drowned out by an abrupt explosion of noise. The Germans had opened fire on us; suddenly it seemed like they were all around us, in a cacophony of machine guns, and mortar shells. 'The truce is finished!' I shouted to Bartek over the racket.

Amongst the noise and chaos I tried to remember what we had been taught – only fire the Bren gun in short bursts; four or five rounds at a time, that's all; just count a couple of seconds and then stop firing for another few seconds. That way we could get about a minute of firing before we had to reload with another magazine and it would help stop the barrel getting too hot and jamming.

A shell exploded noisily about thirty metres or so ahead of us, showering a spray of earth and wood into the air. It was mayhem all around us; the dull rhythmic thudding of the machine guns firing, and the high pitched whistling sound of the bullets flying past us, with the bloody shells exploding all around, and shrapnel hitting the trees that surrounded us and the top of the trench. The Germans were firing the shells from mortars and there was a lot of smoke, dust and earth being thrown up from the explosions, onto us and into the trench. You couldn't even see the sun. 'We're sitting like bloody rabbits in a hole!', I yelled to Bartek, holding on to my helmet as the blast wave hit us from a shell that exploded nearby.

I couldn't see anything clearly through the trees and the smoke and dust, but I kept firing thinking that I would keep the Germans suppressed, if nothing else. The Bren gun vibrated and roared in my hands like some kind of a wild animal. I fired it in the direction of the Germans, towards the direction of Arnhem to the east, where I could hear the sounds of the German machine guns coming from.

The Nazi machine guns had a much faster rate of fire than ours and I hoped that might mean they would go through their ammunition faster too. I could see the other trenches, where Big Mietek and the other Polish and British paratroopers were also sheltering and firing back at the Nazis. In the bedlam, I could even see one of the British officers trying to send off a message by carrier pigeon. Good luck flying back to England in this, I thought to myself.

Every minute or so we would stop to reload a new magazine, Bartek pulling the used magazine out of the top of the gun and replacing it with another one. Then Bartek changed the barrel; it was starting to get red hot and we didn't want the bullets to stick. He lifted the catch, then wrapped his jacket around his hand to protect it from the heat, and pulled the barrel forward and out from the gun. Placing it to one side, he then took the spare barrel out of his equipment bag and inserted it back into the gun.

The area to our left was taking a pounding. The paras in the trenches there were being pummelled with mortar shells; you could hardly see them through a haze of dirt and dust. I'm not sure how long it lasted for, maybe ten minutes, twenty minutes, I'm not sure. Maybe it was only a few minutes. Time passes in a strange way in those kinds of situation. Then, suddenly, almost as quickly as it had started, the German firing stopped and the woods again fell silent.

Bartek and I sat there without talking for a few minutes. The sweat was dripping off my brow with the effort of trying to hold the Bren gun steady and fire it. 'Do you have any cigarettes, Staszek?' Bartek asked me. I had to half lip-read him; the sounds of the explosions were still ringing in my ears and making it hard to hear.

I didn't want to smoke so I swapped him my weekly ration of 50 or 100 cigarettes for the handful of sweets that he had. When he took them, I could see that his hand was shaking. He lit up the first cigarette straight away inhaling deeply, so that the cigarette glowed brightly. He smoked it quickly, the ash drooping more and more from the end of the cigarette, and then falling to the ground, and he then lit another cigarette from the end of the cigarette that he had just finished.

I remembered how nervous he had been when he first jumped out the plane back at Ringway in Manchester and how he had given me a photo of himself in uniform once we had all become fully qualified paratroopers. In those days it had been a kind of tradition in the brigade to give photos of ourselves to close colleagues and friends as a memento and to write a few words on the back.

The German guns were still silent. Captain Kobak came over and told us to get ready to move out. Our section would be moving forward, ahead of the British lines, to help defend a key crossroads. I wondered to myself whether going ahead of the lines was a great idea but kept my thoughts to myself. Kobak led us for a few hundred metres through the trees, past houses pock-marked with bullet holes, through gardens, along streets. It looked like it had been a leafy, well-to-do suburb, but now many of the houses were gutted, with their windows blown out, and the streets were covered with wrecked cars, downed telegraph wires, tree branches and rubble.

We ran quickly across any open areas and sheltered behind any cover that we could find: trees, walls, vehicles. There were dead bodies here and there in the streets and in the woods – both Germans and Allied soldiers. They couldn't remove the dead as there was too much gunfire and shelling. There were snipers everywhere.

Kobak brought us to a house near a crossroads. It was a two-storey house, with a smaller third storey in the attic. It should have been a nice building; it was painted white and you could see pretty white wooden shutters still hanging to the sides of the large six-paned windows. But many of these had been blown out and the sides of the building were now dirty and riddled with bullet holes. It was on a street called Utrechtseweg near where it intersected with another street called Stationsweg. The street names sounded familiar and then I realised that this was the crossroads which the British paratrooper had been telling me about earlier, where the heavy fighting had been.

Utrechtseweg was the main street between Oosterbeek and Arnhem. When the British paras had landed here at first, the Dutch had come out cheering to welcome them, waving orange flags. But now it was like no man's land. The Dutch were sheltering in their cellars, and the Allies were sheltering in the houses or in trenches. We got inside the house just in time. No sooner were we inside than the German guns started again.

The whole situation around Arnhem was touch and go. The Germans had retaken Arnhem Bridge and were using improvised battle groups, that they called kampfgruppe, but our ground troops from XXX Corps were close. We needed to defend this area for as long as we could to give XXX Corps time to get over to us. We positioned ourselves near the windows so that we could get a good shot over the road and up towards the crossroads; but all the time making sure that we weren't seen by anyone. There were tanks in the area that could blow us to bits and snipers watching out for any movement.

Many of the windows were already broken or blown out, but we cleared away any sharp shards and knocked out more panes with the butts of our rifles where we needed to in order to get clear shots. I could see across the Utrechtseweg to the houses and gardens on the other side. If I came right up to the window then I could see up the road to the crossroads, but

I tried to stay further back, so that the Nazis wouldn't see me. Control of many of the houses had been changing hands back and forth regularly between us and the Germans, depending on how the fighting was going; some of them had been turned into first aid houses.

The firing continued from tanks, machine guns, rifles and mortars. From my vantage point, I could see some Germans and tanks in the distance. Puffs of smoke were coming from the barrels of the tanks, as they fired towards the British and Polish positions or towards some of the buildings where they suspected paratroopers might be hiding. There was one German soldier, far away, who was shooting. I could barely see him in the distance, but took aim with my rifle. Looking carefully along the gun sight, I slowed my breathing and heart rate as much as I could and fired. I don't know if I hit him, but the shooting stopped.

Then, a few minutes later, a German soldier approached along the road and passed by outside. He was a young German with a machine gun. He was close. It was an easy shot. I could see his face clearly and I could see him looking all around him nervously, as he walked along. My first thought was to shoot him in the back as he walked away up the street. But it didn't feel right. And then I thought no, I should just shoot him in the leg, just to wound him, but not to kill him. I raised my rifle to take aim, but again I wasn't sure and I hesitated. And then, finally, I just thought: *let him go; just let him go.*

I don't know why I let him go when I didn't let others go. Maybe it's fate, I thought to myself. Maybe if I spare you, then you will spare me. Or maybe you'll be the one that shoots me in the end. Like that British paratrooper said, maybe it's all just pure luck.

After the German soldier disappeared up the road, the guns again fell silent.

We couldn't see anything happening outside and Bartek signalled to us that he was going to move closer to the window to get a better look. He stood up, and went up closer to the window, poking his head out, so that he could see up the street to the crossroads. He turned back round and started to speak, then suddenly slumped forward, a look of shock on his face. He collapsed onto the ground with a thump, lying on his side, with his arms and legs all askew.

'Bartek!' I shouted, running across to him. I pushed his helmet back from his face. His eyes were wide; staring. 'Ugh…ugh,' he tried to speak but no words came out. The side of his head was covered in blood, which ran down his ears and the side of his face and neck, soaking into his army uniform.

'Bartek!' I said again, choking up. 'Jesus Christ, Bartek hang in there, we'll get help!' And I looked around at the others, but I knew that it was too late and then I felt his body go limp, and he stopped trying to speak and I saw his eyes lose their focus and lose their spark, and then it was all over.

Just like that. Gone. And I thought about his wife and child back in Poland, and found myself crying; for him, for them and for all of us. Mietek came over and closed his eyes and we laid him out straight. I covered him with a blanket that was in the room, and then I slumped back against the wall.

I pulled out the photo he had given me back in the UK. I turned it over. On the back he had written 'To Staszek, for the memories.'

Chapter 31

The Crossroads

We spent a restless night in the house. Bartek's body in the corner loomed out of the shadows and entered our dreams in the brief moments that we were able to rest. We took it in turns to keep watch from the windows and to make sure that the Nazis were not mounting an attack along the street. But we didn't see anything until the next morning, on the 25th. Then, a low rumble started to build, coming along the road from the direction of Arnhem. I poked my head over the window sill and could see a large vehicle coming towards us, kicking up dust into the air behind it. As it got closer, I could see that it was a tank.

Could it be one of ours? Had XXX Corps managed to get across the river? Or was it one of the Nazi tanks? Then, for a brief moment, the dust cleared slightly and I got a clear sight of the marking on its side. There was a black cross, surrounded with a white border; the emblem of the Wehrmacht, the German armed forces.

Panzers! It was a Tiger tank. Tanks could blow us sky high if they found us in here. The noise of the tank grew louder as it drew closer and closer to us. I could hear the caterpillar tracks squeaking and clanking and squealing as they rotated. Kobak crawled over to the window, next to me, passing close by the body of Bartek.

The tank was now almost outside, the house was shaking as it rumbled over the ground, crushing the rubble and tree branches under it as it went. Then suddenly it stopped, just outside the next house down from us. It just sat there, silent and menacing, like a vast metal beast brooding in the street.

Sheltered inside the house, we weren't sure what we should do. Was it best to hope the tank would move on after time, or should we take advantage of this moment to try to take it out, but then risk the tank opening fire on us? Looking down at my left leg, I saw my Hawkins anti-tank grenade, strapped just above the ankle. It was about 6 inches by 3 inches, metal, with a dark maroon colour paint on it. I wondered whether I could somehow crawl outside and put my Hawkins grenade under the tank. The tank's armour was thinner at the sides and the rear where the engine was. The Hawkins grenade could be used like a mine – when the tank drove over it, the charge would be detonated.

I told Kobak about my plan and he sat without answering for a few seconds, considering the options. Eventually he responded, shaking his head. 'Better not. The tank might head off in the other direction and not set it off, so you would risk your life for nothing.'

I looked out at the tank again, still stationary, about 20 metres down the road from us. Then, suddenly, I saw the roof hatch on the turret start to open, and I ducked back down again quickly as one of the soldiers stood up out of the hatch. There was silence in our room; all you could hear was the sounds of people breathing heavily. Then, a loud voice came from outside. 'English here?' It was the soldier from the tank. 'English here?' the voice called out again. 'This is the English army. We have come to help you. Any English here?'

We looked at each other with confusion. Wasn't this a German tank? Why was he speaking in English? Why was he saying that he wanted to help?

Kobak motioned with his hands for everyone to remain hidden and then I realised that it was a trick. I remembered what had happened to Tice. The Germans were pretending to be British to fool us into revealing ourselves, so they could fire on us. We all looked at each other; nobody moved. I desperately wanted to look out the window to see what the soldier was doing, but I didn't dare risk it in case he saw me. I couldn't hear anything from outside. How many of them were there? Was he still in the tank, or was he coming out of the tank? Was he on the street? Looking at the houses? Was he going to come into our house and find us?

Then, outside I heard the echoing sound of metal clanging down on metal; could it be the roof hatch on the tank being closed? And then the tank engine revved, and I could hear it starting to move again, rumbling and squealing, along the street, past our house and then continuing further along, until it was out of our sight and hearing.

I took a deep breath and exhaled slowly after the tank left. There was a quiet lull in the street, and I could hear birdsong coming in through the broken glass of the window beside me. Mietek put his head back against the wall, staring up at the ceiling.

* * *

The captain decided that we needed to get more information on what was happening. We couldn't get good radio communication and we didn't know what the situation was like outside now; whether the British were still in the same positions as yesterday or if the Germans had pushed the Allies back, or if we had pushed the Germans back.

Kobak would go back over the road to where the British paratroopers were, then bring back news about what we would do. He pointed to Big Mietek. 'I want you to come with me.' I would stay behind with Jurek, on high alert for any signs of the Germans and we would give covering fire when Kobak and Mietek crossed the road.

Big Mietek and Kobak gathered up their guns, and Jurek and I settled ourselves into positions beside the windows where we could cover them as best as we could. As they left the house, running out onto the road, we opened fire towards the German positions to try to cover their movements. Then they disappeared across and down the road and into the trees on the other side.

Jurek and I stayed in position for around one hour, waiting for the return of the others. Then, just when I was beginning to wonder what had happened to them, we saw Big Mietek and Kobak, running up the road from the direction of the trees about one hundred metres away. They were making their way quickly towards us, running around the side of a burned out wreck of a car, then jumping over the rubble and tree branches on the street.

They were making good progress and had almost reached the safety of the house but then, suddenly, a shot rang out and Kobak fell to the ground, just ahead of Mietek. Mietek abruptly stopped, looking around himself with his eyes and mouth wide open, and then down at the body of Kobak beside him, which wasn't moving.

Then I saw Mietek bend over and grab Kobak under his shoulders and he started trying to pull him up the street, towards our house door. But it was desperately slow going; Mietek was walking backwards in small shuffling steps, his body arching backwards, trying to pull as hard as he could and heave Kobak off the street. Then, another shot rang out from the same place as before and, just beside Mietek's foot, a small puff of dust and smoke rose up from the ground, as the bullet ricocheted off the road surface.

Mietek jumped away instinctively from the shot and then, with one last look at Kobak, who still hadn't moved, he turned his back on him and ran as fast as he could towards our house, shoulder-barging the door open, so that it crashed against the wall as he ran in and then slamming it shut again behind him.

'Damn them all! Fuck this whole damn war!' Big Mietek shouted, breathing heavily, sweat on his forehead. He was standing at the door to the room where Jurek and I were stationed. He leaned back against the wall, and slowly slumped down to the ground, his knees up at his chest.

I looked around the room, with the broken windows and the body of Bartek in the corner, covered by the blanket, at Jurek sitting beside the window, and at Big Mietek sitting in the other corner staring at the floor, with his head on his knees.

The body of Kobak outside hadn't moved. I didn't give them the details, how I had seen Kobak collapse to the ground instantly, how there was a pool of blood gathering beside his body, and how when Mietek tried to drag his body, there had been a thin trail of blood left on the road behind him. We had to decide whether to go out and get Kobak's body, but we soon realised there was nothing that we could do. There was too much gunfire, and the Germans would be looking out for us. Mietek had almost been shot already.

And I wondered who had shot Kobak, and whether it had even been the guy that I had let go the other day.

* * *

Mietek took a deep breath and looked up. 'We got the damn orders,' he told us.

Another crossing of the Rhine had been attempted the previous night, to bring more support over to us. More of the Poles and also some of the British, from the Dorset Regiment of XXX Corps. They had wanted to try it with boats again and some amphibious trucks, but it hadn't been successful. They didn't have enough boats and they didn't judge the currents correctly so only a handful of the Dorsets had got across, the rest were swept too far downstream and were captured.

It had been decided that the crossing of the Rhine by the British Second Army was no longer feasible for the time being, so there had been a change of plan. The order had come through that there would be a retreat from Oosterbeek, called Operation Berlin.

The British and Polish paratroopers would retreat back over the Rhine that night, under cover of darkness. In the meantime, we had to sit tight and defend our positions. The Germans had been increasing their attacks and had started bringing in Tiger tanks. They had pushed through some of our lines, and the British and Polish had been fighting hard so that we didn't get cut off from the river.

That evening, a heavy downpour started. The rain fell from the sky in heavy sheets that obscured our vision, and it gathered in large puddles on the roads and pavements. I hoped that the bad weather would help to conceal us a bit. About 9pm a British paratrooper arrived, to take us down to the river. We would be evacuated in order – first those who were furthest to the north, followed afterwards by those closer to the river. Some men would remain in place all night; mainly the wounded soldiers. They would provide covering fire for us.

The Allies had done everything we could to conceal our plans from the Nazis. We were sending out fake wireless transmissions so that the Germans would think we were still there, and everyone was staying in their positions until the last minute. If the Germans suspected anything it was hoped that they would think we were trying to make another resupply mission, not that we were trying to evacuate everyone. XXX Corps would provide an artillery barrage and machine gun fire to keep the Nazis suppressed, and the Canadian Engineers would organise the boats for the crossing.

Mietek, Jurek and I followed the British paratrooper out of the house leaving the body of Bartek behind. Then out onto the road and past Kobak. He was lying face down, his arms and legs spread-eagled at awkward angles; the blood that had oozed out of him was being gradually washed away by the rain. We stayed in the shadows, which the gloom of the storm helped to deepen, the rain falling heavily around us, and helping to muffle any sound that we made.

The British paratrooper led us along the road, past one of the first aid houses which had a flag with a red cross hanging outside it. It was quiet that night; there was nobody firing on us. He led us across the road and through the trees, past the trenches and down towards the river. Every so often we came across figures who silently helped guide us in the right direction, and there was some tape tied to trees to aid us on the right path.

We went in single file and as we walked I wondered anxiously about what would await us by the river. Whether it would be like last time, with German machine guns and shells, or whether the rain might protect us a bit. I wondered if all the boats would be ready and if there would be enough of them.

As we approached the Rhine my eyes were becoming used to the dark, and when we came out of the tree line and onto the marsh land and the muddy shore, I could see that there were hundreds of people there. The scene was illuminated by red tracer shells being fired from XXX Corps across the river. The paratroopers were sitting and lying in the mud, in small groups of ten or fifteen; sitting silently, or whispering quietly to each other. Some of them had tried to camouflage themselves by blackening their faces with mud.

They were patiently waiting for the boats. I could see two or three boats there, on the shore. Small, flat-bottomed metal boats, called storm boats, which had an outboard motor on the back. Under normal circumstances they could carry about ten people, but it was more like fifteen men that were climbing onto each one that night, and when they were fully loaded the boats sat low in the water, so low that I wondered whether they would get across the river without sinking.

There were a few other boats already on the river, boats packed with men making their way to the southern shore, and empty boats driven by the Canadian engineers making their way back across the two hundred yards or so of water to where we were waiting. We took our places on the bank, soaked and shivering from the rain, alongside another group of British paratroopers, to wait for our turn. We sat silently, listening to the sounds of the artillery and machine gun fire from XXX Corps on the other side of the river, or mortar fire from the Germans, or the sound of the storm boats' outboard motors, which sounded so loud right next to us that I felt sure that the Germans must know that we were there.

Sometimes a German mortar shell landed close and we had to crouch down into the mud and cover our heads, but they didn't hit us; maybe the rain and the darkness were protecting us. We waited for hours in the mud and the rain. The boats went back and forth all night, carrying a total of more than two thousand paratroopers. Sometimes a boat's engine would stall in the middle of the river and then the soldiers would paddle with their rifles, while the engineer desperately tried to restart the engine; sometimes an overladen boat would start to sink, or a boat would capsize if it hit a sandbank, and the men would bail out into the fast flowing river and try to swim for it. Weighed down by their clothes and equipment, not all of them made it.

But for every boat that made it successfully back and forth across the river, more men arrived on the muddy shore beside us. 'They're not getting us across fast enough!' I whispered to Mietek who was sitting just in front of me. 'There are still hundreds of us here! If we're not across before dawn, the Germans are going to see us and we're not going to have a chance!'

One by one the waiting groups were told that it was their turn and they would then clamber aboard; the boat sinking low in the water with the number of people, and set off across the river; but still we weren't taken.

Men started to get anxious. 'What's happening? What's the delay?' we asked each other. Some said that there was a shortage of boats; some said that the boats had been caught by the strong currents and drifted too far down the river to be used; some said that half the boats couldn't be used as they were too far west – they were mistakenly placed at crossing points which turned out to be controlled by the Germans.

Time passed and the sky in the east started to lighten ever so slightly, the first sign that dawn was coming. It was only at around 5am that an officer eventually came over to our group and told us it was our turn to get into a boat. We made our way down the slope towards the river's edge, slipping and squelching through the mud until the water was lapping at our feet. I was towards the back of the line, next to one of the British paratroopers and just behind Big Mietek and Jurek. The men in front started to climb onto the boat, and we all gradually shuffled forwards, awaiting our turn supervised by the officer. Two men on the boat, then four, then six, then eight; all British paratroopers so far; then Mietek and Jurek; that made ten, then another two British paratroopers and another two. Fourteen on the boat, and I was next, alongside the last remaining British paratrooper.

It was a tight squeeze, the boat was crowded and very low in the water. Some of the waves were almost coming up to the gunwale and coming inside the boat. I stepped into the water, and grabbed the side of the boat, ready to swing my leg over the side. The Englishman on the other side did the same. But just as we were about to clamber into the boat, the supervising officer put an arm on my shoulder. 'It's too full, you can't get on. You neither,' he added to the Englishman on the other side. The British para was desperate: 'I've got to fucking get across! I've got to go!'

The boat was already starting to move off, as the Canadian engineer in charge of the boat throttled up the motor. I could see Big Mietek and Jurek looking back at me with an expression of shock on their faces.

'Where's the next one? I've been waiting all bloody night!' the para exclaimed; he was getting really agitated, and was looking all around for where another boat might be. He was starting to go crazy. He looked around again; our boat with Mietek and Jurek was now about 20 or 30 metres out into the river and I could just make out their faces in the gloom. There was one other boat near to us on the bank, but it was now full with other paratroopers. Some boats were making their way across the river towards the other bank, and there were some boats at the other side, but there were no boats travelling back across the river towards our side.

'I can't fucking stay here!' the para cried out, 'It's getting too light! They're going to stop the crossings! The bloody Nazis will get us!'

And, before I could say anything he was running into the river; up to his knees in the water, then up to his waist, still with his full kit on. Then further out into the river, and you could see the strong current start to take him and he was being swept downstream. You could see him try to fight against it, but his equipment was heavy and dragging him down and then his head was starting to sink below the water. He bobbed up again as he splashed his arms and legs maniacally, but then next time he was below the water for longer, and above the water for less time, and then the time after that below water for even longer and the time after that he didn't come up at all.

The sky continued to get brighter in the east, dawn was definitely coming now and as the visibility got better, I could hear an increase in the German firing towards us. They could see what was happening now, and were beginning to realise that it wasn't a resupply mission, it was everyone escaping. As the firing increased, I had to make a quick decision. Could I swim it? Maybe if I took off some of my equipment I could do it?

There were still hundreds of other paratroopers on the north bank, all around me. As the reality of the situation dawned on them, we all had the same decision to make. Some of them launched themselves into the river, and were swept away or under the water like the first paratrooper; others were taking off their clothes, and then trying to swim the river naked. I didn't have time to see if anyone would make it all the way to the other shore. Others ran and hid from the German firing, getting away from the open terrain next to the river and taking refuge amongst the trees.

I decided that I couldn't risk swimming it. There was too much German fire, the river was too wide and the water looked too deep and too fast.

Chapter 32

The House with the Red Cross

I decided that I had to get away from the river. It was just too dangerous to stay there with the German machine gun fire and shelling.

I didn't want to go back to the trenches or to the house at the crossroads. I knew that the Germans would soon realise that we were gone, and would come looking for anyone that had been left behind. Maybe they would take us prisoner, or worse maybe they would just shoot us. Kobak had told us that there are rules and laws for how prisoners of war are treated, but they are not always followed and he hadn't been sure how the Germans would treat the Poles, as they had invaded Poland and considered it part of their territory rather than a separate country.

Then I remembered the aid house, with the red cross outside, which we had passed on the way to the river from the crossroads. *As good there as anywhere*, I thought to myself.

I made my way back there. It was a small house with bullet-marked white walls and a grey sloped roof, from which many of the tiles had fallen, leaving behind holes and the bare wooden rafters. There were two bodies lying outside on stretchers beside a glass conservatory, with their helmets pushed down over their faces. I walked past them up to the slightly ajar front door, pushed on it and went in.

The house belonged to a local family who had been sheltering in the cellar, and it had been turned into a makeshift first aid centre. Inside there were wounded of all nationalities: German, British and Dutch. There were lots of men there, taking up all the available space. There was a smell of death and antiseptic. Some doctors were there, but they could hardly do anything in those conditions; they hardly had any equipment or medicines or resources. Table linen was being used for bandages and the injured were covered with coats instead of blankets. There was one wounded German, lying on the floor in his uniform, with a blood-soaked bandage around his head, who was roaring out in pain all the time.

I decided to take out the trigger from my rifle and I dumped it, along with all the rest of my equipment, in a corner of the room. I felt I might be less likely to be shot by the Germans like this. I stayed the rest of the day there and then the night, listening to the shouting and yelling of the German soldier. Everyone slept on the floor as there was hardly any space. In the morning the wounded German was quiet and dead.

Around 10am some Germans came to the house; they were searching for paratroopers. I was standing beside the window and saw them approaching towards the house. When a German officer passed by, he saw me at the window, and he pointed his revolver towards me through the glass. I stepped back quickly and he never fired.

The Germans entered the house; a small ragtag group of three or four of them in khaki uniforms of different types. Most of them looked young except for one older man. The officer was the only one with a metal helmet and had a pair of binoculars around his neck. The others were wearing cloth caps and carried grenades or guns by their side. They looked around the room, gesticulating and pointing at the wounded men, and talking to each other. I couldn't overhear what they were saying. They searched the house and gathered together the few uninjured Allied paratroopers that could walk, including me. 'What are you going to do with us?' I asked one of them. He didn't answer and just pulled me by the arm towards the front door.

They took us outside, myself and two other British paratroopers. Outside there was a group of about twenty other paratroopers that they had already collected. I was the only Pole there. One of the Germans stayed with us while the other Nazis walked off, to continue their search in the other houses, streets and gardens. He was the older man with grey stubble on his face, which he had not had time to shave off during the previous days of battle, and he looked tired and weary. He was wearing a green camouflage jacket and the buttons of his jacket and shirt were undone around his neck, which was covered with dirt and grime.

'Come,' he signalled, with a wave of his arm, and led us off through the streets. We walked silently in three rows, through Oosterbeek, then along the road to Arnhem.

There were heaps of dead British soldiers that the Germans had stacked up at the side of the road. If they were on the road, the tanks just drove over the body, squashing it; you could smell decaying flesh. I saw one para who had landed on electric lines and been burnt to death; he was charred black. The Germans had just left him up there.

When I thought the guard wasn't looking I decided to fling away my army book to the side of the road. I didn't want the Germans to know I was a Polish paratrooper, in case they would want to take revenge. The Polish and British uniforms were similar, so I hoped I would pass as British. We passed lots of other German soldiers on the road. Some were in tanks, others were walking. Some were gathering up equipment that had been abandoned by the British; some were looting the houses, taking out furniture and other household items, and piling them up on the roadside.

One young German soldier on the road came up to our group and started speaking to our guard. The young soldier had a surly face and wasn't wearing a helmet; he had blond hair, which was short at the sides and slightly longer and wavy on top. He was wearing a smart uniform with black lapels on the jacket, on which was printed two letters, SS, that looked like lightning bolts. He continued talking to the old soldier who was saying nothing. Then the young soldier started to raise his voice angrily. He pointed towards me and shouted again. The old soldier shook his head.

We were all watching the two of them. What did the young soldier want with me? My heart then jumped, as he pointed towards me again and, making a shape of a gun with his thumb and forefinger, said 'fire!' to the older soldier. The older soldier said nothing for what seemed like forever, and his young companion again shouted a stream of words at him. Our guard turned around and looked at me. I looked back and, just for a second, our gaze met.

He swung back around, then gave a curt 'nein' to the younger man, then waved us off along the road again, and I could feel the young soldier staring at me hatefully as we passed.

* * *

We walked behind the old soldier for around half an hour along the Utrechtseweg street. He took us to a big house, which sat high up about half a mile outside Arnhem. There was a jeep outside which had a red cross painted on it. 'Wait here,' the German soldier said to us all, motioning inside the building. 'SS guards are here,' he continued, and pointed to the German soldiers who were stationed at the entrance to the garden and around the perimeter of the house. 'Don't escape, or they will shoot,' and he lightly touched the gun at his side.

We went inside and I could see that it was another kind of first aid house. There were wounded men lying on the floor, and a British army doctor who was helping to look after the patients. I sat down against the wall. The floor was wooden and hard, but I was tired and, after a few minutes, I could feel my eyes starting to close and then I fell asleep. When I woke up, the doctor had come over and was standing near me, changing the dressings on one of the patients. When he saw that I was awake he started talking to me.

He told me how he had helped set up this emergency first aid station when the battle started, but when the Germans started pushing back they found themselves on the front line. They had come under mortar fire and some of the patients were even more badly wounded because of that. This house had ended up in the area controlled by the Germans, but they had been allowed to continue working and he had stayed behind after the evacuation to look after the patients.

He did some basic operations, or gave the patients morphine when they needed it. There were a lot of wounded there, but not many staff. Supplies like dressings, morphine and water were running low too. The doctor only had three Dutch nurses to help out, one male and two female. The doctor asked if I could help him out and I agreed.

We had to work by paraffin Tilly lamps as all the electricity was cut off. The first patient I helped with was a man who had shrapnel in his stomach. We needed to take out the shrapnel so that he wouldn't get gangrene. I helped to hold up the patient's head while the doctor injected some morphine into the man's arm, and then he used something like a small chisel to get all of the small pieces of metal out. He put iodine on the wound, to help reduce the chance of infection, and a bandage on top. The doctor scribbled details of what he had done on a tie-on label which he attached to the man's jacket.

Every day, the Germans came round and they took away all of the wounded and any paratroopers that they had captured and brought to the house. They took the badly wounded to hospital, or if they were healthy enough, they would be taken for interrogation or taken by truck to a prisoner of war camp. Each time they only left the doctor and his three

Dutch helpers. But every time that the Germans came I hid in the toilet, so that I wouldn't be taken.

I managed to stay in the house for a few days like this but then, one day, the doctor followed me to where I was hiding in the toilet. 'Look, if you want to escape, you need to do it tonight,' he whispered to me. 'Tomorrow the Germans are going to close this whole place down and they're going to take us all away, me included.'

I wondered how I could get away. I had picked up an inflatable swimming lifebelt from a wounded young British paratrooper in the house, to replace the one that I had thrown away earlier along with all my other equipment. I had asked the paratrooper quietly if he wanted to escape with me, but he had thought he would be better in hospital or as a prisoner. He had started shouting, 'No! I don't want to escape!' so I had taken the lifebelt and left quickly, before one of the SS guards outside heard him and I got into trouble. I told the doctor that I was planning on using it to swim the Rhine.

'God bless you,' he said, simply.

* * *

All that afternoon, I wondered how best to put my plan into action. Even if I was lucky enough that the Germans didn't spot me crossing the Rhine and open fire on me, I remembered from before how wide and fast-flowing the river was. Even with a lifebelt on, and without all my kit to weigh me down, I would still be swept downstream. And how to even get to the river in the first place? The house was still surrounded by the Germans; there was no way out that I could see.

Later that afternoon the male nurse came up to me, while I was standing quietly beside the window, looking out at the SS guards surrounding the house. He was a young man, a teenager and tall; all the Dutch seemed to be tall. He had light brown hair and wore a white shirt with a grey woollen jumper on top. He came up close to me, beside the window and whispered to me: 'Do you want to escape?' I looked at him with shock, then nodded.

'I'm with the Dutch underground,' he said. 'You can call me Willem. One of the other nurses is my sister and the second girl is a friend. I think we can get you out this afternoon, before this place is closed down.'

He put his hand on my shoulder: 'We're going to go out right past the guards. Wait here and I'll bring another bike and civilian clothes for you, and then we'll leave the building together. When we go out, I'll speak Dutch to you. You don't answer.'

Chapter 33

Escape

Willem came back around one hour later, handing me some navy blue overalls to change into from my army clothes. He was waiting near the front door, beside the two girls. They were all young, maybe 17 or 18. 'We've got the bikes ready out there,' he said, pointing to four bikes that were leaning against the outside wall of the house. 'Now remember,' he added, 'just follow us; I'll talk to you, but you don't say anything!'

The four of us left the building and got onto the bikes. I could see the SS guards out of the corner of my eye, but didn't look directly at them; there was a group of them near the entrance to the house, standing around talking to each other and laughing. I remembered what Kobak had said, that if a soldier is caught in civilian clothes, he is treated like a criminal or a spy and likely executed. I tried to put this out of my mind and just concentrated on staying close to the other three. The young man was keeping up a constant chatter to me in Dutch, of which I could understand nothing. We were getting closer and closer to the SS guards, then we were right beside them; I could see the SS marks on their lapels, the dirt on their trousers and the mud on their boots.

One of them turned slightly to look at us as we went past, shifting his rifle a little in his arms; I thought for a moment that he was going to put out his arm and stop us, but he said nothing and then he turned back to his colleagues, as they all started laughing at some joke that someone had said. Then we were past them and out on the road, cycling west away from Arnhem.

We didn't take the Utrechtseweg road to Oosterbeek this time, but took a route in a slightly more northerly direction along a road signposted for a town called Ede; through small towns and the Dutch countryside, away from the gutted buildings and debris-strewn roads of Oosterbeek and Arnhem.

We had been cycling for around ten or fifteen minutes and hadn't met many people on the roads, neither Dutch nor German; then, in the distance I could see coming into view, high up on a banking, maybe three or four Panzer tanks. There were about ten soldiers standing beside them; the light was glinting off the binoculars of one of them, as he looked out over the land towards the river and then to the British positions on the other side.

The road that we were on led over to where they were positioned, passing about twenty metres away from them at its closest point, before it curved away again. That's the danger point, I thought to myself. If we can get past that point then we should be OK. The others were still slightly ahead of me, the two girls in front and the young man behind. The Germans seemed to be ignoring us as we approached their position; they were still surveying the landscape with their binoculars.

I kept pedalling along the flat road, as calmly as I could. Then, just as we were about to reach the closest point to them, my foot suddenly slipped forward and there was a cracking sound as the pedal moved forward rapidly. I put my foot back on the pedal and pushed again, but it just spun round without any force, and I could feel the bike slowing down. I looked down with horror and I could see that the chain had come off! It was hanging loosely down away from the chain-ring at the front.

The Germans were right above me now standing beside their tanks. My bike gradually coasted to a halt; the other three hadn't noticed what had happened and were still cycling on ahead!

'Damn it!' I swore to myself, and a cold sweat started to come over me, as I knew that the Germans were just a few metres away. I cursed my bad luck; why the hell did this have to happen here, of all places. What should I do? I couldn't speak any Dutch and I didn't want to call out to the others and draw more attention to myself. All I could do was try to fix it and hope to God that the Germans would ignore me. Remaining as composed as I could, I got off the bike and tried to fix the chain, my hands shaking. The chain had become wedged in between the bike and the pedal, so I had to pull it hard and work it from side to side to loosen it and then lever it back over the chain ring. It felt like it was taking forever to fix.

I didn't dare look at the Germans on the banking! Were they watching me? My heart beating hard, I swung my leg back over the bike and started cycling again. Were they going to catch me? My apprehension was almost unbearable and my heart was in my mouth, but I still didn't risk looking back at them. The chain seemed to be holding, so after ten or twenty metres I stole a glance out of the corner of my eye. Thank God, they didn't seem to be paying any attention; nobody stopped us.

* * *

I kept cycling and soon managed to catch up with the others with my hands still shaking from the shock of what had just happened. When we reached the outskirts of a small village, the two girls left us and the young man continued with me until we reached a house in the village. It was a pretty house with wooden shutters and white-washed walls, surrounded by a neat garden with grass and flowers, but some of the glass in the windows and front door had been broken as a result of all the artillery firing, and the shards of glass lay on the path and around the garden.

It was the house of a local doctor who was helping the Dutch resistance. He was waiting in the kitchen when I arrived and Willem introduced us. The doctor worked in one of the hospitals; he was living at the hospital too, along with his family so would not be in the house much. The doctor told me to take whatever I needed in the house, and gave me one of his suits to wear. It was a good fit, but a little bit long in the trousers. I rolled up the ends of the trouser legs and tucked them underneath so that they didn't drag on the floor.

There were two other English paratroopers also hiding out in the house. They were slightly older than I was. One was red-haired and the other had dark hair.

Willem told us that he would come back in the evening with some supplies for us. There were Germans all around looking for paratroopers, so he would give a password so that we would know it was him. He told us that anyone who came that we could trust would say 'friend' before they came in the door, and we would have to acknowledge it to let everyone know that it was safe. 'If anyone comes to the house who you don't know, and who doesn't give the password then you have to dispose of them,' he said.

The dark-haired British paratrooper was a friendly guy from London, called Jones. The Dutch underground had helped him escape in his stocking feet after the Germans had taken his boots away. 'The Poles were good to me,' he told me, when he found out where I was from. Earlier in the war he had been captured by the Germans in North Africa, in Tunisia in November 1942, on a mission to destroy German aircraft at an airfield there, called Oudna. The Germans took him as a prisoner of war to eastern Poland, which they were occupying at that time and put him to work on a farm. The Poles helped look after him, trying to smuggle him extra food and supplies. When the Soviets advanced into the east of Poland he had been sent back to the UK.

The red-haired paratrooper, called Baker, was not so friendly. 'Bloody Poles!' he suddenly cried out from his chair. He glared at me, leaning forward in his chair with his hands on his knees. 'You fucking Poles started the war.'

'You'd be here, Poles or no Poles,' I replied. 'Hitler would come to Britain.' Jones turned to him: 'You shut your mouth. You talk a lot of fucking rubbish, you do.'

* * *

We stayed in the house there for about three days. At night, we slept either on blankets and coats on the floor in the cellar, or in the attic, where there was a single bed. Each night Willem would come to bring us food. We would hear his footsteps coming up to the house; at the kitchen door he would say 'friend' so we knew it was OK, and we would let him in. There was some food in the house too, we would eat apples or pears preserved in jars.

Willem sometimes brought bread which he stole from the Germans. He gave me a photo of him with three of his friends. They were in a music group and used to play folk music around the local cafes and bars. All four people in the photograph were dressed in traditional Dutch clothes. Two of the men were dressed in trousers and jackets, with neckerchiefs and hats, while the other two men were dressed like Dutch women! 'Haha, it's for a joke,' Willem told me with a laugh. In the photograph, Willem was sitting, holding a guitar with a long striped skirt, a dark apron, black men's leather shoes and a woman's embroidered headscarf!

On the third day the doctor came back to the house. He was getting worried as by now the Germans were suspicious about hidden paratroopers and were starting to search all of the local homes. Dutch civilians and the

Dutch underground were hiding around 300 or 400 allied soldiers in the woods and houses around there. The doctor told the three of us that he would take us to the hospital where he worked, and where he thought it might be safer. 'There is a cellar there where you can stay until the British Second Army comes,' he told us.

The doctor drove us over to the hospital in his van and parked in the garage there. We waited in the van while he went in. A lot of the German wounded were taken to this hospital, and it was a few miles away from the doctor's house. It was a good bit into German territory, while the house had been close to the front line.

After about half an hour, he came back out again from the hospital, carrying some food which he gave to us in the back of the van. He looked anxious; he had just told his wife about the plan for us to stay in the cellar in the hospital, and she hadn't agreed with it. It turned out that she hadn't known we were staying in the house either. 'She's worried that if you get caught, then all of us will get shot,' he said. I thought to myself that he was probably right.

The doctor told us that he would drive us back to the house again. Despite the risks, he still wanted to help us. For the next two nights nobody came. We heard nothing from Willem or the doctor, and day by day my anxiety was building about what might be happening. Were the Germans still searching all the houses? Had they found out about Willem and the doctor? Were we just going to try to keep on hiding, until hopefully the Allies might make it across the river to us; or were we somehow going to try to get back to them?

Then, on the third day, what I had been dreading happened. We were sitting in the attic when we suddenly heard noises outside. We all sat up straight; I could hear the sound of footsteps outside, cracking glass underfoot as somebody walked around the house breaking the shards of glass that lay on the ground from the shattered windows and doors.

Then we heard German voices and the handle of the front door being turned! There was no time to escape. We all looked desperately around the attic for somewhere to hide. There was a single bed there and lots of other junk and bits and pieces. Jones hid himself behind the wardrobe, wedging himself between the back of the wardrobe and the wall. Baker ran over to the corner where the roof sloped down low and there was lots of junk piled up. He crouched down and hid amongst old chairs and tables, an old rocking horse that must have belonged to the children, coats, blankets, prams.

I started to panic! I couldn't see anywhere else to go! There wasn't room to hide under the single bed and wouldn't that be the first place they would look anyway? Where could I go?! I could hear the Germans in the kitchen downstairs. I hoped that we had left things tidy, so they wouldn't suspect we were there. I could hear them talking to each other and opening and closing drawers, then moving through to the lounge which was near the stairs that led up to the attic.

I looked around myself again frantically; near where Baker was hiding there was an old pram, and a long black winter coat. I flung the coat over the pram and hid below, my heart thumping. The coat almost came to the ground, but not quite; it was maybe six inches or so short; I could see out just at the very bottom on to the wooden floor. Then I heard the German footsteps on the stairs, stomping up in their boots and it was then I remembered, my God, that we had left some apples on the stairs, that we had collected from the trees in the garden. Surely they would see them and surely they would suspect something; but they didn't seem to realise. The footsteps continued up the stairs without halting and then they were coming into the room. There were two of them. From under the hem of the coat I could see their black boots as they came closer, they were standing right next to the pram!

I crouched as low as I could and made myself as small as I could under the black coat, trying to keep myself as far away from the edge of the coat as possible, so that they wouldn't see me.

Just don't move a muscle; don't make a sound; don't make a bloody sound. My heart was pounding in my chest and in my ears, like it was shaking my whole body. I was trying my best to control my breathing. The slightest sound could give us away. The slightest sound. The smallest bloody sound. My breathing is too heavy. Can they hear it? And my heart that is beating like a drum and pounding in my head. Can they hear that too?

The two Germans sat down heavily on the side of the bed. One sighed as he leaned forward, and picked up a pair of women's boots that were lying nearby. 'Heinz,' he said 'these would be good boots for your sister.' Heinz gave a sound of approval. 'Cigarette?' They sat a while talking and smoking.

I scarcely dared to breathe. I can see this damn Heinz's feet right next to me! I can hear him turning those boots in his hands. He's smoking a damn cigarette now! Why won't they just leave! Do they know we're here?!

After a few minutes, one of them got up and went back downstairs. He yelled from the kitchen: 'Heinz, come, come!' But Heinz didn't move. He just sat on the bed.

He must know something! We'll surely be caught. Heinz – move, you bugger! Don't let them lift up this coat and look under it. Is he going to look behind the wardrobe? Or look in the pile of junk where Baker is hiding? If he finds any of us then it's game over for everyone.

Heinz sat quietly five minutes more on the bed. Then, eventually, he went downstairs taking the women's boots with him.

Chapter 34

The Dutch Underground

Heinz... I would never forget that name.

As the adrenaline in my body started to subside, I began to feel light-headed and my legs started to feel weak. I was worried that they might give way at any moment, so I sat down next to Jones. I knew how close we had been to being captured, and I knew that I didn't want to push our luck in the house for much longer.

That night, a young lady arrived at the front door. She gave the password, 'friend', and we let her in. She told us that Willem had been on his way but then the SS started following him so he had passed the job on to her.

It felt like the net around us was tightening more and more. We told her about what had happened to us earlier that day, when the two German soldiers had come into the house, and we had almost been found in the attic. We told her that next time we might not be so lucky and we urgently needed to get out of the house.

We didn't see anyone for another few days then, after we had been in the doctor's house for about a week, the young lady came back again, in the evening after dark. Her name was Maria and she told us that she would take us over to her mother's house. She looked nervous. I could see that her hands were shaking as she spoke. She quietly led us out of the house and a short distance through the village to a small cottage. It seemed like a quiet night, and we didn't see any Germans on the way. When we arrived, there was a plump middle-aged lady in her late 40s, sitting in the kitchen reading a book.

She looked up and smiled at us and Maria when we came in, but then her expression began to change as the situation was explained to her, and Maria told her who we were. Then, as Maria told her the plan for us to stay there, she started crying and shouting hysterically. 'We're going to be shot!' she howled. 'If the Germans find us, they will shoot all of us! Why did you bring these men here!' She was making so much noise that I felt sure everyone in the village would hear her and that she would attract the attention of the Germans!

'Get us out of here!' I said to Maria. 'And tell her to calm down! She's going to bring all the Germans here!' But I couldn't blame the woman for being afraid; we all knew what the situation would be for all of us if we were caught.

Maria hastily said something to her mother and hugged her and then we all hurried out of the house. Maria looked around frantically, in case anyone had overheard us, but the village still seemed to be quiet. 'I'll take you somewhere else. Stay close to me. Come quietly!' Maria then took us along the road, round a sharp right turn, and on to another nearby house in the village, where she introduced us to an older woman and two teenage girls, maybe aged 18 or 19, who lived there. 'These are my aunt and cousins,' she said to us. 'You can stay here tonight with them.'

After the introductions, the older lady soon went to bed but the two girls brought us some bread, sandwiches and some tea and stayed to chat. They seemed to be taking a shine to Jones and me, although Baker went and sat on a couch in the corner, curling himself into a ball; he didn't say much, as usual.

The two girls asked us lots of questions, smiling and laughing, always offering us more food and tea. 'Will you come back here after the war? Do you have a wife, Staszek? What do you think about Dutch girls?' But despite how friendly they were, believe me, I wasn't thinking about girls right then; I just wanted to survive.

We stayed overnight there, Jones, Baker and I sharing the couch. The thought of having a proper bed never even came into my head. As long as it was dry, I would happily put my head down and sleep anywhere.

* * *

The next morning, the older sister came into the lounge. Jones and I were already up, while Baker was still lying on the couch. She told us that she would take us on to yet another house in the village where an old man and woman lived. The couple lived on their own and were maybe in their late seventies. They were a kindly couple, with grey hair and ruddy cheeks, from a lifetime spent outdoors. They said that they had a son but they hadn't seen him for a few weeks. He was with the Dutch underground too, helping the paratroopers, but they weren't sure what had happened to him.

'The Germans use torture on their prisoners to try to get information on the underground,' the old lady told us sadly. She looked tired, like she hadn't slept much over the past few days. 'They slam doors on their hands, or put needles under their nails. They know that there are paratroopers being hidden around here. The Nazis want to take the captured paras away to their prison camps in Germany.'

'Come with me,' the old man said. He led us over to a wardrobe that was in the corner of the kitchen. He unlocked the wardrobe and flung the doors wide open. 'Take anything you want!' I looked inside with astonishment. The wardrobe was full of guns! There were British rifles, French revolvers. I thought I could even see some American guns. I wondered what we should take. On one hand it would be good to have something to protect ourselves with, but if the Nazis found us with weapons then it might mean even more trouble if we were caught. So in the end we thanked our host, but declined his offer.

We stayed in this house for two days. We shared a single bed; the two Englishmen were at one end, and I was in the middle, at the other end. I made sure to turn more towards Jones than Baker; he was a strange guy.

On the morning of the third day, the old man told us that somebody else would come to take us on from there.

Our next contact from the Dutch underground was a man in his 40s called Hans. He had a dark complexion for a Dutch person, with dark hair and dark brown eyes. He took us on to the next destination by bike.

'Be careful,' he said, as we left the old couple's cottage. 'Lots of Germans pass by this place taking their horses to a nearby blacksmiths.' As we started cycling, I could see German soldiers through the trees, leading their horses via the footpaths in the forest.

We all kept pedalling as calmly as we could. Surely the Germans would be looking out for paratroopers like us by now? My memory flashed back to what had happened the last time that I was on a bike, and I prayed that the chain wouldn't come off my bike on this occasion, as we got closer to the Germans. *Please God, don't let it happen again.* When we were only ten or twenty metres away, I could smell the horses and hear the Germans talking to each other. I didn't dare look at them and just focused on Hans ahead. Left leg, right leg, left, right, just keep pedalling, just don't look, and just pedal gently so that the damn chain doesn't come off. And then I took a deep breath and pedalled again, and then we were past the Germans, and they were still talking with each other and, *thank you God for hearing my prayer*, they hadn't taken any notice of us.

We carried on cycling through the forest away from the Germans and the blacksmiths. After a while, Hans stopped and turned to us. 'We're going to split up now,' he said. 'It's easier to hide one person than to hide three.'

He took me on to a farm which was near one of the main roads in the area. There was a large farmhouse and behind the farmhouse there was a windmill; it had a thatched roof and its wooden sails were slowly turning in the wind. To the side there was a wooden shed for storing grain and produce.

'You can sleep in the shed, son,' said the farmer, coming out to greet us. He gave a smile, a cigarette hanging low from the left side of his mouth. He was wearing some old work clothes which had mud stains down the front, and his face was weather-beaten. 'It should be comfortable enough. I'll look after you here until the British Second Army comes.'

He brought me some food: bread, cheese and coffee. The Dutch didn't have much food themselves, so even this was difficult to get hold of. The underground had to steal some from the German army as the Nazis controlled a lot of the farms and the supply of food.

But in the end, I only stayed at that farm for one night. In the morning the farmer came rushing into the shed to wake me up; but I was already awake. I couldn't sleep for more than an hour or two. I would lie there, all sorts of thoughts racing through my head, about what was going to happen to me; if I would ever get back to the UK, if I would even survive, if the Germans would find me. Then, if I eventually drifted off, I would find myself in dreams with parachutes and tanks and guns, and German soldiers goose-stepping and doing Nazi salutes, and Nazis searching the houses and the farms and finding my shed, where I had heard them coming and was hiding in the hay, but then they started bayoneting the hay to check if someone was there, and then I would wake up with a jolt breathing heavily in a cold sweat.

The farmer told me that another person from the underground would come and take me away. 'It's not safe here anymore!' he said frantically. 'Germans are searching all the homes in the neighbourhood. They know we're hiding paras under their noses. They'll be here soon. We need to get you out of here immediately!' His smiles of yesterday had been replaced by a desperate look of worry.

Soon there arrived yet another person from the Dutch underground. He took me away from the main road, off through the forest. He was a young man who said he came from one of the local villages. He had blond hair that was combed back from his forehead and a nose that curved down at the end, like the beak of an eagle. 'It's best you don't know my name,' he said to me. We walked through the forest for maybe one and a half hours. We picked our way through bushes and trees, then crossed a road, then back into the forest on the other side, passing through high bracken, and arrived at a point maybe 800 yards away from the road.

'Many of the houses aren't safe now, and the others have already got paratroopers hiding,' he told me. 'We need to hide you in the forest for a few days until we can find somewhere else safe that you can stay.'

We dug a hole in the ground to a depth of between one and two metres, and lined it with straw, then we interlocked sticks over the hole to make a roof. We covered the sticks with earth and piled it high with lots of bracken to make it waterproof.

The man said 'I'm leaving you now and you won't see me again. A Dutch policeman will look after you. He will have a navy blue uniform. If you see him coming from this direction,' he pointed in the direction of the road, 'he will give three whistles. If you don't hear those whistles, you must clear out quick.'

I got dry bracken and blocked up the entrance at night so that I wouldn't be spotted. I didn't have any blankets, but it was warm enough inside lying on the straw. I felt very alone. I missed the company of Jones, but at that moment I might even have been thankful to have Baker there. It was a long night, feeling constantly on edge and without much sleep. I tried to keep my mind off the situation that I was in, to only think about positive things, and to keep telling myself that it was going to be all right, but it was almost impossible. I passed the hours slipping in and out of a kind of semi-consciousness, listening out for any sound coming from the forest, jumping anxiously whenever an animal passed nearby or a branch cracked. I gradually watched the sky grow lighter as dawn approached.

The next morning, I was sitting in the hole, looking out, feeling tired and anxious, when I saw the head of a policeman coming through the trees. He whistled and I came out of the hole. He was clean-shaven with sharp cheekbones and was wearing a dark blue uniform with shiny metal buttons down the front. He was carrying a good bit of bread. 'I've managed to get this from the German hospital,' he told me, 'and I've got some water too. I'll come the next day with more food. If something happens to me, someone will take over and do the same routine.'

But nobody came the next day. So I just stayed in the hole, or sat quietly in the sun beside it so that I wouldn't be spotted.

On the third day the policeman came again. He brought a kind of watery beetroot soup in a dixie. I stayed there in the forest for a number of days. I kept a look out, but I didn't see any other people. Just the policeman coming for a few minutes each day to bring me some food and water.

It was hard, being on my own day after day. I was constantly on a hair trigger, and looking out for danger; not knowing what would happen to me from one day to the next, or from one hour to the next. Knowing that there were hundreds or thousands of German soldiers out there who were looking for me, who wanted to kill me, or shoot me, or at the very least wanted to take me away and throw me in some Nazi prison camp. Not knowing if anyone was coming to help.

My mind started to play tricks on me. I wondered whether the army had forgotten about me. Maybe they were focusing on other goals, like getting to Berlin, and now they were just leaving us here to fend for ourselves. There were just a few of us here, after all, so maybe they had bigger priorities. Maybe nobody was ever going to come to help us. Maybe all of the Dutch underground were going to be captured and then nobody could bring any food or water here, and then I'd gradually die from starvation. Or maybe the Germans would come to my shelter one night, when I was sleeping, and then they would drag me out of here before I had time to escape.

I thought about Isa, back in Scotland. I wondered what she was doing, and if she had been told that I hadn't made it back over the river with the others. What would she be thinking? Would she think that I had been killed? I tried to distract myself with stupid games, like seeing how many leaves I could count on a branch, or how many bird calls I could hear. Anything to stop thinking about all the bad things that could happen. But it was worse at night when the darkness came down and I could hardly see anything and every shadow became a German, and every sound was a Nazi soldier.

I was in that hideout in the forest for more than a week. After about ten days, the policeman came up to visit me for a last time. He shook my hand. 'Another man is going to be taking over from me,' he said. I wanted to ask him so many questions. Who is coming now? Where will I go? I've been stuck here for weeks – is there any plan to get us back to the UK? When will I get out of here? The policeman shook his head. 'Just try to be patient. He'll come in the evening. God bless you, my friend. I wish you all the best.'

That evening, just as the sun was starting to go down, another young Dutch man came to my hide-out. 'We're going to go deeper into the forest. I'm going to take you to a hut where there are other paras hiding,' he told me.

Chapter 35

Last Chance

We walked for around half an hour through the forest. The light was getting low, and was casting long shadows through the trees. You could see dust and small flies swirling and dancing in the golden light of the setting sun. We approached a wooden hut which had a kind of decking outside. The Dutch man led me up a couple of stairs and then told me that he had to leave, but that somebody would be back the next day. I entered the hut and could see two familiar-looking men in there. One dark-haired and the other red-haired.

It felt so good to see Jones again, after all the days that I had spent on my own in the forest, not knowing what might happen or if I would ever see a friendly face again. Baker hadn't shaved for a few days and was growing a beard; he had bags under his eyes from too many days and nights of half-sleeping. He looked like how I felt; weeks of hiding and living on the edge was starting to take its toll on all of us.

Inside the hut there was just one room. In Baker's corner there was a wooden table, with a few old chairs spread around it in a disorganised way. Then in the opposite corner there was a single bed with a cast iron bed frame. The bed was unmade with no sheets, and the blankets piled up to one side beside a discoloured pillow.

I didn't want to sit beside Baker so I went over to the bed to sit down. As I approached, I could see the mattress looked dirty, and I decided that I would turn it over, in the hope that the other side would be better. I lifted one side up, and as I stood the mattress on its side, I could see a gun lying underneath. It was an American Colt pistol. I picked it up. It was beautifully balanced, and a dark metallic colour, like the colour of storm clouds before a thunder storm. It was an automatic so it could fire fast, although there was only one bullet inside it.

I turned the gun over in my hand, then I slipped it into the side of my shoe, under my sock. Even though it only had one bullet, I thought that I might be able to get more. And I knew what the Germans might do if we were caught; so I would keep this one bullet for myself just in case.

I couldn't relax. There were too many thoughts racing round my head. You never knew if somebody was going to come or if a German soldier was going to find you. Someone could come at any moment, and if that happened we would get shot or taken to some prison camp; we would never get back home.

I decided that I would sleep outside on the deck. If you slept inside you couldn't hear so well what was going on. If you were outside you got a better chance to buzz off if anyone came. Jones joined me, and we decided that we would take it in turns to keep watch. It was a fresh October night but the skies were quite overcast, so the temperature was not too chilly, and we were warm enough under our blankets. There was a light breeze and from the decking I could see some clouds moving past overhead through the trees, and the moon occasionally coming out from behind some gaps in the clouds.

I was on high alert, straining to catch the slightest sound or movement in the forest. It felt like there was potential danger in every movement of tree branches in the wind, or in every rustling noise coming from the undergrowth. After an hour or two of watching, I heard a branch snap to my right and I gave a jump. What was that noise? I stared in that direction, but I couldn't see anything; it was too dark. Or could I? Was there really something there or was I just imagining things? Surely it was just some small nocturnal animal making its way through the forest? I fingered the gun down in my shoes, checking that it was still there.

Baker was snoring inside and the bed occasionally creaked as he turned around in his sleep. On the decking beside me, Jones was also sleeping.

Then, a few minutes later, I heard another branch cracking. I stared again. Was that a shadow over there? A shadow that was somehow darker than the surrounding forest? Then, suddenly the moon came out from behind the clouds again and, yes, I felt sure I could see the silhouette of something larger moving through the forest! I caught my breath when I saw that it was a man coming in the direction of our hut. Had he seen us? Did he know we were here? Who was he? The Dutch resistance had never come in the middle of the night like this before.

My hand reached down again towards the Colt pistol in the side of my shoe and I could feel its reassuring outline under my socks. As the man got closer still, I could hear him breathing heavily, making hard work of the dense bushes and shrubs in the dark. He looked like he was well-dressed, wearing a suit with a white shirt and a tie.

Once he was within about 15 metres, I called out to him: 'Stop!' He stopped suddenly, staring at me. 'Hands up!' I called out again, and I mimed putting my hands up in the air. He followed my instruction silently, slowly putting his hands up, still staring at me intently.

I pulled out the Colt pistol from my shoe, got up carefully from the decking and made my way towards him. I didn't take my eyes off him. I was ready for any sudden move that he might make, but he stood motionless and silent, just watching me. I searched him, using my left hand and keeping my right hand ready with the Colt. I looked in his jacket pockets and his trouser pockets, but he didn't have any documents and he didn't have any weapons.

'Who are you?' I asked him. He didn't answer. I tried again. 'What is your name?' I tried in English, then Polish and some German and Russian – every language I knew, but nothing. Still no answer; he only shook his head, looking at me. Who was this man? Did he really not understand, or was it just that he didn't want to communicate?

I woke Jones up, but he was just as confused by this man as I was. We didn't know if he could be a spy, so we decided that we better hold on to him until the Dutch underground came back again.

* * *

The next morning, the man from the Dutch underground arrived back at the hut. His name was Joost, and he was a tall, wiry man, maybe in his late 20s. He brought more Allied soldiers with him. There was an American soldier, then an English major came and another two British paratroopers, so that there were seven of us in total.

We told Joost about the stranger who had come to the hut the previous night. We had taken him inside and watched over him for the rest of the night. Joost went over to speak to him, but then it turned out that the man couldn't speak Dutch either. It was a real mystery. How was it possible that he couldn't understand any of these languages? How could he not speak English or German or Dutch? Or even Polish? Was he having us on? Was he going to listen to everything we said and then sneak off and tell the Germans? No-one could decide where he could be from. There was a discussion about what we should do with him.

'We should dispose of this guy,' said Baker, staring at us with wide eyes. 'Best not to take any chances. We've all been risking our lives here for weeks now! I'm not going to kick the bucket because of him!'

'But maybe he had been trying to escape and had been living in the hut before we came?' Jones replied.

Joost wasn't sure what to do with him; he hadn't heard of him before. He decided to take him away so that the higher ranks of the underground could try to work out who he was.

We stayed in the hut for about two weeks. It was good to be with other people again, but everyone was anxious, everyone was hungry, everyone was tired from never being able to relax, never knowing if this day was going to be our last and if we would be caught or killed. We were tired from being stuck, hiding behind enemy lines for week after week, in holes and sheds and huts, with no idea if, when, or how we might get out; worried if the people who were helping us would get caught and shot too. You could feel it in the air and see it in people's faces.

Every few days Joost, or somebody else from the Dutch underground, would bring us some food: bread, and cheese and some water. Maybe two or three days would pass when we didn't get any food and we were all gradually getting weaker. I sometimes searched the forest for apples and, when it rained, you could catch water on a leaf and then drink it.

One day, the Dutch underground brought Jones and me some letters. I looked at mine, but I couldn't make head or tail of it, as I wasn't good at reading, so Jones helped me. The letters were from the two sisters who had helped look after us back in the cottage in the village a few weeks before.

They had written that they were thinking about us a lot and were wondering if we were OK, if we were staying safe and getting enough food and water. Apparently the Germans were starting to crack down more on the Dutch underground and had ordered all the residents of the villages near Arnhem to leave their homes by 22 October. The girls had been trying to organise with the leaders of the underground to be able to come to bring some food and water to us in the hut, but it had not been possible yet, and they hoped that we could come back and see them after the war was over.

'Well, they're kind of love letters actually,' Jones concluded with a grin.

* * *

A couple of days after this, Joost arrived with one other man from the Dutch underground, carrying more supplies with them. They brought some guns, ammunition and army clothes; not full uniforms, but just odds and ends for each person.

Everyone got a Sten gun and some ammunition. I took a red British paras beret. Baker took some trousers, but then wanted to swap them with me. He wanted the suit from the doctor's house that I was wearing, but I refused.

Joost spoke to us from the door of the hut: 'It doesn't look like the British Second Army is going to cross the Rhine any time soon, so it has been decided that we are going to evacuate all of you back across the river. The Germans are getting more suspicious of us every day and we can't delay any longer. We're going to go tonight, in a few hours, the night of 22 October.'

I suddenly felt an almost overwhelming mixture of excitement and nerves. This was it! This was going to be our chance to get back home! But for sure it was not going to be easy; how on earth would we get safely past all the Germans. Would we be able to sneak past them, or would we have to try to shoot our way out somehow? I anxiously remembered back to our initial drop into the Netherlands and our first crossing of the Rhine, and all the machine guns and mortar fire that the Germans could bring if they found us. Surely we wouldn't have a chance against that.

The evacuation was called Operation Pegasus. If successful, it was going to be the largest escape from occupied territory in the war, getting more than one hundred paratroopers back across the river.

One of the resistance members ran a transport company which often carried out tasks for the Red Cross. He had organised a lorry to transport us from our starting point near a village called Oud Reemst, south-west through the German lines to the rendezvous point in the forest near a village called Renkum, a few kilometres west of Arnhem, which was as close as they could get to the Rhine with a lorry. We would then need to walk about five kilometres to the river, avoiding German patrols. Boats should be waiting for us there to take us back across. The British Army would supply the rowing boats and there would also be some American paratroopers in the boats in case there was any fighting.

There were a lot of Germans in the area after all the fighting around Arnhem. They patrolled right up to the Rhine but their main line, which had most of their tanks and artillery was a bit behind the river, maybe a couple of hours walk. The roads were going to be crowded with all the civilians that the Germans had told to evacuate from Arnhem so it was hoped we would have less chance of being checked. There would be women from the Dutch underground stationed every few miles along the road, with bicycles. If anything was wrong, they would signal it to us by pretending to repair their bicycle.

Our truck would be painted all white with a red cross logo, so it looked like a medical transport. 'It is against the Geneva Convention to transport armed soldiers in Red Cross trucks,' Joost said. 'So if you get stopped and the Germans want to search the lorry – you know what to do – shoot them and run to the Rhine.'

Around an hour after dark the lorry arrived, just as Joost had described. We all climbed aboard and slipped under the canvas tarpaulin in the back. The heavy engine of the lorry revved, and we shuddered forwards, being rattled from side to side on the metal floor as it drove over the rutted country road through the forest. I couldn't see anything from under the tarpaulin, but after about five or ten minutes the truck made a turn and I felt us move onto a smoother road. Everyone lay without saying a word, staring at the floor in front of them, listening for any sound of danger from outside. I held my Sten gun tightly beside me.

Then, in the distance I started to hear another sound over the engine of the lorry. It became louder and clearer; the unmistakable rattling and creaking sounds of tanks moving past us on the road: German tanks! I felt a sudden rush of nerves and adrenaline, as the rumbling German tanks shook our lorry.

I could hear some German voices outside, shouting at each other. Then, suddenly, our truck seemed to be slowing down! If they stopped us, it would be terrible. I knew we would need to jump out quickly and take our chances at trying to shoot our way out of whatever situation we might find ourselves in. But then the odds would be against us ever reaching the Rhine, or getting out alive. I looked at Jones and held his gaze for a moment; I knew we were both thinking the same thing.

Our lorry slowed down again and I held my breath. Was this going to be it? After Siberia and the Middle East and Arnhem, was it all going to end like this? In a desperate shoot-out? I adjusted my body again, turning slightly to the side in a crouched position, ready to spring up as quickly as I could. Jones did the same beside me.

But then, just when I thought that we were surely going to stop, our lorry revved louder and speeded up again, and we were leaving behind the German voices and the German tanks and nobody had stopped us. The road became quiet again and I slumped back against the side of the lorry with a sigh of relief.

We travelled for a good while, maybe one or two hours. Then, eventually, the lorry gradually slowed down and stopped. *Time to get out*, I thought to myself. *We've reached the rendezvous point.*

Wordlessly, we climbed out of the lorry. There were some other paratroopers from the Airborne Division there, and we were organised into single file sections each led by a guide, who started to lead us towards the Rhine. It was about 9pm by now and very dark. We couldn't use any torches, so just had to rely on any light that came from the moon. Jones was walking behind me and sometimes put his hand on my shoulder to help him go the right way. It was hard going as we were all hungry, and we had lost strength after being in hiding for weeks.

We had to walk very slowly and quietly for a couple of hours to reach the Rhine and had to go carefully as there were German patrols about, as well as German machine gun nests. Sometimes we had to cross main roads, and we would then cross them one at a time on our stomachs. We avoided open ground as much as possible due to the patrols.

While we were walking through the forest, the major that had been in our hut kept running back and forth from the front of our line, making a racket each time he did so. 'You're making too much noise!' he hissed to us. 'Keep quiet!' After the major came back for the third or fourth time, I was so on edge that I couldn't hold my tongue any longer, even if he was a major. 'You're the one making all the noise, with all your running back here!' The major didn't run back from the front of the line any more after that.

Around midnight I could see that we were approaching the Rhine. Jones and I found ourselves getting separated from the others in our group. We crossed the last road and came out from the forest onto the floodplain beside the river. The floodplain was exposed land where it would be easy for the Germans to spot us; I didn't want to hang about there.

Then I heard an American voice calling out to us. He was about twenty yards to our right beside a boat; they were waiting for us. Jones and I quickly ran over to where the American was, clambered inside the boat and grabbed the oars. 'Let's go!' Our freedom was so close, I just wanted to get out of there.

The American wanted to wait, to see if any other paratroopers turned up, but I was so nervous that I just wanted to leave as quickly as possible. 'No. No more, let's go!' I said. I didn't know where the others were, but I knew that there were other boats which could take them. I felt sure that if we waited something would happen to ruin it all.

We started rowing. Me on one side and Jones on the other. I was rowing so hard that I was making the boat go squint! We were halfway across, then three quarters; the other shore was getting closer. There was the tracer fire from the Allies overhead and some sporadic German firing, but it was not close to where we were. We were going to make it!

We landed on the south bank of the Rhine, in the zone controlled by the Allies. They had tied white tape to bushes and trees to indicate a path that led up from the river to a farmhouse. At this house, we met up with all the other escapees again, except for the major – he must have been taken somewhere else. It didn't seem real, it felt like a dream to be there, safe, to be surrounded by smiling faces and by the other men from the hut in the forest. It didn't seem right to see them amongst the everyday table and chairs and plates and crockery of a Dutch farmhouse, and part of me kept thinking that something was going to go wrong, that someone would jump out and say it had been a mistake, that we still weren't safe or that we had to cross back over the Rhine and go back into combat.

I met an American there who loaded me up with cigarettes and chocolates and then we were taken by jeep to the British zone HQ. The Germans must have known that this road was used at night as they were firing shells all around us. I don't know how it was possible that we weren't hit.

When we arrived we were told to leave our things and go shower, and we were then issued with a nice clean uniform. We were all bloody dirty; we had been about five weeks in total behind German lines, just living from one day to the next, not knowing what would happen next and I hadn't washed in all that time. I washed my hair four or five times with soap. We didn't have shampoo in those days.

Then we were taken for a meal and afterwards brought into a hall. The six of us that had been in the hut had to sit at the front. Men from military intelligence put up a map on the wall and we had to tell them everything that we could about the German forces that we had seen.

We were then taken to Brussels and from there flown to Lincolnshire, near Stamford. We had a meal in the canteen and the lady in the canteen had tears in her eyes as she gave us some food. It was the lady who had given me the extra chocolate before I left. 'You're back, dear! Oh, welcome back! We thought that you weren't going to make it!'

The six of us then split up: me, the American, Jones, Baker and the two other British paratroopers. Jones and I hugged each other strongly. It was an emotional time and I was really sorry to see him go, and vice versa. We had been through so much together.

I was taken in a jeep back to the Polish paratroopers at Stamford. The mood was sombre there. Many paratroopers had been killed and our brigade had lost a quarter of its fighting strength – almost 600 casualties. We had all lost close friends and colleagues. To add insult to injury, there was a rumour going round that despite risking our lives we were now being criticised by the British, and that attempts were being made to turn Sosabowski and the Polish Brigade into the scapegoats for the failure of the operation to achieve all its goals. Operation Market Garden had captured the bridges at Eindhoven and Nijmegen, but the failure to capture the bridge over the Rhine at Arnhem meant that the war could not now be finished before the end of 1944.

'Welcome back,' the officer said to me without smiling, as I arrived back at the camp. 'It's been reported to me that you didn't salute an officer before you left for Arnhem, so it has been decided that you will have seven days CB.'

CB – confined to barracks. It was just sitting in a room by yourself – like prison. *You dirty buggers*, I thought to himself, *I fought for the country and that's the thanks I get. What if I'd died?*

After my CB finished I got two weeks holiday and I went back up to Scotland to visit Isa. She said that I looked like a skinned rabbit after Arnhem, as I had lost so much weight there. You can imagine how emotional we both were when we saw each other again; we were both crying and shaking as we hugged each other tightly, neither wanting to let the other go. It was thinking about her that had kept me going through the worst moments in Arnhem, when I had been on my own, not knowing if the Nazis would find me, or if I would survive, or if I would see her again. I knew that I didn't want to lose her.

Isa had been informed that I was missing in action. After so many weeks away she had feared the worst.

After she had calmed down, she told me to sit down and looked me in the eye. 'Well, now it's my turn – I've got some news for you,' she told me. 'You're going to be a father!'

Epilogue

The failure to take the bridge at Arnhem meant that the war dragged on for longer. It was only in May 1945 that the Nazis finally surrendered.

I knew that I couldn't return to Poland after the war. By around February 1945 the Soviets had occupied all of the pre-war territory of Poland. They took control of the country and put a communist government in charge. Where I was born wasn't even in Poland anymore. The boundaries had changed and it was in the Soviet Union. Nowadays it is in the country of Ukraine.

After the war ended, I was sent to help occupy Germany as part of the British Army of the Rhine (BAOR). It was in a place called Bramsche which was near Osnabruck, beside the Dutch border.

My group stayed in dorms in what had been a German army camp. There were thousands of refugees there: Poles, Yugoslavs, Czechs and some Russians. We helped keep them under control, like the police. There was lots of fighting between nationalities. The refugees used to make vodka from potatoes and some blinded themselves with it or went crazy, as it was so raw and not purified. Others went to nearby farms, stealing pigs. I found a Nazi Iron Cross medal lying on the floor in one of the farms, after we had to go there to bring back some Russian refugees.

Memories of the war were still very fresh and it was a strange feeling to go to Germany as an occupying force, when we had been fighting the Nazis just a few months before. At times I felt uncomfortable, at times resentful, at times thankful that it was all over. You couldn't forget what had happened that quickly, nor your friends and colleagues that had been killed. We weren't allowed to speak to any Germans or we would be court-marshalled.

We were there until early 1947 when I was given two years extended leave – but I was still a reserve and could be called up at any time due to the Cold War. I went to work on one of the local farms near where we had done our paratrooper training in Scotland, in a small village called Boarhills. Isa and I moved there in March 1947 and it was the worst snow that anyone could remember. It came right up to the tops of the walls around the fields and the only way to get food was to drive into St Andrews with the tractor. Then eventually, in 1948 I got demobbed up in Dundee at the army office. When I was demobbed, they gave me civilian clothes – sports jacket, shirt and trousers and a hat that looked like the US mafia. They gave me a gratuity of £26 which I put in the bank.

My son, Stanley, was born in 1945. I asked for our son to be named after me. Stanley's birth was recorded with the registrar who also worked in the post office. 'If you don't marry Isa later, with a son sharing your name, you will go to court,' the registrar said. 'I promise I'll marry her,' I replied.

Once the war ended we didn't need permission from the army any more to get married, so of course that was when they gave us permission. We got married by a Protestant minister. We had the wedding in the house – it was a common thing in those days. Isa didn't have a white dress, just a nice blue frock that she could use again. I wore one of the suits that a German tailor had made me back in Bramsche.

A man had come up to me one day in Bramsche, offering me a seven-valve wireless radio in exchange for cigarettes. He said that his father had a clothes factory that had been closed down by the British. He offered to arrange to make clothes for me in exchange for coffee beans and cigarettes. He showed me where the tailor lived – all the fabric materials and equipment were kept behind a secret wall in his house that you swung around, to keep them secret from the British and the Germans. Isa had stayed back in Scotland during this time working in the farmhouse, and I got her to write to the cigarette factory in Liverpool to send the cigarettes to me – I got cheap cigarettes as I was with the overseas forces. Isa sent the coffee beans herself and in return, the tailor made me one dark suit and one light suit.

On the way back to Scotland from Bramsche, I travelled via France. I went into a bakery to try to get some bread, but the lady working there couldn't understand any English and eventually, exasperated, I started walking out, swearing to myself in Polish in frustration: 'dupa!'

'Ah, du pain! du pain!' she cried out, and to my amazement went away to gather some bread! We were all in stitches, laughing, that a swear word in Polish would mean the same as the French word for bread.

My daughter, Isobel, was born in 1947 and was a little, red-haired baby. I was so happy to have one boy and one girl. 'That's enough now,' I said to Isa. I didn't want a large family like rabbits, like I was born into, as we never had enough money or time.

I never gave up making enquiries and trying to find the rest of my family; I gradually managed to find out what had happened to the others. My father and Rozia had survived, and were eventually released from the camp in Siberia; they were sent to a town called Jelenia Gora after the war. All the borders of Poland had been moved to the west after the war and Jelenia Gora was in the west of Poland, in an area that had been German before the war. I found them through the International Red Cross. They were given five hectares of land and a house as compensation. My father went to work in a factory.

We tried to arrange to meet each other but by now the Cold War had started and it was not easy to travel between Poland and the UK. It was many years until I could see them again. I only saw my father once more in my life when I managed to finally visit them in 1967. My father offered me his house, but I refused: 'Give it to Rozia,' I told him. On the way back home, at the East German-Polish border, the border guards checked under our car with big mirrors and took out the seats. I didn't even know myself that they came out.

My sister Stefka had been safe when the Soviets invaded as she was a woman and married to a Ukrainian man. She wasn't taken away to Siberia like we were, but when the Germans invaded they had taken Stefka's family to Germany to work on a farm near Hannover. She was then in a displaced persons camp nearby before moving to live in Zielona Gora, another area in the west of Poland.

My brother Edek had been taken from his house by the Soviets just like we had, but he had managed to escape at one of the train stations by hiding behind a big tree. He would later be captured by the Germans and after the war he went to live in Lublin.

Billy survived the battle at Monte Cassino and stayed on in the UK, like me. He lived in the south of England on the Isle of Wight.

As for the other paratroopers, Big Mietek's boat never made it to the other side. He ended up being captured by the Nazis and after the war he went to a place for recovering PoWs in Grantown on Spey, a town in Scotland.

Andrzej, who had jumped out of the aeroplane, ended up landing safely. I met him later in Bramsche, and he told me that he had stayed in the area where he landed and sold army blankets for the rest of the war.

I still don't know what happened to Jurek.

Sosabowski was controversially removed from his command in December 1944. After the war he went to work in a factory in England. Other workers who knew who he was used to salute him, but the communist Polish government stripped him of his Polish citizenship, and the British Army wouldn't give him a pension.

As for me, I could never entirely forget what had happened to me during the war – how could I? I don't think that anybody would forget such events, especially when so young. Even after the war, there was the constant, numbing reminder that I would never really be able to see my family in Poland again. But by then, I had a new family and so I focused all my energy on supporting and raising them, and I successfully built a new and happy life in Scotland.

At the end of the war, I had my whole life ahead of me. But that, as they say, is another story.